For the Beauty of the Earth

For the Beauty of the Earth

Birding, Opera and Other Journeys

Thomas Urquhart

SHOEMAKER & HOARD
WASHINGTON, D.C.

Library of Congress Cataloging-in-Publication Data

Urquhart, Thomas (Thomas A.)
  For beauty of the earth : birding, opera, and other journeys /
Thomas Urquhart.
     p. cm.
  ISBN 1-59376-017-5
  1. Bird watching—Anecdotes. 2. Natural history—Anecdotes.
3. Opera—Anecdotes. 4. Urquhart, Thomas (Thomas A.)
5. Urquhart, Thomas
(Thomas A.)—Travel. I. Title.
QL677.5 .U76 2004
508—dc22
                                    2003027124
ISBN 1-59376-017-5

Text design by Gopa & Ted2, Inc.
Printed in the United States of America
Text set in Goudy

 Shoemaker & Hoard
A Division of Avalon Publishing Group Inc.
Distributed by Publishers Group West

10 9 8 7 6 5 4 3 2 1

Contents

*It is perhaps a more fortunate destiny to have a taste
for collecting shells than to be born a millionaire.*
—Robert Louis Stevenson

For the Beauty of the Earth

Prologue

"Make the Boy a Naturalist"

"Make the Boy a Naturalist"

Gie me ae spark o' Nature's fire,
That's a' the learning I desire.
—Robert Burns

I CAN IMAGINE no better piece of advice for raising a child than Captain Robert Falcon Scott's last message to his wife, sent from his final, fatal expedition to the South Pole: "Make the boy a naturalist." He was, of course, referring to his infant son, Peter. Few pieces of parental instruction can have been so well observed or so fortunate, few careers as illustrious as this boy's turned out to be, as wildlife artist, conservationist and environmental educator.[1]

When I was at boarding school in England during the late 1950s, framed prints of Peter Scott's paintings of waterfowl flying in at dusk or dawn were a familiar genre all their own; what would headmasters' studies have been like without them? I remember the excitement of my first visit to his new Wildfowl Trust at Slimbridge. As a budding birdwatcher, I was faced with the dilemma over which of the many waterfowl species splashing in the pools I could legitimately "count." Certainly, there were some fabulous birds—the nearly extinct Nene or Hawaiian goose, which was one of Sir Peter's early rescue efforts, for instance—but these were clearly captive, and even as a child I knew instinctively that away from

---

1 At a conference on world conservation, I once heard Sir Peter speak of his first trip, late in life, to Antarctica. Even in the face of his British understatement and restraint, no one in the audience could mistake the emotional impact the visit had had on him. So personal a moment was in sharp contrast to the rest of the conference, which seemed to be a caricature of international bureaucrats at their rain dances. That same year, 1984, when as deputy director of the International Council for Bird Preservation (now Birdlife International) I was looking for a name for the new magazine, it was Peter Scott's suggestion, *World Birdwatch*, that won the day.

their native habitats they had no place on my life-list. On the other hand, swimming among these exotics were shovelers and shelduck that had voluntarily made Slimbridge their home. These were fair game. More problematic was the stunning Mandarin duck. Originally a native of China, the birds were imported to ornament English ponds with their oriental beauty, and a healthy wild population now thrives in Britain, far healthier than in China, where the Mandarin duck is severely endangered by loss of habitat.

I like to think that this early sorting out of home versus exotic birds laid the groundwork for a worldview that is the thesis of this book: that the gentleness of our everyday home turf—our gardens and fields and parks—is as important to save as the undoubtedly stirring lonelinesses of peaks and forests. Thanks to Thoreau's oft-quoted maxim[2] that in wildness is the preservation of the world, wilderness enjoys a lusty advocacy as being alone fit for inspiration. Certainly places whose elemental grandeur is undiluted by obvious human presence are to be prized. But few of us have had our relationship with nature forged in such spots. The bonds of familiarity that sustain the vast majority of us and shape our thoughts and actions are with the nature we see every day. It is nature we have left our mark on, to be sure, but is the wildlife of hedgerow or pasture, for instance, any the less interesting for that?

Natural history has had its spell on me for as long as I can remember. But I cannot really call myself a naturalist, not at least in the sense that Peter Scott was. When it comes to natural history, I am a true amateur, or, as Webster puts it: "1: a devotee, admirer 2: one who engages in a pursuit, study, science or sport as a pastime rather than as a profession 3: one lacking in experience and competence in an art or science." In cheerfully pleading guilty to all three charges, I feel a certain kinship with T. H. White, who introduced his observations of sporting life in the English countryside of the mid-thirties so:

This book cannot pretend to be written by a naturalist, and it is not for naturalists. It is a book about things, for people who have lost them; because it has

---

2 It is as often misquoted, "wildness" being replaced by "wilderness."

given me pleasure to rediscover my things, and I should like to shew them to other people who might be pleased as well. It has turned into a book about the tangible side of country life. People, I felt, ought to pay more attention to the temperature of their baths, and the way they fill their pipes, and the birds who are squandering their song for a chance audience, and the spectacles of nature that give food for the pleasures of rumination, and the construction of fires, and the time to drink sherry, and the season at which a hot water bottle improves upon the comfort of warming one's own bed.[3]

I can subscribe completely to everything in this statement; all these "things" are important, but especially "the spectacles of nature that give food for the pleasures of rumination." And I want to share some "things" of my own, some experiences that have resonated with me and that illustrate some of the joys that come from a fascination with animals, nature and the land. A few of them I found in wilderness. For the most part, though, my outdoors were never far from human habitation. I was brought up in the city, where an outdoor expedition meant a walk in the park.

I don't remember the origins of my interest in natural history; I don't think it came from any parental decree. Rather some might say that the love of nature is something you stand to lose more than find. With this in mind, Rachel Carson wished to endow all children with "a sense of wonder so indestructible that it would last throughout life." In nurturing a child's interest in nature, Carson wrote, "It is not half so important to know as to feel. If facts are the seeds that later produce knowledge and wisdom, then the emotions and the impressions of the senses are the fertile soil in which the seeds must grow." This is balm to the amateur's soul. It speaks of days in the woods rather than hours in the library, and it is in no way limited to a child's experience.

A chance encounter, however fleeting, with a wild creature in the

3 *England Have My Bones.*

field produces an emotional response, and the process of identifying the animal in one's brain is akin more to feeling than to knowing. British bird-watchers have a wonderful word to size up all at once that combination of attributes—behavior, shape, size, etc.—that is so much more than the sum of its parts. Usually spelled "jizz," it derives from RAF slang used in plane spotting in the Second World War: General Impression Shape and Size.[4] It is something ineffable that cannot be taught, only absorbed through experience. Jizz is an intuition and one of a naturalist's little perfections.

By comparison, an up-close and impersonal look that unveils every spot or marking, feather or number of teeth is hardly worth the toss. I remember once drifting down a tributary of the Amazon being stalked by an ocelot. Night had fallen, and the animal's silhouette would appear and disappear amid the overhanging vegetation on the bank as it followed us, as mysteriously as the Cheshire Cat. Sometimes we could see the outline of its head, sometimes its body or its tail, sometimes we caught the shine of its eyes; but never once did we see it whole. It was an unforgettable encounter. But when the animal was later treed in the glare of our flashlights, it was just a scared cat; all its mystery was gone, and the experience sullied forever.

My acceptance of this gift of a "sense of wonder" goes back to my earliest childhood memory: watching woolly caterpillars crawling over a gray stone statue in a garden. There is something rather satisfying about a first memory that foreshadows so nicely the unabashedly humanistic love of nature that has dominated my life. It was the first summer after

---

4 One evening on safari in the Okavango Delta, Ken Newman, the dean of South African ornithologists and author of the standby *Newman's Birds of Southern Africa*, regaled me with the story of his "plane-spotting caper" in the Second World War. After he had been turned down on medical grounds for active flying duty in the RAF, he told me "there was a sudden cry for guys who could identify aeroplanes. We were a small group of hot-stuff plane spotters; very elite! Trouble was that the rule of thumb ID at that time was that if the plane had rounded wingtips it was allied, if it had square wingtips it was German! Suddenly the Yanks arrived with Hellcats, Thunderbolts and Mustangs, all of which had square wingtips. Everyone from fighter aircraft to merchant ship gunners was shooting the hell out of American planes: not a very welcoming gesture! In the meantime the Germans introduced their new Focke-Wolf fighter which had rounded wings. Our job was that of teaching aircraft identification, and in a hurry!"

the family arrived in America from England, and I would have been less than two.

If those furry caterpillars were witness to the awakening of my "sense of wonder," I feel sure it was our beloved Nanny who nurtured it and took my nature education under her wing. In a play based on the memoirs of the French writer Colette, there comes a moment when she recalls her mother's fascination with nature: "Regarde ça!" she would exclaim to the young Colette, pointing at a butterfly or a flower. When I saw that play as an adult, a memory of our Nanny and the red bird— my first cardinal—came into my head. My mother had decorated our dining room chairs with cardinals and cherries based on Audubon's picture, but it was Nanny who showed me a live one in our garden and pointed out the gorgeous contrast of black around its red beak.

Whether found or innate, early on, my natural history bent became the organizing principle of my interests. It was enough to impress the grown-ups in my life. At the end of the school year, my second-grade teacher wrote at the top of a list of early-reader books recommended for holiday reading, "I hesitate to suggest one of these for Thomas; his mind runs to deeper things." So the books I ended up with for the holidays were not about Dick and Jane but the Ice Age and the Norse myths. For most of the year, my outdoor explorations were confined to New York City. I could find the Ice Age, if not the Vikings, in the smooth but scarred patina of the rocks of Central Park. On excursions to Jones Beach we collected gold and orange jingle shells, which my mother made into beautiful flowers displayed under a glass dome in our hall. Once every year, we would find a sea horse amidst the wrack, which she would also turn into an artistic creation. I was disappointed, however, when I found that a hike along the old Indian trail known as Broadway was unlikely to yield up either birds or arrowheads anymore. On the other hand, some of our friends had houses in the country—upstate New York or Connecticut—and weekends spent visiting them always produced their own memorable encounters with wild creatures such as skunks or raccoons or deer. Once, the dog's frenzied barking brought us to a big old snapping turtle that lunged at anything that moved. Another time, a friend and I mapped the little stream that ran through the woods behind his house. It was fall, and the woods were yellow; the project occupied us morning to night until the weekend was over.

Above all, New York had *the* Natural History Museum. I spent many a city-bound weekend exploring its halls with my best friend, and every time, there were new surprises to discover. He was the great-grandson of Theodore Roosevelt, and the splendid equestrian statue of the 26th president, flanked on foot by a Zulu and a Red Indian, outside the main entrance seemed to confer upon us a sense of personal ownership of which we, if no one else, were keenly aware. The marvelous displays of animals in every kind of habitat from faraway lands were the entrance into a magic world. To this day, there is a "certain Slant of light, winter afternoons," as Emily Dickinson describes it, that summons up for me at once the diorama of a pack of wolves loping through the baleful glow of a snowy dusk. Certain social situations do the same thing: the attitude and expression of some of the animals brought together in a chance meeting around the water hole or in a forest clearing made it evident that the designer of these exhibits had a great sense of humor. The museum kindled and largely satisfied a yearning for exotic places, and when we had done with its corridors, the outcrops and fields of Central Park would become the Serengeti and we its lions or antelopes.

My father's career was the United Nations, which was why we lived in New York. To provide a nondenominational place of worship for the delegates, Secretary General Dag Hammarskjöld set aside a Meditation Room in the new headquarters building on the East River.[5] The room was not large, and it was dominated by an enormous block of iron ore from his native Sweden. I can't remember how many tons it weighed, but it was said they had to drive a steel support right into the bedrock of Manhattan so that the building could bear its weight. Its horizontal surface was smooth, and it made a kind of altar, which was struck by a

---

5 ". . . (T)here are simple things which speak to us all with the same language. We have sought for such things and we believe that we have found them in the shaft of light striking the shimmering surface of solid rock.

"So, in the middle of the room we see a symbol of how, daily, the light of the skies gives life to the earth on which we stand, a symbol to many of us of how the light of the spirit gives life to matter."

From the statement by Dag Hammarskjold written for the dedication of the Meditation Room.

single ray of white light. This was the only illumination in an otherwise dark room. I will never forget the awe I felt as a child in the presence of such a grand theatrical gesture, which I perceived to be about nature. Along with the museum, the Meditation Room became another favorite though less frequented spot.

At home, I had my own "museum," a collection of nests and shells and rocks housed behind sliding glass doors in a mahogany cabinet that reached to the ceiling. There were fossil ammonites and belemnites collected from the cliffs of Lyme Regis in Dorset, England, where my father was born. There were shells from all over, bought or traded with friends who had traveled further afield than I had. And there was a set of dinosaurs that came in boxes that were themselves painted dioramas, brought back by my father from a little shop in Paris that specialized in tin models.

My collection steadily grew and grew until it was finally "deaccessioned" by my parents when I left home for boarding school in England. If I could have back just one item from my old museum, it would be the fired clay model of a dodo that was made for me by a school friend's extremely artistic German au pair. I can see it clearly to this day, the bulky gray-blue body, the yellow feet and beak, the exquisitely painted little plume of a tail, and in front of it, nestled in a scrape of the earth, a single large egg. Even as a boy, I always took it as a personal affront that I would never meet a live dodo in the wild. Years later, I visited Mauritius, the only home the dodo ever had, to inspect a conservation education project I was managing there. Another model dodo, made of local wood, now sits on my desk as a souvenir of that visit, as a symbol that there is still hope for some of the other endangered birds on that wonderful island, and as a personal memento of "the voice that used to squawk and squeak," as Hilaire Belloc put it.

One of my school friends—a delightfully eccentric fellow who would come to school with a live garter snake concealed in his pocket and surreptitiously show him off in the middle of class—gave me a Siamese fighting fish for my birthday one year. He knew I collected something, couldn't remember what, and decided the fish was the answer. We named this beautiful bright red creature with flaring gills and fins Jimmie, and he launched my aquarium. It thrived for several years. Neon tetras and black mollies flashed through faux coral; I introduced beautiful water plants; my guppies even bred. The end came when I added a couple of carnivorous Amazonian fish with some snails to keep the tank clean. The snails' response to the immediate outbreak of hostilities from their cohabitants was to secrete a goo that spread over the entire surface of the tank, suffocating the fish. After that, I went back to collecting inanimate objects.

Summer produced the best opportunities for collecting, with my prizes to be borne back in triumph to my museum in the fall. Some years, we spent the holidays in America. At first we went to Cape Cod, and so I got to know the woods and beaches, fields and ponds of the New England coast. To this day, the smell of low tide in a salt marsh reminds me of the mudflats where I would watch fiddler crabs bolt into their holes and catch them if I could. My mother was a born hunter-gatherer, and we collected Irish moss for seaweed pudding and beach plums for jam or jelly. Later, when we rented a place on Penobscot Bay in Maine, my parents would duck dive for scallops in the harbor. It was the year I was ten, and the Maine view—smooth, ocean-washed granite framed by the jagged outlines of the forest and the blue-green of the sea—engraved itself into my memory. That summer was like a premonition of the future time when conservation would bring me back to live in Maine. The building, Down East Farm, has gone and its fields have been subdivided, but I have a clear memory of it still: an old white clapboard farmhouse set in fields rolling down to an inlet from Eggemoggin Reach. There was an old rowboat to take us to the small rocky islets for picnics and seals that would follow us as we rowed. There was a minute horseshoe crab, which I kept in the bilge in the bottom of the boat, and an immense black snake that lived beneath the disused chicken coop. There was also a beautiful bouquet of stems with bright, shiny leaves arranged in threes, picked and presented proudly to me by our Scottish au pair one day after she had been out for a walk, which took me to the Blue Hill general hospital with a mighty case of poison ivy.

Every other year, my father, as a U.N. diplomat, got "home leave," and we went to England. There our home was Amberley, one of the most picturesque villages in the country, with its thatched cottages, immemorial elms and the twice-daily procession of the farmer's cows down the village street on their way to and from the farmyard and the meadows. Its rose-covered walls and thatched roofs still inspire painters, and its scenes still appear on calendars and in books about the English Village Beautiful.

The same natural beauty of its surroundings that made Amberley-God-Knows, to give it its full Victorian name, so attractive to artists made it a paradise for a budding naturalist. The village is in the Sussex Weald, perched between a range of rolling chalk hills, the South Downs, and the Amberley Wild Brooks. Through these, and through a gap in the Downs, the River Arun runs to the sea. Amberley was, and always will be, my spiritual home, and I like to think of the Arun as the spring that watered my love of nature and from which it still flows.

The Amberley Wild Brooks were known simply as "the marshes." In the reeds that lined the dikes, herons stalked their prey and moorhens nested. Here grew the marsh woundwort, which we once gathered and made into a potion to cure my mother's mother's vertigo. (She gamely drank the syrupy brew, but it made her condition no better.) The fields frequently flooded even in summer if it was a rainy one; they became virtually a lake during the winter, and from the air one might think one had already reached the coast ten miles further south. Then masses of duck—mallard, teal and widgeon—would come, and there was good shooting. One village wag used to tell of being out one foggy night and hearing the throb of great wings beating. Hurriedly loading his muzzle-loader, he aimed into the fog in the direction of the sound and pulled the trigger. At his feet fell three swans, royally protected birds that have belonged to the Crown since medieval times, skewered through the neck with his ramrod. In his haste, he had forgotten to remove it before firing. According to the tale, he gave one swan to the vicar, one to the gardener at the castle and one to the owner of the pub.

If the Wild Brooks were the quintessential "haunts of coot and hern," on the Downs one entered the windblown world of the Wheatear. John Masefield, the poet laureate, must have known the Downs well to capture their magic so beautifully:[6]

6 "Up on the Downs," John Masefield.

Up on the downs the red-eyed kestrels hover,
Eyeing the grass.
The field-mouse flits like a shadow into cover
As their shadows pass.

Men are burning the gorse on the down's shoulder;
A drift of smoke
Glitters with fire and hangs, and the skies smoulder,
And the lungs choke.

Once the tribe did thus on the downs, on these downs burning
Men in the frame,
Crying to the gods of the downs till their brains were turning
And the gods came.

And today on the downs, in the wind, the hawks, the grasses,
In blood and air,
Something passes me and cries as it passes,
On the chalk downland bare.

The Downs have felt the hand of man since the Stone Age, and it was here that I absorbed the first foundations of my belief in good steward-ship, long before I knew that a steward existed anywhere except on board the Cunard liners we traveled to England on. In the fifties, the Downs were being fenced and plowed, and on our frequent walks I only had to listen to my parents as they came across yet another new fence in a field they remembered as open to know that changes were taking place right before my eyes. Then came myxomatosis, the hideous disease with which rabbits were deliberately infected to eradicate them from agricultural lands. It spread uncontrollably. Dead and dying rabbits were everywhere, their eyes horribly swollen. When we found them, my siblings and I would club them to put them out of their misery.

However, the newly plowed fields offered one bonus: a never-ending source for archeological and natural discovery. Stone and pottery relics of the various human cultures that had lived on the hills since time immemorial lay all over the place. Nodules of iron pyrite stood out from the dominant chalk and flint, their rust-colored crust, when cracked open, revealing a mass of steely spindles radiating out from the core. Occasionally we found fossils of sea urchins from the Cretaceous era when the Downs were formed under the sea.

❧❦☙

In order to get into boarding school, I left my family in New York to live with friends of my parents in London for a year, while I was "crammed" for the entrance exam to Westminster School. That fall, I had my first real experience of bird hunting. My host was a member of an organized pheasant shoot in Suffolk, and I would accompany him into the field. Richard Jefferies captured the flavor of this sport in his classic, *The Gamekeeper at Home,* and although he wrote it in the nineteenth century, in many respects the world he depicted was totally recognizable in 1957. The gamekeeper he describes could indeed have been the one who greeted us every Saturday. "In personal appearance he would be a tall man were it not that he has contracted a slight stoop in the passage of years, not from weakness or decay of nature, but because men who walk must lean forward somewhat, which has a tendency to round the shoulders. . . . His neck has become the colour of mahogany, sun and tempest have left their indelible marks upon his face; and he speaks from the depths of his broad chest, as men do who talk much in the open air, shouting across the fields and through the copses." At the beginning of the day, this god would take from his pocket a little silver container, about the size of a matchbox, in which were silver sticks, every one with a number at its base. Then each of the shooters, clad in tweed from their hats to their plus fours, would pick one from the box, and so would be assigned his position in the line of guns.

My position was with the beaters driving the game towards the sportsmen. As Jefferies says of the organized pheasant drive, "The difficulty is to prevent them [the pheasants] from wandering off in the early morning; and men are stationed like sentinels at the usual points of egress to drive them back. The beaters are usually men who have previously been employed in the woods and possess local knowledge of the ground, and are instructed in their duties long before: nothing must be left to the spur of the moment." The local men were a fount of information.

An entry from my notebook reads: "October 26, 1957—Tendring Hall Estate—H. Brooke trod on a hen pheasants tail. Pheasant got up and flew away leaving tail underfoot." In the back of someone's Land-Rover, I was introduced to a merlin kept for falconry, and heard about the rabbit's instinct to crouch under a barbed wire fence and the destruction this habit can wreak on a diving falcon's wings; the general use of barbed wire fences was having a severe impact on the sport itself. On another occasion, the famous horse painter Alfred Munnings, out for a ride, stopped by the pub where we were having lunch and told a story about George the Fifth. (I am afraid I don't remember the story, but I think it had to do with the King's reputation for bad language—and probably his lack of interest in aesthetics.) There was the time that the same "H. Brooke" got hit on the head by the pheasant he had just shot; I happened to be taking a photograph of him at that split second. (It came out, but very blurred.) I learned how to dispatch a wounded bird by squeezing it between the wings (but I could never bring myself to bite its head, which is what the gamekeepers and some of the sportsmen did). And I heard one of the most musical sounds of my life, the tinkle, infinitesimally soft but clear as a bell, of the chimes of the gamekeeper's watch, which, according to Jefferies, "tells him the time in the densest darkness of the woods. On pressing a spring and holding it near the ear, it strikes the hour last past, then the quarters which have since elapsed: so that even when he cannot see an inch before his face he knows the time within fifteen minutes at the outside, which is near enough for practical purposes."

Joining the shoot was an astoundingly new experience in natural history and a wonderful way to get outdoors, but at the end of the first day, when I surveyed the rows of dead birds and animals, I felt very strange and guilty. Reconciling the visceral enjoyment of the sport with all those corpses is still a puzzler. T. H. White touches on this quandary with pitiless accuracy in the context of "sitting shots." "One [the sitting shot] is a concrete assassination of beauty, the other [on the wing] is a creation of beauty—the beautiful aim. Shooting sitting is not unsporting, but unsatisfactory. It produces no elation and so leaves time for remorse to breed. No art has compensated the destruction which one is left to contemplate. A mere dead hare: horrible. But a hare cut over so that he somersaults with his head on the ground: beauty."

I quickly got caught up in the excitement of the shoot: the sounds of the beaters chirruping to their dogs, thwacking their sticks against tree trunks and kale stalks, whistling and hollering to get the game up; the steadily increasing anticipation from the beginning of the drive: when would they start to fly, would there be any birds in the field; then a pheasant taking off, followed by another and another, and the shotguns' sharp reports growing more rapid until all was suddenly quiet again. But what I remember with the keenest pleasure of all is the raw smell, the rusty color and the feel of an English autumn, less brilliant but infinitely more penetrating than the New England falls I had been used to: the damp bracken[7] where the birds would sit tight till the last minute before rocketing into the air; the fields of sugar beet where they would crouch and run until one more nervous than the rest would break cover and fly; and above all the covert shoot where the birds would fly out of the park, high and fast over the majestic oaks. "The beauty of the park," extols Jefferies, "consists in its 'breadth' as an artist would say — the meadows with their green frames of hedges are cabinet pictures, lovely, but small; this is life size, a broad cartoon from the hand of nature."

In the rarefied intellectual atmosphere of Westminster, I began to take an interest in classical music, and opera especially became an obsession. It started with a performance of *Lohengrin* conducted by Otto Klemperer at the Royal Opera House, Covent Garden. As the ethereal music of the prelude emerges out of the blue, Wagner imagined an angel descending closer and closer until it touches the earth. At that moment the cool shimmer of the strings briefly acquires the golden glow of the brass.

7 Rudyard Kipling's British centurion knew it too: "You'll go where laurel crowns are won, but will you e'er forget / The scent of hawthorn in the sun, or bracken in the wet?"

When I read Thomas Mann's *Buddenbrooks* several months later, I recognized his description of young Hanno's response to *Lohengrin* as my own. "The sweet, exalted splendour of the music had borne him away upon its wings." The sound emerging from the glow of the pit in the darkened opera house was a moment of discovery from which there could be no turning back.

Covent Garden was entering the glorious years when Georg Solti was its music director. The next season opened with a new production of *Götterdämmerung*. The Norns' discourse in the prologue reawakened my love of the sagas, and the powerful swell of the Rhine motif as it captured the music of Siegfried's impetuous search for adventure swept me up as well. I determined to make music my career. Starting on the bottom rung of the ladder, I spent a few months before going up to Oxford working for a fearsome old lady, a veritable gorgon, who ran a theater ticket agency. She had the reputation of being able to get her special customers tickets for anything. This she did simply by terrorizing the poor backroom boys like me. Sitting on high stools like Dickensian clerks, we worked around a huge central table divided by a wall of ledgers representing the agency's seating allocations for the different theaters. We would inscribe the reservations as they were called in from the various offices around London, and Heaven help the miserable clerk who inadvertently let go of any seats Miss Parker might have had her eye on.

Although I had got into Oxford on my biology skills (my slide of the mouthparts of the cockroach for the entrance exam was deemed sensational!), I found that the course would not be oriented to what we now call conservation biology but was designed to point toward a career in medicine. This I knew I did not want to do. What I wanted to do was to go to the opera. So the authorities allowed me to read, or major in, geography.

For the most part, I felt little rapport with the subject. The exceptions were a course on historical geography—the re-creation of the land as it was during a given period of human use—and especially the English landscape architecture of the eighteenth century. Otherwise, an excerpt from my notes of a geology class discussion over a series of specimens tells it all: "Number 73, Pegmatite—Granite with intergrowth of felspar and quartz. . . . The rock jars my memory. The sound of the stream, pink-ish because of the pebbles in its bed; one or two dead leaves at the bot-tom. I had that dream often many years ago. Were there these pink translucent rocks? . . . I would not share the beauty of this world. The natural paths are broken by icy quartz. In little pock marks filled with rain are coloured pebbles treasured by the Indians. In larger holes, the water soothes." As F. Scott Fitzgerald wrote after a similarly gushy out-burst from Gatsby, "Through all he said, even through his appalling sen-timentality, I was reminded of something—an elusive rhythm, a fragment of lost words, that I had heard somewhere a long time ago."

But the summers were full of opera. During the long vacation, I cov-ered British opera festivals as a critic for *Opera News*, the magazine of the Metropolitan Opera. I went to the Wagner Festival in Bayreuth. Espe-cially memorably, Glyndebourne, the opera house nestled in the South Downs, was a picturesque drive from Amberley, and I saw almost every production. My mother would make a fabulous picnic for dinner during the intermission, with the best Sèvres china and damask napkins packed in a wooden trug. We would stake out a spot at the end of the lawn next to the ha-ha, the hidden ditch much beloved by English landscape archi-tects, that separated the operagoers in evening dress from the safely graz-ing sheep and the Downs beyond. Inside the theater, there was a bat that would wake up after the intermission and fly about; it made a point of appearing in the graveyard scene in *Don Giovanni*. Sometimes the sun shone, and sometimes it didn't; but I only remember once when it rained so hard we had to retreat to the car for our picnic. It was torrential. Gey-sers of water were shooting up between the flagstones, and the manage-ment had to make duck-boards out of flats from the productions that were over. The Sèvres, too, came to an end one evening when, late for the opera, we took a humpbacked bridge too fast, tossing the trug and its contents in the air.

The first summer after coming down from Oxford, I spent a weekend with my father, who was then researching his biography of Dag Ham-marskjöld, in a rambling old farmhouse in southern Sweden. We woke to a beautiful morning with more than a hint of autumn in the air. I went for a walk along the shore of one of the many inlets from the sea that perforate that part of the Swedish coast. To my great excitement, at the end of the path a Viking gravestone rose haphazardly out of a clearing in the bracken. The last wild rose blossoms of summer were blowing over it, and overhead a flight of cranes was heading south for the winter. Valhalla or Nature: I was about to make my choice. After unsuccessfully hunting for a job as a recording producer in London for a year, I returned to New York and went to work for Leopold Stokowski's American Symphony Orchestra.

At the time I was working for him, Stokowski, then well into his eighties, was making plans to retire to England. While scouting out a suitable house, he came to stay with us in Amberley. Every afternoon he would retire to bed for a nap, leaving the door of his bedroom open so that he could summon his traveling companion if necessary. His room was off the busiest corridor in the house, and as the household tiptoed past it one could just see, and not fail to notice, two stockinged feet stretched out on the counterpane. No one minded the self-imposed curfew, but my mother was heard to complain gently, "It's those *feet* I find so depressing." On another occasion, when friends came to stay and the Maestro graciously tried to correct their five-year-old daughter in her piano practicing, the child told him to "fuck off." "Little girls," he responded with scarcely concealed horror, "should not say such things."

The American Symphony gave memorable performances with different conductors of three symphonies by Gustav Mahler: Igor Markevitch led an account of the First that radiated *mittel-Europischer* style until the final pages where he inexplicably cut several crucial angst-defying bars. Jascha Horenstein's Ninth had all the authority of a conductor who had started his musical studies in Vienna the year Mahler died. Stokowski himself conducted the Second Symphony—the Resurrection—and it was a revelation. All vanity shed away, the performance rang with a musical truth to which few have access other than a conductor nearly ninety.

I stayed in the world of arts administration for nearly ten years. Long before my career did, however, my heart was leading me back to natural history. As the resurgence of my old interests built up, more and more omens—flights of geese, soaring hawks—pointed the way. And then I met a woman, a writer whose feeling for nature was as deep as my own (and who had kept frogs in her bed as a child, or so I was informed by her former au pair on our wedding day). As soon as we were married, we moved from Boston into the country, and I started a journal illustrated by poems and other quotations appropriate to the moment and generally to do with natural history. The next year, I went to work for the Massachusetts Audubon Society. Ever since, nature and our experiences on the land have played a dominant role in our lives at work as well as play.

So what makes a naturalist? From watching the reactions to wildlife and nature in my children when they were very young, it is clear that Rachel Carson was right: the "sense of wonder" is something innate that needs to be nurtured, not something external that needs to be instilled. Carson herself prescribed "the companionship of at least one adult who can share it, rediscovering with him the joy, excitement and mystery of the world we live in." As it grows stronger, this sense of wonder, deriving from and responding to nature, seems to breed its own delights until experiences come tumbling one over another, and the course for a lifetime is set.

Over the years, Mother Nature has been an endless and almost ubiquitous source of joy and comfort for me. She has also been a prism through which to consider works of art. Nature and the arts have been the twin mainstays of my lifelong interests, two baroque columns whose voluptuous ornaments can easily distract one from their central purpose of holding up the world. My enjoyment of music, painting and literature has also deepened my appreciation of the natural world. "A rock pile ceases to be a rock pile the moment a single man contemplates it, bearing within him the image of a cathedral," wrote Antoine de Saint-Exupéry. In a discussion with Maine's poet laureate, Kate Barnes, she spoke of Goethe's assessment of nature and art, and later sent me the following quote that says it all: "*Wem die Natur ihr offenbares Geheimnis zu*

enthüllen anfängt, der empfindet eine unwiderstehliche Sehnsucht nach ihrer
würdigesten Auslegerin, der Kunst."[8]

When it is in balance, the relationship between man and nature is
more intensely moving to me even than the awe I have felt on a wild
mountain or in a virgin forest, great and unforgettable though those
moments have been. T. S. Eliot provides a nice counterpoint to Thoreau
in his opinion that "it is not necessarily those lands which are the most
fertile or most favored in climate that seem to me the happiest, but those
in which a long struggle of adaptation between man and his environment has brought out the best qualities in both." My love of nature is
unashamedly humanistic. Just as the caterpillars crawling over a statue in
our garden when I was a baby might have been exploring the strokes of
the artisan who sculpted it, I am "happiest" when approaching nature
through human artifacts and the grandeur of the one is matched by the
inspiration of the other. For better or worse, we are part of the landscape,
and we must find our place in it. I realized that in the anciently cultivated
Downland around Amberley, but the mental ground was tilled in New
York's Central Park and the American Museum of Natural History.

8 He to whom Nature begins to reveal her open secret will feel irresistible yearning for her
most worthy interpreter, Art.

Home

In the Beginning Was the Bird

The Brave Days of Old

Landscape, with Man

If Music Be the Spice of Life

In the Beginning Was the Bird

Do you ne'er think what wondrous beings these?
Do you ne'er think who made them, and who taught
The dialect they speak, where melodies
Alone are the interpreters of thought?
—Henry Wadsworth Longfellow, "Birds of Killingworth"

IT'S SPRING, and my neighborhood is like a battleground that recalls the worst excesses of the Wars of the Roses.

Over the course of the winter there has been relative peace. The cardinal that added a dash of color to the bare bushes around my yard, and a relative newcomer himself, might deplore more recent immigrants like those drab arrivistes, the house finches, but animosities at the feeder were discreet. True, the local barons—led by the sharp-shinned hawks—exacted their tribute, taking the odd chickadee. One morning I crossed paths with a merlin flying in fast and low over the bay to make a lightning raid on a feeder at the end of a narrow chute between two houses. But in general, law and order were maintained, allowing for a more or less stable world. Restlessness was limited to the song, plaintive in the bright, cold landscape, of a chickadee impatient for longer days.

But now the legions from the south have arrived, and they are an unruly lot. Their coming has brought about a general collapse in civility even among the local tribes. At my window, a robin is locked in an endless pugilistic round with its own reflection until the pane is smeared with feathers and the bird itself punch-drunk. The mockingbird that on winter mornings kept my spirits up trying out his repertoire is now surly. From the peak of our neighbor's roof, he lets out an evil hiss before taking off straight as an arrow after an oriole that has designs on a maple he counts his own. From the treetops the calls of the cardinals, now the neighborhood heralds in their scarlet finery, come on like bugles from the tents of warring camps, and a flicker laughs its contempt at the challenge. Even hummingbirds are now duelists, locked in a tight circle as they feint and parry with their rapier beaks on their way up to dizzying heights. When a crow flies overhead, two grackles scramble like fighter pilots to harry it until the intruder is well out of their airspace. In the meadow beyond, rapine is everywhere. Not even the most modest bobolink miss is safe to wander abroad. No sooner has she left the safety of the ground than a lusty male, puffed up in his heraldic suit of black and white and gold, is after her, chasing her into the equivalent of some dark doorway in the tall grass. And all the while, English sparrows brawl under a split-wood fence, in the manner of Breughelian peasants at a kermesse.

In the eyes of family and friends an interest in birds is my defining attribute, and I am not normally so churlish where they are concerned. But there are days in the spring when their activity starts too early for me. It was 4:52 this morning when outside my window the cardinal bid the world to rise, and unlike the electronic kind, there is no "snooze" button for the avian alarm clock. He was soon followed by the rest of the dawn chorus.

When I was in college, I came across a poem called "Dawn Chorus"[1] in the Sunday paper and liked it so much I cut it out and have kept it in my wallet ever since:

> There comes a moment when the tide turns;
> Light has won again. The birds stop singing
> For a long moment, then begin again
> On a much more casual note. They've done it:
> Dragged back day, tipped cool light
> Over the lock of dawn with the nervous force
> Of their throats. Some strength of mine
> Was sapped to bring that toneless even glare

1 Ruth Fainlight.

And settle the question: after each dawn's
Struggle, in the clear white of exhaustion,
Insomniacs float down wide canals of sleep.

But today the dawn chorus brought no "wide canals of sleep." From my pillow I found myself naming each new songster as it chimed in. I didn't want to, I didn't mean to, I just had to. Unbidden, my brain leapt into action, putting sleep to flight in the process. There was nothing for it but to get up and go for a walk around our neighborhood, a dyspeptic spectator to all these shenanigans.[2] But with the sweetness of the lilac ushering in a parade of springtime memories, I was soon feeling privileged to be enjoying the daybreak. Never had the well-known lawns and bushes, pristine in their new leaves sparkling after a night's rain, seemed so entrancing. And never again would season, hour, weather and a host of other imperceptible variables combine to exactly the same effect. The oriole, now hanging at eye level and letting me take in his gorgeous plumage at leisure, ensured that I was seeing my neighborhood once again for the first and only time: I would never forget this moment.

My mother was the one who first focused my natural history interests on birds. The year I was in second grade, she decided that I should keep a bird list as a project for the summer holidays. It was a good choice since we were going to England, and it would seem a little exotic when I returned to my school in New York in the fall. I still have the exercise book she bought for the enterprise, still adorned with feathers and full of childish

2 It is not only slumber that the willful interruption of birds drives away. Allen Morgan, who brought the venerable Massachusetts Audubon Society into the environmental era in the 1960s and '70s, brought the same fierce competitive drive to tennis, which he took up in middle age, as he had applied to birding all his life. He once told me he hated playing out-of-doors because the automatic process of identifying any bird that came into view, no matter how common, distracted him from his game. In mid-serve, a swallow . . . and a split second later, a fault. By contrast, a golfer I know loves to hear the songs of birds on the links; they help him concentrate on his shot. And therein lies the difference: he is not a birder and can let the song flood innocently into his brain without caring to know who sang it.

notes in rather curious spelling. The first bird I entered wasn't exotic at all—the common or garden sparrow. I'd known sparrows all my life. But thanks to my list, I was *seeing* a *house* sparrow for the first time, and under those conditions, the male is really quite a handsome bird with its chestnut back and striking black mask and bib. In the sparrow's case, familiarity has truly bred contempt.[3] Not so the second visitor, who came to our kitchen door in search of the breadcrumbs I put out. The chaffinch is common enough in English gardens, but he has a better reputation. With his combination of slate blue nape, rosy red breast and the prominent white epaulettes as he flies, he is still one of my favorites.[4]

That was my start as a bird-watcher, and it is a hobby I have pursued more or less ever since. I started with an old bird-book that must have belonged to my mother when she was a child. It guided me beyond the birds we saw regularly in the garden at Amberley—thrushes, blackbird, robin and goldfinch—to the species that were terra incognita even to the grown-ups. Impatient with the text, I gained little ornithological knowledge but a frenetic desire to see each of the birds depicted in the color pictures. Prowling around the hedges that broke up a hodgepodge of flower beds and lawns, I imagined seeing the most improbable species. The plate of the hoopoe exerted a special fascination, and I fully expected to find this Mediterranean bird flying about our quintessentially English garden.

But I happily settled for the handsome goldfinches that flitted about the apple arbor, a dappled tunnel between beds of roses. It opened onto a terrace with an immaculate lawn, the domain of pied wagtails that bobbed about among the tiny daisies in the green. Beyond, there was an apple orchard that yielded enormous green apples—hard and inedible

---

3 This attitude has been encouraged, and redeemed, in scripture: "Are not two sparrows sold for a farthing? And one of them shall not fall to the ground without your Father." (Matthew 10: 29)

4 In *The Charm of Birds*, Viscount Grey of Fallodon describes the song of the chaffinch fondly if snobbishly: "I have known people complain of the persistent iteration of the chaffinch's song, and I must admit that it does suggest a happiness that is a little trivial and commonplace. If the chaffinch were human one can imagine that he would say 'Cheerio!' as a greeting to a friend."

until cooked—and stretched to a wood at the end of the property whence came the cry of the green woodpecker or yaffle. The orchard is no more, blown to bits by the hurricane that devastated southeastern England in 1987, and the arbor has succumbed to old age and changing horticultural tastes. But in my memory, the garden at Amberley comes together in a riot of the senses: the smell of box and the scent of innumerable roses, the color of the delphiniums and hollyhocks, and birdsong—the flutelike blackbird, the bonhomie of the chaffinch, and from the treetops, the repetitive phrase in 5/4 time of the chiffchaff. And these are the birds that I delight to find again when I visit England.

When I was a little older, my parents gave me an airgun. The first time I took aim at a bird in the garden—it was a sparrow sitting in a pear tree, and so I was arguably destroying a pest—to my amazement I hit it, and it dropped out of the tree, stone dead. The pellet had gone straight through its head. Then on closer inspection it turned out to be a hedge sparrow or dunnock, which isn't a sparrow at all, and the thrill turned to remorse. From then on, the only birds I stalked with my airgun were wood pigeons, certified destroyers of crops, which my grandfather's cook turned into delicious pies and stews. When I was sixteen, I did some shooting with a 20-bore shotgun in Scotland, but aside from the odd lucky shot, I never got good enough to be comfortable with bird shooting, much as I had enjoyed my Saturdays with the beaters. But at the time, it was an engaging avenue to learning more about the birds I was chasing.

By the time I went to boarding school in England, bird-watching had become the chief amusement of my holidays. My grandfather, my mother's father, gave me my first pair of binoculars on my thirteenth birthday, and they at once became as much a part of me as the emblems of their martyrdom are of the saints in Renaissance art. Not only was Amberley the perfect place for birding, but birding led me to know that anciently tended countryside on an intimate level I would never have otherwise found. One valley in particular, tucked in the Downs, held a special magic: on its rounded flanks where wheatears flicked their tails, centuries of sheep had cropped the turf close, which in turn revealed in graceful profile the geological architecture of the land. No wild crag could have been more satisfying to my eyes.

It was again my grandfather who taught me one spring how to blow the birds' eggs I found in the hedgerows along the cow pasture and the dikes that divided the Wild Brooks. He fashioned an instrument out of an old glass medicine dropper, bending it at right angles over an alcohol flame. With infinite patience, he showed me how to take a needle and make a hole at one end of the egg, as small as possible, just enough to insert the tip of the pipette. If the egg was fresh, the unformed innards could be extruded by gently blowing into the hole, and a near-perfect shell would be added to my collection.

Spring rambles became a natural Easter egg hunt in which my most often found prizes were greenish blue streaked with brown from the blackbird, a symphony of light and dark brown from the moorhen, white with just a hint of pink in the mass of twigs that makes a wood pigeon's nest and the true "birds'-egg blue" splashed haphazardly with black of the song thrush. Egg-collecting is very much frowned on now. The loss of the actual egg is not so much the trouble; if the bird is still laying, she will quickly replace the missing treasure with a new one, as far as we know without even noticing the loss. However, the scent left by human marauders can give away the location of its nest to the sitting bird's natural predators, spelling the end of the whole clutch or worse.

Still, I wonder what can replace the outdoor fun of egg-collecting, the astonishment that these natural works of art can inspire when found and examined in the hand and the entrée into the world of natural history they provided. The French naturalist Jean-Henri Fabre, writing at the very end of the nineteenth century, waxed eloquent about the power of birds' eggs to fascinate the young. Having admitted some of the local children into his study in which "a thousand curious things are arranged,"[5] he noticed that while they politely admired his collection of exotic seashells, "It is quite another story with the boxes in which the birds'-eggs of the district are arranged. . . . Now their cheeks flush with

5 It still exists in a little village outside Orange. An aging custodian who lives on the premises will open the house for you and let you shuffle quite unsupervised past case after case of all manner of specimens just as Fabre had left them. It is still captivating, and when you have had enough of the dusty interior, you can refresh yourself with a walk in the wonderful

excitement and they whisper, in one another's ears, which they would choose of the finest group in the box. There is no amazement now, but ingenuous admiration. It is true that the egg recalls the nest and the young birds, those incomparable joys of childhood. Nevertheless, a rush of reverent emotion evoked by the beautiful may be read on their faces. The gems of the sea astound my little visitors; the simple beauty of the eggs arouses a more human ecstasy." And in my own case, these "incomparable joys of childhood" provided some of my fondest memories of a grandfather who was at most other times terrifying to children.

I also learned that birding expeditions have from time to time their embarrassing side. The first summer after I went to boarding school, my parents took me to the south of France and threw in a couple of days bird-watching as compensation for a heavy tour of French cathedrals and chateaux. On a beach near St. Tropez, while focusing my binoculars on a purple heron (my first), I found I was in the midst of a nudist colony. And at school, I was still very unworldly when the Divinity master took the ornithological club to visit a sewage treatment plant. There were plenty of birds — great-crested grebes, waterfowl of all sorts — and a vast number of things that looked like shed skins floating in the water. I drew the chaplain's attention to these with unsuspecting curiosity, but he replied somewhat distractedly that we didn't need to dwell on them as "they were not of the animal kingdom." Most mortifying of all was one summer afternoon walking with my parents around the pond in St. James's Park, no great distance from school. Suddenly an avian squabble blew up at our feet. A female mallard had grabbed a sparrow by its neck and was waddling as fast as it could toward the lake. To my intense embarrassment (suppose someone from school should see), both my parents bounded across the ankle-high fence ("Don't Walk on the Grass") shouting at the predator. My father tried to hook it with the end of his umbrella, but it was too late. The duck was by this time well out of range

---

wild garden that he created out of a bit of wasteland in the Provençal countryside. He called his refuge the Harmas: "the name given in this district, to an untilled, pebbly expanse abandoned to the vegetation of the thyme. It is too poor to repay the work of the plough; but the sheep passes there in spring, when it has chanced to rain and a little grass shoots up."

in the water where it proceeded to drown the unfortunate sparrow, leaving me alone on the path and ashamed of my self-consciousness.

I got to hone my bird-watching skills on the other side of the Atlantic as well. Back in New York for the Easter holidays one year, I had left my binoculars in England. So when I advanced on The Ramble in Central Park, it was armed with my mother's mother-of-pearl opera glasses. The Ramble is a treasure trove for bird-watchers, especially in spring. I quickly found a group of die-hard birders who took me under their wing. One was a dentist with a strong southern accent, another was a Park Avenue doctor and the most colorful was a mapmaker from the Lower East Side, whose bushy beard had earned him the moniker Castro. They were a godsend, both for their knowledge of the birds just beginning to return for the summer and for their superior spotting equipment with which they were very generous throughout my vacation. They were just as generous when I returned at Christmas and took me out on the Audubon Christmas Bird Count. So I was very pleased when I had the chance to return the favor. Just before I had to return to school, there was great excitement when a very rare lesser white-fronted goose showed up from northern Europe on Jones Beach; its photograph made the *New York Times*: "First of Kind Seen on Continent" ran the headline. For some reason, of my birding friends only Castro was around, and he could not drive. So I enlisted my mother as chauffeur, and out we went and found it.

My daily visits to Central Park produced many "life" birds and also the occasion for the first real money I ever earned. A columnist for *The Observer*, the English Sunday newspaper, was a frequent visitor to our house, and he asked me to help him with some local color for a column he was writing about Central Park. When his article came out, he described the park as "a vast rectangle . . . cut, like a skylight, into the richest part of the city . . . walled in by a tumultuous rampart of skyscrapers." Thanks to me, London learned that "you can find groups of bird-watchers, serious and scholarly, kind and easy people who exchange information as others do stamps. Central Park is on one of the two main north-south highways for migratory birds. It is a sudden oasis in the desert of stone and noise. So here they can find birds with crisp American names like grackles, cardinals, towhees and flickers. Or they may come upon a gold-crested kinglet or even a xanthochroic chickadee. And the watchers go home as pleased as if they had made money." He added a footnote to the word "xanthochroic": "This, I am told, means possessing the tendency to turn yellow." It was a nice wink at me.

After that my birding activities went into remission for a while. Consumed by my new interest in music, I left my binoculars in their case hanging on a peg in that oubliette of old houses, the cupboard under the stairs. The only new bird I came across was the forest bird in *Siegfried* when I made my first pilgrimage to Bayreuth. But although my life-list lay thrust in the back of a drawer, birds continued to add an incidental extra of interest whenever I traveled.[6] Flocks of evening grosbeaks brightened the winter I first came to live in America as an adult. Back in Amberley after an absence of several years, I spotted a pair of bullfinches in the overgrown garden—the first time I had seen them there. In another way I could tell my old interest was only dormant: where other people might see a tit, I knew whether it was a blue, great or coal; a hawk didn't exist unless I could tell it was a sharp-shin or Cooper's; and if I simply had no idea, I still made a beeline for my old field guide.

And I started collecting antique prints of birds, Audubons and Goulds as well as anonymous artists whose subjects caught my fancy. On a visit to the Berkshires, a fall of warblers in their springtime best dazzled me. That summer, I spent a lot of time in a house (it was really a shack) on stilts in an estuary in Wells, Maine. I woke one morning to find a flock of glossy ibis, dark and hunchbacked, feeding in the salt pans just outside my window. Stalking over the spartina with their startlingly prehistoric aspect, they looked like visitors from another geological era as well as migrants from the south. Further off, a pair of white waders were decorously stalking their prey. As one moved almost imperceptibly forward, it raised a dainty claw out of the water, and automatically I strained to see whether it was black (an immature little blue heron) or gold (a snowy

6 Thanks to some nifty computer software, I have been assiduously reconstructing my life-list—four decades of sporadic bird-watching—by searching in my old guides and journals for odd bits of paper and old envelopes on which I might have scribbled the names of birds seen on journeys to exotic places. And now that I have it "up and running," I am more aware of the regular visitors to my yard.

egret). I was getting hooked again. The salt marsh's primeval landscape was working its magic, too: the changing play of light on the sodden salt marsh hay, the ebb and flow of the tides and the right moment to pick up the fork and bucket and go out to dig for clams. As the mud squelched up between my toes, it was easy to feel in the presence of creation itself. I could not know that twenty-five years later, the protection of that same estuary would loom large in my work at the Maine Audubon Society.

Soon after we were married, my wife and I visited her sister who was working in a biological station in the Camargue, the great delta of the Rhône River, and living in another ramshackle building, a run-down old *mas* or farmhouse. Our first morning, we were greeted by a family of Little Owls: the incident started when one of the nestlings, like a large ball of dirty cotton wool, fell onto the bed in which we were sleeping. The mother soon appeared, peering nervously through the hole in the ceiling and hissing instructions to her offspring. It was the first time I had been in the Camargue since that trip to the south of France with my parents. Now I was back, rubbing shoulders with the ornithologists who had brought the flamingos back to the area. One morning we watched them, a pink cloud in the distance, from the battlements of Aigues Mortes from where St. Louis and his Crusaders departed for the Holy Land. Late that afternoon we counted seventy pairs of marsh harriers flying in to roost for the night, making a vast reed-bed as busy as an airport. At dusk we visited a cave in the hills where the eagle owl hooted for her mate as he started the evening hunt on enormous but silent wings. And I finally saw my first hoopoe. When I approached too close, he fanned his crest in alarm, and then what had been a pinky, cinnamon-colored bird turned into a flying zebra, the white and black bars on his wings flapping their lazy butterfly beat across the land.[7] We celebrated that event in a room whose ceiling was pockmarked from the impact of champagne corks

---

7 According to an ancient Eastern tale, the hoopoe was once King Solomon's messenger. "One day King Solomon was oppressed by the heat of the sun, and the Hoopoe came and made for him of their wings an umbrella and a sheltering. So pleased was Solomon he said to these birds, 'Ask anything you wish, and I will give it.' Foolish indeed were they, and asked to be allowed to wear a golden crown just like his. So each hoopoe went out with a golden

celebrating the staff's significant sightings, or *coches*, each one circled, noted and dated.

That summer, working at a theater in the Berkshires, I would listen to the descending song, like a double-helix, of the veery as it wafted into my office from the woods outside. I used to bicycle the half dozen miles to the theater from where we were staying through the farmland of the Tyringham valley, one of the prettiest spots in the world. One day, I rode past a recently killed flicker lying by the road. I stopped to pick it up and was entranced by the exquisite colors and patterns on its feathers. I thought of it a dozen years later when I heard Roger Tory Peterson describe how at an impressionable age, it was a close encounter with a flicker that turned him into an ornithologist. "There was this bundle of brown feathers in a tree. I thought it was dead. I poked it and it burst into color, with the red on the back of its head and the gold on its wing. It was the contrast, you see, between something I thought was dead and something so alive. Like a resurrection."

And so my interest in birds was resurrected, too, not by a rarity like the white-fronted goose, but by the birds of our backyard like that beautiful flicker. When the theater closed at the end of the summer, I decided it was time to trade in the performing arts for conservation, and I went to work for the Massachusetts Audubon Society. It was a very conscious return to my natural history roots. At a philosophical level, if our aspirations as a species are to be realized in the arts, we need a clean environment to live in. It is a more refined pyramid of need than Brecht's *"Erst kommt das Fressen, dann kommt die Moral,"*[8] but a pyramid, nonetheless, and I wanted my work to be closer to its base. And at a personal level, the environment offered me a chance to be more closely involved in the issues, whereas the absence of any performing skills would always relegate me to playing an administrative rather than a creative role in the arts.

---

crown, and were immediately set upon and slain in great numbers by the avaricious, who hitherto had not considered them worthy of attention." Arvind Nehra, *Letters of an Indian Judge to an English Gentlewoman.*

8 First comes the grub, then come the morals.

It was Mass Audubon that started the Audubon movement in 1896, when two Boston ladies launched a campaign to get their friends to stop wearing egret plumes. Feathers good enough for a lady's hat had to be taken during the breeding season when they are at their finest. Thus the killing of a single bird could take with it a whole generation and threaten the species itself. Mass Audubon went on to become the largest conservation organization in Massachusetts (and one of the largest in the country). From a storefront at the foot of Boston's Beacon Hill, it had moved out to an imposing brick mansion in the suburb of Lincoln, a town justly proud of its carefully conserved landscape. If I had had any doubts about this shift in career, they were dispelled the first day as I climbed the grand staircase past original elephant folio prints from Audubon's *The Birds of America,* hand-colored by Robert Havell. It was this work, well-known to the Boston ladies, from which the new movement had taken its name. In keeping with Mass Audubon's mission—as if to galvanize us in our work—the pictures chosen were of the birds that had become extinct since John James had painted them: passenger pigeon, Carolina parakeet, Labrador duck and ivory-billed woodpecker. In these works, my twin interests of art and nature were combined.

I hadn't been in my new job a week before the not-so-subtle distinction between bird-watcher and ornithologist was borne in on me. Used to being the resident expert on things avian, I was quickly humbled by the Mass Audubon crowd. Nothing makes a person feel quite so sheepish as loudly "calling" an osprey that a split-second later turns into a black-backed gull.[9] Of course, it is just as frustrating not to make the call first when you turn out to be right, but that is a sin of omission (with no one to razz you) rather than very public commission.

When we were living in England, my wife, who is quick to mark down

---

9 Note to tyros: circling high in the sky, the birds have a superficial resemblance, but if you have the slightest question in your mind, it's always the gull. You will know with certainty when it is the osprey. That said, even Audubon directors make the wrong call sometimes!

an English foible when she sees one, wrote a provocative "letter from abroad" for the Boston Globe. She professed to find British bird-watching an "elitist sport" and compared it negatively with its more "companionable" American form. Her star witness was Jerry Bertrand, Allen Morgan's successor as head of Mass Audubon, who among other things told her, "You get dumped on for calling a bird wrong [in England]—something I'm never ashamed to do." Which makes birding with Jerry so thrilling as well as enjoyable an experience. Even the best bird-watchers make mistakes . . . and birders in pubs and bars still chortle over them and make famous such calls as "So-and-so's tinamou," which turned out to be a domestic chicken.

In bird-watching, there is a well-defined gradient ranging from keenness, through expertness, to sheer manic compulsiveness. The British, who were generally speaking the original bird-watchers,[10] have a word for the last: the "twitcher." You know you are out with a twitcher when in the depths of some woody dell you hear this kind of question: "Who needs a short-toed tree creeper?" (for their year/month/day/whatever list, understood[11]). The implication is that he has the bird in his "bins" and will point it out to you if you "need" it (i.e., have not already seen one). Some say the term "twitcher" describes the display of uncontrollable excitement when the looked-for bird is found, rather like the agitation that nestlings exhibit when they beseech their parent for a nice worm or sand eel. I tend to think of it as an expressionistic description of the rapid-fire "ticks" with which the twitcher confirms his sightings in his tattered field guide.[12] And yes, twitchers are predominantly male; there

10 On August 7, 1778, Gilbert White wrote from Selbourne: "A good ornithologist should be able to distinguish birds by their air as well as by their colours and shape; on the ground as well as on the wing, and in the bush as well as in the hand. For, though it must not be said that every species of bird has a manner peculiar to itself, yet there is somewhat in most genera at least, that at first sight discriminates them, and enables a judicious observer to pronounce upon them with some certainty."

11 I once watched with some amusement as a notorious twitcher paced and fumed at the bald eagle on which his telescope was trained a mile away on frozen Quabbin Reservoir, willing the bird to cross the county line only yards from where it was tearing at a deer carcass so that he could add it to his county list.

12 According to Bird Watching, a British magazine, the term "comes from the most extreme

are exceptions, but traditionally bird-watching has been a manly pur-suit.[13] It is easy to smile at a twitcher obsessed with his lists, but noting the species one comes across according to place (the backyard list) or time (the annual list) is not a bad way to keep exploring the familiar—knowing it better—instead of taking it for granted.

The earliest reference to birding I know of comes from Shakespeare. "I do invite you tomorrow morning to my house to breakfast; after we'll a-birding together," says Master Page to assuage Ford's jealous mood in *The Merry Wives of Windsor*.[14] Shakespeare's sport is a convivial activity designed to soothe the soul. (It also serves to clear the way for the plot, Falstaff's supposed tryst with his wife: "He's a-birding, sweet Sir John.") This more relaxed approach is where I am most comfortable. I don't mind admitting that there are certain groups of birds I can't be bothered with on my own. I am happy to leave them to others to sort out. For example, I don't get very much further with American sparrows than the obvious ones like chipping or song or white-throated. And just as some people don't do windows, I draw the line at gulls. For each gull you must know at least three birds—juvenile, first year, as well as adult—and however different these phases may be from one another, they are ago-nizingly similar stage by stage to all the other gulls, or so it seems to me. Such a practical if lazy approach to bird-watching is rather more com-mon than one might expect, even among experts. Spotting a drab little

cases in which some twitchers exhibit heightened anxiety, displays of extreme nervous energy and mood swings from elation to despair. 'Twitching' often involves long distance travel in the single-minded pursuit of rare birds. In many instances regardless of expense, safety, domestic bliss and, in some cases, the law!" *Bird Watching*, May 1994.

13 See Ann Harries's *Manly Pursuits*, an engaging historical novel in which Cecil Rhodes, Oscar Wilde, Dr. Leander Jameson, Lewis Carroll, and Rudyard Kipling are linked in a nar-rative spun around Rhodes's wish to hear British birdsong in the African veldt before he died.

14 Page adds, "I have a fine hawk for the bush," so we can assume the expedition was more than just a bird-watching one. Hunting and birding were intimately linked until quite recently when superior optics made a shot unnecessary if all one wanted was to admire. Just think of Audubon himself whose first impulse on seeing a bird was to shoot it, although, as his memoirs make clear, his love for birds from a very early age was as great as any twitcher's, and his understanding probably a good deal greater. To this day, the argument rages among scientists over the necessity of "collecting" even endangered species.

bird skulking along the shores of a magnificent lake in northern Greece one day, I asked a friend — a professional ornithologist who knows all there is to be known about the Dalmatian pelican — its name. For answer he gave a Gallic shrug, opining that he studies pelicans only because they are big enough to recognize.

Which is not to say that I cannot be quite easily infected with the twitcher's obsessive excitement when I am with other "birders out on a spree." That was the disgruntled comment from a Maine Audubon member who had joined me and a friend on an expedition to Monhegan, an island ten miles off the coast of Maine. It was the first field trip I had led for Maine Audubon, and I assumed — forgivably, I think — that I had an eager band of birders with me. Fall migration was in full swing. As we made our way to Black Head on the northern end of the island, birds were everywhere. In one opening in the woods, a young merlin put on a terrific show giving a flicker a run for its money among the spruces. But that was nothing to what awaited us at the tip of the island where wave after wave of migrating warblers were coming ashore. Poised to meet them were another couple of merlins who were having a banquet. It was a spellbinding display of nature and her intractable (and, if you were an exhausted warbler, cataclysmic) ways. This conscienceless capriciousness is the chasm separating our species from the natural world; across it never the twain shall meet, but peering into it there is much to admire and learn from. My friend and I could not take our eyes — or binoculars — off the spectacle. Eventually one of us looked round only to find that our entire group had melted away and returned to the hotel.

◆§§◆

I should have learned the lesson some years earlier — on a trip to France with two dozen birders — that not everyone carrying binoculars and a Peterson field guide has limitless patience. Our itinerary took us through the Alps, and although it was mid-May, it was beginning to snow by the time we reached our last stop before lunch. Only a couple of the hardiest left the bus with me, but it was a noble cause: to find the elusive wall creeper (which would be a long-sought life bird for me). We promised we would give it twenty minutes and then return, successful or not. As we slogged up the side of the mountain, a pair of ptarmigan got up, giving us a respectable look at them before flying over a ridge. But where was the wall creeper? We looked at our watches, and decided we had just enough time to go as far as a likely-looking outcrop a hundred yards ahead; if it wasn't there, we would turn back. Once there, however, we spied only a little further off some even more likely wall creeper habitat. And so it went, like the stereotypic male not stopping for directions: just one more turn, then if I don't recognize the road I will ask the way. In the heat of the chase, we lost all thought of our comrades on the bus. Our tenacity was eventually rewarded: *Tichodroma muraria* put in a brief but exquisite appearance. And at the same moment there came from afar the most extraordinary racket. Turning, we looked back to the road where one of the ladies, crazed with hunger, was smiting the side of the bus with a wrench borrowed from the driver's tool-kit. Momentarily paralyzed by such an abrupt shift in reality, we could only stare as thud after thud, each one a split-second after the stroke, reverberated across the valley. It was as a chastened leader that I climbed aboard the bus some time later, but inside I glowed with triumph: I had seen the wall creeper.

How do you know when to call a halt to the search or tear your eyes way from some grand performance? Watching birds is one of those pastimes that will fill all the time and space available, and it is as well to have at least plenty of time on your side. Wildlife does not perform for us on cue, and excursions into the world of nature are as unpredictable as anything I know. A host of setbacks, of which weather is the most minor, wait on your advance into the field. If you are looking for a particular bird that is either shy or rare, the chances of being disappointed are quite high. And at the end of the day, when failure stares you in the face, the consolation that you have still the future excitement of finding it to look forward to is cold comfort.

At which point my puritan side will have me believe that bird-watching would be an uninteresting sport indeed if I could always count on finding the bird straightaway. The fun is in the pursuit, he says, and the loss of the sense of challenge and adventure would dampen my enjoyment. It may be so, but on a cold rainy day? One December morning at an ungodly hour I rolled out of bed and into a van carrying a bunch of excited bird-watchers eager to check out reports of the first calliope hummingbird ever seen in the state of New York (and in December at that). When we arrived at the appointed spot, an urban park at the tip of Manhattan, and as the light turned from night to murk, I wondered pessimistically how we would ever spot our bird, a creature no bigger than a large moth. Then as if on cue, the bird flew more or less between raindrops right up to where we stood. It proceeded to hang around us for twenty minutes investigating the weary remains of a few flowers until it was time for us to leave. Would my sense of satisfaction have been any greater had we "thrashed" the patch all morning before putting it up? With hot coffee waiting for us back at the hotel, I doubt it.

But so cooperative a bird is in my experience the exception. Instead of playing the odds around a particular quest, I would rather broaden my horizons. Too pointed a search limits what one would otherwise bring back in terms of experience. The tale of an old Nantucket sea captain who returned empty-handed from a long whaling trip is instructive. Temporarily forgetting his Quaker manners, he exploded, "We never saw a single wall-eyed, son-of-a-seacook, blankety-blankety whale." Then remembering that he was in the meeting house, he added quickly: "But we had a very fine sail." Anticipation of anything more specific than a great day out runs the risk of disappointment.

Above all as we set off into the woods or along the shore, a singular goal is unnecessary as a measure of success when all of nature is out there to explore. We should take her as she comes instead of letting dreams of rarities or thoughts of adding to the life-list attempt to control the order of her appearance. Moments when light, place and accidental encounter come together in an unforgettable epiphany happen when least expected; surprise is part of their charm. It is worth cultivating a state of mind that is open to such experiences, but it is one that is easily frightened away by over-expectations.

By the same token, the happenstance of chance encounters can make us celebrate the familiar, helping us to get the best out of our everyday surroundings instead of overlooking them. As a fairly faithful runner, I have a route near my home, and one of the things that keeps me at it is that every day it shows me something new. Occasionally it will be a flower that has just bloomed, but nine times out of ten, it will be concerned with birds: a racket of crows pinning down a barred owl trying to relax, a gathering of ducks that keep me tuned to the seasons or an infrequent visitor that adds a new dimension to my familiar landscape. To encounter all that so easily makes one realize how much we are missing as we surrender to the hurly-burly of daily schedules that drive us from pillar to post. An unknown bird I passed on the highway the other day —I thought it might have been a shrike—made a mute statement about being in the moment. Was it a shrike? I would like to have stopped, but I was in a hurry to get nowhere in particular. The truth of its identity prickled my consciousness for a day or two. Apart from that, I missed the chance for a healing moment that could have

> . . . *given my heart*
> *A change of mood*
> *And saved some part*
> *Of a day I had rued*

as Robert Frost found when a crow dusted him with snow as he walked beneath the tree it was perching in.

ᘛᗰᘚ

As a calliope hummingbird in New York City attests, one great advantage of bird-watching as a hobby is that it can be pursued almost anywhere. You don't have to head for the wilderness. Birders can (and do— see note on twitchers) travel far afield after exotic species and places, but there is almost always plenty to see right at home. As a city boy, I learned that nature can be found in the most seemingly unlikely places—The Ramble in Central Park, for instance, or the floodlights around Cleopatra's Needle behind the Metropolitan Museum where the first pioneer house finches built their nests. A fall of brightly colored warblers in spring can turn a dusty urban park into a lush wilderness, as Wendell Berry points out in his poem "The Wild."

In the empty lot — a place
not natural, but wild — among
the trash of human absence,

the slough and shamble
of the city's seasons, a few
old locusts bloom.

A few woods birds
fly and sing
in the new foliage

warblers and tanagers, birds
wild as leaves; in a million
each one would be rare,

new to the eyes. A man
couldn't make a habit
of such color,

such flights and singing.
But they're the habit of this
wasted place. In them

the ground is wise. They are
its remembrance of what it is.

I was recently in just such a place as this, a couple of blocks that, two years before, had been even more of a wasteland, an illegal dump on the south side of Chicago. Abetted by a community leader who had a vision for a more wholesome neighborhood, a team of kids from the local school were in the process of reclaiming it. They had been on a school field trip to one of the many forest preserves that ring the city and came back inspired. Their enthusiasm turned to disappointment when they realized that one outing in nature was all that their school could afford.

And so they decided to clean up the empty lot and build their own nature preserve for their own community. Already a cardinal was brightening the landscape, the butterflies were coming back to feed on the native prairie flowers they had planted and, for a triumphant moment, a peregrine eyed us from above as it soared over this patch of recovering ground. A HUD program once ran a television ad in which a city dweller said, "I knew the neighborhood was coming back when I heard the birds again." Such is the power of Mother Nature, and birds are her prophets.

Of all the different phyla, birds possess a unique fascination for us humans. They frequent our myths — for example Athena's owl, Odin's ravens — and serve as enduring symbols like the dove in the Bible from Noah's Ark to the Holy Ghost. On a less elevated plane, many more people watch birds, at least to some degree, than they do, for instance, butterflies. Because there are twice as many different species of bird as there are of mammals, the amateur naturalist is able to enjoy the additional variety, without getting to the mind-numbing numbers of plants and invertebrates. From the cranes kept as a status symbol by tribesmen in Pakistan, to the chickadees visiting literally millions of feeders in the United States — to, I am sorry to say, the honey buzzards shot as they migrate across the Straits of Messina to enhance the virility of Calabrian hunters — birds enjoy (or pay for) a closer relationship with our species than any other nondomesticated order of animal. Even TV mob boss Tony Soprano is moved to tears by a family of ducks in his swimming pool.

No doubt part of the reason is that the majority of birds are diurnal and highly visible; and they are ubiquitous. When I applied for a job at the International Council for Bird Preservation (ICBP)[15] I was asked to define the appeal of birds in a hundred and fifty words, which ultimately became the introduction for the ICBP's brochure.

Wherever we live, birds stand out from the rest of the animal kingdom, uniquely capturing our imagination. Their flight is a universal symbol of freedom, and

---

15 Now Birdlife International.

their songs, colors and displays have inspired human beings throughout the ages . . . Birds are an international treasure we cannot afford to waste. On their wings the imagination of all mankind can soar.

Leonardo captioned his drawing of a bird sitting in a cage, "Thoughts turn towards hope." According to his contemporary biographer, Vasari, he would buy birds in the market just for the pleasure of setting them free.[16]

In earliest times, at least in the temperate parts of the world, our species learned to calculate with considerable accuracy the solstices and equinoxes, and they devised rituals to ensure that the earth would stay on its course. In their rock alignments, monuments like Stonehenge and Maes Howe preserve a record of our ancestors' knowledge of the sun's annual trajectory. They must also have marked the year's progress by the seasonal arrival of migratory birds from the north or south and their subsequent departure the other side of the solstice. This changing of the guard continues to invite us to celebrate the changes of the year, long after the shortening and lengthening of days ceased to be mysteries. And if we are in danger of taking our patch for granted, the arriving birds, especially in their breeding best, can quickly revive our interest. We anticipate the first swallow and mark the date of its arrival; as each new warbler arrives, we note its appearance. As in my backyard, spring comes with considerable fanfare; no matter how fickle the weather, the songs and colors of our summer visitors assure us that the planet is still on its course.

Where we greeted the swallow's arrival with singular precision as if it were returning to our private Capistrano, departure is a collective phenomenon that builds over weeks as if to milk our melancholy sense of time passing. When I was a child, the lines of swallows on the telephone wires were as much a sign of the summer holidays ending as were the ripening apples in the orchard. But my sense of loss is now mitigated by the excitement of the changing seasons and by the spectacle of the omens of departure as they build: waders start massing along the tide-line

16 *The Notebooks of Leonardo da Vinci.*

(though our summer may be scarcely half over), kettles of hawks make leaden fall skies come alive and, as the Earth completes one more circle, rafts of waterfowl gather in the bay at winter's end, ready to head for their breeding grounds in the north. An awareness of these comings and goings connects us spiritually to nature's cycles and makes something enduring of our backyards. When *we* do the migrating, capable of flying faster and farther than any bird, we miss the season's changes and sacrifice for the year part of our connection to the land.

While academic painters were painting sentimental pictures of swallows leaving and young lovers' regret (Scottish concertgoers will find a lovely example in Edinburgh's Usher Hall), coalminers were taking a canary with them into the pits to test for poisonous gases. Because of its immediate connection with human health, this avian image has become the metaphor for early signs of environmental degradation. However, it was the killing of birds for their plumage that got the conservation movement rolling and gave it its first success. The organizations that formed to save the birds from the milliners—Audubon in the United States, the Royal Society for the Protection of Birds (RSPB) in Britain—are today among the oldest and most respected conservation groups in the world. In this sense it can truly be said that "in the beginning was the bird." Later on, with aigrettes no longer in fashion, these organizations took on a new adversary, market gunners. At the turn of the century, to bring sufficient quantities of birds to growing city markets, hunters would blaze away into the huge flocks of migrating waterfowl using punt guns—basically a cannon mounted on a skiff. Since most of the ducks and geese being massacred were migratory species whose range could span continents, they needed to be protected along the entire length of their journey. By the 1920s, market gunning had been abolished, and in the process conservation had been taken out of the backyard and into the international arena; ICBP was founded in 1922.

Birds spawned the next great step forward in conservation, too. This time it was not a campaign to stop something but rather practical encouragement and guidance from one of conservation's great visionaries, Roger Tory Peterson. It goes without saying that he was first and foremost a birder, and his breakthrough *Field Guide to the Birds* with its system for identifying birds by highlighting their most obvious field marks made bird-watchers out of a generation. No one knows for sure, but somewhere between 12 and 13 million copies have been printed since it was published in 1934.[17]

Having been lucky enough to go birding with Peterson in the Camargue when I worked for ICBP, I invited him to speak at the American launch of *Save the Birds* (a book on international bird conservation for which he had written a chapter) at Maine Audubon. In addition to his easy, gentle manner at the various events—book-signings, receptions, bird walks—two memories are especially clear. When it was time to leave, he was deep in conversation with several of us about the spread of the house finch across America. Evidently, having got a foothold on the East Coast, the two populations of this originally western bird had expanded toward one another until scarcely 500 miles between them was house-finch-free. The great man was already running late for his next appointment, but nothing would hurry him away from so enthralling a discussion. If the subject was birds, he would talk to anyone and at any length.

The other memory came from an earlier panel discussion when he recalled learning of the death of his friend James Fisher, the English "Peterson." His eyes grew misty as he told of a dream he had had of Fisher surrounded by radiant light. When I heard of Roger's death in 1996, I could not but remember this, and wonder if the world's "next" great ornithologist was somewhere mourning Roger's passing. A friend gave me the answer. There is no one such person. Roger Tory Peterson's legacy is that instead of passing the baton to another individual, he passed it on to millions of people for whom he opened the doors of bird-watching and natural history. In the fulsome words of ABC's Peter Jennings, Peterson "turned the skies into a cathedral for the worship of living things," and he did it for people all over the world.

17 Roger Tory Peterson Institute.

In the tropical countries of the developing world, where conservation is trying hard to take hold against fearful human problems, birds are once more in the vanguard, just as they were in Europe and America a century ago. That is the underpinning of Birdlife International's conservation programs. On the island of Mauritius I worked with an energetic young Hindu who was starting a conservation education program to complement the remarkable efforts to save three endemic birds now reduced to pitiful numbers. It was sobering to capture in the viewfinder of my camera almost all of the remnants of wild Mauritius, a few mountainsides that represented virtually the entire habitat of the Mauritius kestrel, and to see the invasive strangler figs literally clawing their way up the sides of the valley. The dozen pink pigeons feeding in the branches of an endemic tree represented more than half the wild population. Most precarious of all was perhaps the sole surviving pair of echo parakeets. Key to the success of the Wildlife Clubs of Mauritius was the growing sense of national pride in these three birds, which occur nowhere else in the world.

Some ecologists maintain that the time has come for triage, and that in order to save the most of the world's biological diversity, we should focus our attention on so-called centers of endemism, which occur on continents, and leave the relatively impoverished islands to their own devices. (Looked at another way, when the world's most competitive birders set out to beat the world record for birds seen in one year, they ignore all but the larger islands, even though each may have its own unique set of species, because islands don't have the bang for the buck in terms of numbers.) From the point of view of a strictly scientific zero-sum game, this is doubtless true. But such a strategy ignores the value of the birds to island nations as symbols of pride on which a conservation ethic can be built.

My Mauritian visit gave me insights into the conservation problems of the part of the world where 75 percent of the world's endangered birds are to be found, the developing countries of the Tropics. Nonetheless, of all the goods that bird-watching bestows, in the end the first and most obvious are the opportunities found at home in the everyday—even, in Wendell Berry's phrase, "the habit of this wasted space." If this is curious in a sport that would seem to thrive on finding something new, the familiar is at the heart of a paradox in other ways as well. To me, it is axiomatic that one is most likely to see something wonderful when least expecting it. Looking too hard restricts the field of vision. Time after time, while my mind is apparently wandering, an almost imperceptible nuance will attract my attention. A pale bundle in a tree as I speed along the highway was absent from the trees already passed, and that is enough for eye to connect with brain and in a split-second produce a red-tailed hawk watching the median strip for its next meal. My mind wasn't wandering after all; instead, relieving the brain of its daily distractions, it remained clear and secretly alert. This kind of awareness of the whole transcends more focused searching. It allows subliminal differences that would otherwise be blotted out by overattention—a twig moving with a motion it shouldn't; the shape, no matter how small, whose precision jars the pattern around it—to attract the gaze. Suddenly the bird materializes, as does the image in one of those "Magic Eye" illustrations when with optical muscles relaxed you find exactly the right focus to see the picture hidden within the design. In the case of bird-spotting, it is probably more accurate to say that the focus finds you; anyone who has tramped past the edge of a pool and had a bittern take shape amid a hitherto featureless mass of reeds will know what I mean. Suddenly the bird is blindingly obvious, although a companion may struggle to find it, even knowing that it's there.

An open mind is also the best defense against the temptation to construct a hierarchy or attach a value to one particular sighting over another. Enjoying nature should not be about stars and prima donnas but rather an ensemble effort. What could be more absurd than the frequently heard birder's question, "Anything about?" unless it is the response, "Nope," when there isn't something *new* to look at? Some birders refer to "trash birds," meaning ones that are ubiquitous and therefore uninteresting. Of course we have all done it, at least in our hearts, as we cast a common chickadee from our binoculars and rush them to another site that may turn up something more unusual. Too often, we feel driven by the conflict between the need to see it all and some great stopwatch in the sky. But if we take the time to linger on even a "trash bird," we may well be witness to some bit of avian activity that rekindles a jaded interest. Watch a bird taking materials to build a nest (note the alert, suspicious eye), the arrowlike flight into a hole (how can it be so accurate not to have to brake?) or the sudden change in direction of a flight of birds (how do they synchronize their movements and which one makes the decision?). At the feeder, "just a chickadee" is a miracle: of charm, of tenacity, of biological efficiency.

Aldo Leopold described one such bird—#65290—in terms that combined a naturalist's observation with a humorous touch that appears to spring directly from his subject. The number referred to the band Leopold clamped round its little leg; this particular bird obtained its elevated status by outliving its comrades from the "class of 1937" by a year or two.

When he first entered our trap, he showed no visible evidence of genius. Like his classmates, his valor for suet was greater than his discretion. Like his classmates, he bit my finger while being taken out of the trap. When banded and released he fluttered up to a limb, pecked his new aluminum anklet in mild annoyance, shook his mussed feathers, cursed gently, and hurried away to catch up with the gang. It is doubtful whether he drew any philosophical deductions from his experience (such as "all is not ants' eggs that glitters"), for he was caught again three times that winter.

Such a passage makes me want to peer into the eye of any passing chickadee and try to see what of 65290's personal charm it has inherited.

Nature study in general and bird-watching in particular can be a practice that keeps us fresh and points out when we are getting blasé. It makes us look at the familiar more deeply and learn to cherish what we might take for granted. When my three-year-old son met a blue jay at our feeder for the first time, I remember how excited he was to see something so beautiful. It was a salutary experience to see this bird again for the first time through the eyes of a child.[18] It made me realize what a strikingly

---

18 As Art Linkletter said, "Kids say the darndest things." Shortly after we moved from

colored bird it is, and I thought how exotic it must have seemed to the Pilgrims just off the Mayflower from England, as exotic as a toucan or macaw would be to me.

The point was pressed home again the other day when I came upon an American blue jay exalted in a glass case in the bird section of La Specola, the venerable natural history museum in Florence. *Cyanocitta cristata* is indeed a brighter bird than its European cousin, which I saw flitting about the Boboli Gardens next door. It made me wonder why I should have set such store by seeing, for instance, the Mauritius olive white-eye, a drab enough little bird but down to a hundred or so individuals on a single island, and sneeze at the blue jay. Isn't there something a little perverse about making a virtue out of endangeredness and a bore out of the commonplace, regardless of the intrinsic beauty of either?

When Aldous Huxley, appalled at the avian mortality caused by pesticides, complained that "we are destroying half the basis of English poetry," he was not thinking of the Mauritius olive white-eye. Poets have not on the whole concerned themselves with rare or obscure birds, but rather ones with a particular appeal to some aspect of human values. One need think only of Shelley's "To a Skylark," possibly the most intense exploration of the joy that birds can bring to us mortals. Sadly, larks are in decline in my part of England, and walks across the Downs have become the poorer for it. One may hear a single song where once were many piling trill upon flight, flight upon trill—or in the poet's words, "And singing still dost soar, and soaring ever singest." Thomas Hardy paid homage to poet and the poem's "blithe spirit" when nearly seventy years later he tramped the fields around Leghorn on the Italian coast (where Shelley drowned) in a metaphysical search for the little bird's remains:

> Somewhere afield here something lies
> In Earth's oblivious eyeless trust

England to Maine, my wife took our two-year-old son for a walk in the woods where they heard a towhee calling. "He's saying, 'Drink your tea,'" said my wife. When I joined them a little bit later, the towhee called again, and Alex informed me, "There's the bird that tells you to drink your coffee." It's one of my wife's favorite bits of family lore. She claims it was the moment she realized our son had become an American.

That moved a poet to prophecies —
A pinch of unseen, unguarded dust:

The dust of the lark that Shelley heard,
And made immortal through times to be; —
Though it only lived like another bird,
And knew not its immortality: . . .

As a naturalist, Hardy easily glides from poetic flight of fancy to ecological reality that makes his initial flight of fancy all the more touching.

Lived its meek life; then one day, fell —
A little ball of feather and bone;
And how it perished, when piped farewell,
And where it wastes, are alike unknown.

Maybe it rests in the loam I view,
Maybe it throbs in a myrtle's green,
Maybe it sleeps in the coming hue
Of a grape on the slopes of yon inland scene.

After some flowery imagery comes the punch line:

For it inspired a bard to win
Ecstatic heights in thought and rhyme.

That is one half of the poet's argument on behalf of the value of birds, as inspiration. The other is Longfellow's, also expressed in terms of heights, as wonder:

Sweeter than instrument of man e'er caught!
Whose habitations in the tree-tops even
Are half-way houses on the road to heaven!

I am glad to say that there has been a reaction to the conservation movement's dry rationales, developed in the wake of the World Conservation Strategy,[19] which emphasized nature's material use, as opposed to its spiritual value. My ICBP brochure spoke of "mysteries we have only begun to fathom. [Birds'] behaviour and genetic makeup conceal countless secrets that, when deciphered, may one day benefit humanity." Granted that, as the full dimensions of our environmental dilemma began to materialize out of the smog of industrial success, the language of socio-economics was essential if conservation was to become mainstream. But doing away with inspiration in favor of material trade-offs risked losing something ineffable that could be irrecoverable. At the turn of the last century, an increasing number of conservationists were beginning to reintroduce emotion, if not quite so effusively as Longfellow or Hardy, in their speeches. Audubon Societies base large parts of their programs on the "wow!" experience that can permanently shift a child's attitude toward nature. The most famous example is of course Roger Tory Peterson's flicker, but ask around and anyone for whom nature is in the least bit interesting will have had such an epiphany early in life. Chances are good that most people's "wow!" experience in some way involved a bird, and that it happened not in some vast lost wilderness, but in the backyard. I can still feel the thrill of my childhood discovery of a Baltimore oriole's nest, the extraordinary architecture, hanging from a tree just out of reach. It must have hung there deserted all winter; then came the spring day when the glorious bird itself completed the picture like something out of a fairy tale.

I suppose that in a way I am trying to recapture a little bit of that first astonishment each time I don my binoculars to go bird-watching. But if over the years it has become rarer to find myself mouth-openly surprised, the slack of excitement has been taken up by layers of more complex experience. Birds lead me to see things I had not seen before and to associations that range from the trivial to the poetic to the philosophic. With its slightly retroussé bill, a nuthatch, upside down on a tree trunk, points out a picture-perfect clutch of pinecones fit for a Hallmark card.

19 UNEP-IUCN-WWF, 1980.

The red reflections of a cardinal mirrored in a branch of maple blossoms become a carmine miniature: Narcissus in springtime. A fall of warblers on their way south poses unanswerable questions: with what examples of human weakness masquerading as strength will these tiny travelers have to contend, travelers whose long-distance endurance we cannot conceive?

Twitchers and contemplatives, conservationists and poets, whether we travel all over the world or like Thoreau a "good deal" in our home towns: we mostly have a bit of all of them in our makeup. As a harried politico told me looking out of his window in the State House, "It's my way to smell the roses. I take my binoculars wherever I go. It's a great way to start the day." The charm of birds—if we open ourselves to it—puts much in perspective, not least the true worth of our most familiar landmarks. Ironically for creatures who taught us to defy gravity, they can keep us wonderfully grounded. With more birders, those "kind and easy people" my journalist friend described more than forty years ago, the world would be a better place.

The Brave Days of Old

When the oldest cask is opened,
And the largest lamp is lit;
When the chestnuts glow in the embers,
And the kid turns on the spit;
When young and old in circle
Around the firebrands close;
When the girls are weaving baskets,
And the lads are shaping bows;
When the goodman mends his armour,
And trims his helmet's plume;
When the goodwife's shuttle merrily
Goes flashing through the loom;
With weeping and with laughter
Still is the story told,
How well Horatius kept the bridge
In the brave days of old.

　　—Thomas Babington Macaulay, "Horatius"

WHEN I WAS AT WESTMINSTER, my sport—or "station" in the school argot—was fencing. It provided on the whole an opportunity for philosophical discussions occasionally interrupted by the appearance of the energetic Austrian teacher who was supposed to be in charge. But on one occasion the feast of reason was interrupted by a dapper old gentleman who was being shown round the school by the headmaster. "So you kill people with swords, d'you?" he said. "Prefer guns m'self, heh! heh!" It was Field Marshal Montgomery.

I remembered this the day my son, aged twelve, came home from our local school having been impressed by the celebrity of his teacher's grandfather, a man who earned a place in the history books by inventing a means of detecting submarines.[20] Does everyone meet or is everyone related to someone famous he asked. It is a hard question to answer, not least because of the question within the question: What is so important about fame? As far as our ancestors are concerned, I think we enjoy a celebrated relation more for the precise navigational fix he or she gives us on our position in the sea of time than for any past glory that may reflect upon us. If Sir Thomas Urquhart—my namesake though not a direct ancestor—had been only an eccentric seventeenth-century Scotsman, instead of having played a modest part in the history of his times, he would be harder to visualize, although we might still enjoy the thought of him as a colorful character.

A glorious response to my son's question is in one of my favorite anthems, sung on many occasions in Westminster Abbey when I was at school: "Let us now praise famous men," taken from Ecclesiasticus and set by Vaughan Williams in the heyday of Edwardian choral music. After the "pomp and circumstance" style of the beginning, which celebrates, among others, "Leaders of the people by their counsels," a more elegiac mood sets in. "And some there be who have no memorial, who are perished as though they had never been; their bodies are buried in peace. . . ." They are the people who have contributed to the building of their country and society, and it is their effort, perhaps blind to the possibilities that we now enjoy, that nonetheless should confer an obligation on us. As the music rises in triumph once again—". . . but their name liveth for evermore!"—it always brings a democratic lump to my throat.

But in reality it was not always thus. Based on the hardships of his own childhood in rural France at the beginning of the nineteenth century, Jean-Henri Fabre, who became the father of French entomology, wrote,

---

20 A delightful entry in Leonardo's *Book of Water* concerns submarine warfare. His comments, 500 years old, are apposite today: "How by an appliance many are able to remain for some time under water. How and why I do not describe my method for remaining under water for as long a time as I can remain without food; and this I do not publish or divulge, on account of the evil nature of men, who would practice assassinations at the bottom of the seas by breaking the ships in their lowest parts and sinking them together with the crews who are in them."

"The common people have no history: persecuted by the present, they cannot think of preserving the memory of the past." He continued, "And yet what surpassingly instructive records, comforting too and pious, would be the family papers that should tell us who our forebears were and speak to us of their patient struggles with harsh fate, their stubborn efforts to build up, atom by atom, what we are today. No story would come up with that for individual interest. But, by the very force of things, the home is abandoned; and, when the brood has flown, the nest is no longer recognized."

The stories of my elders were indeed "surpassingly instructive." Family tales, told and retold and probably embellished, contrived to make history, ancient and modern, something infinitely fascinating and alive. The palpable feeling of time as "an ever-rolling stream" peopled by characters drawn from family lore and spiced with their deeds was a priceless bequest. It is a gift I have never taken for granted, but when I first read Fabre's words I realized anew how lucky I have been to have in my own life this extra dimension, in time as well as place, with which to look at wider events. And, made by a great naturalist, they incidentally underline the connection between natural and cultural history. Intuitively, it seems appropriate that a strong sense of history be an inevitable part of the urban naturalist's makeup.

℣

Held in the hand, history was first a regiment of tin soldiers, and the block of flats where my mother's parents lived in London had one redeeming feature from my point of view. From its windows I could watch my collection come alive as the Life Guards exercised their horses every morning. We would hear, before we saw it, the cavalcade clattering up the street as it left the Knightsbridge barracks, a beautiful series of Georgian red-brick buildings just a stone's throw away (now gone). As the troop came into view, the polished breastplates of the soldiers would sparkle, if the sun was shining, and the white horsehair plumes of their helmets would wave in the breeze. In the rain, the soldiers were cloaked, but they still held their swords upright, their arms as rigid as the ones that swung freely from the shoulders of my tin figures (and were always the first parts to get broken).

The apartment building itself was an unprepossessing—though well-built—slab of brick, an aesthetic horror from the thirties. From the street, I could always pick out my grandparents' flat because their balcony was protected by two heavy panes of glass, the gap between them small enough to prevent any unwanted entrance. My grandfather had them installed after a burglary during a particularly bad London fog, one of those legendary aspects of London life, the product of pollution, mostly from coal fires, that were accurately likened to pea soup. So many flats in the building were hit the same night that the police decided it must have been the work of not one but several independent thieves, cat burglars alleged to have been trained in scaling sheer faces in the Commandos during the war. I couldn't help imagining the somewhat comical spectacle, had the fog suddenly lifted, of that ugly façade ornamented by half a dozen spider men at work.

Eventually action was taken to prevent such terrible pollution, and the great pea soup fogs have become a memory. I was at boarding school in London during the last one. Our chemistry master used to come to school each morning on a motorcycle, which we thought rather novel. The first day of the fog, when he strode into the lab, his face was streaked with grime, and the handkerchief he used to cover his nose and mouth during the ride was black. The deaths of several hundred people were blamed on the atmospheric pollution that week.

By that time my grandfather was certainly dying, but the fog hastened his end by several weeks. Earlier in the year, he had broken his hip in a fall, and he was now confined to his bed. His condition notwithstanding, he had the cook, a large, friendly Yugoslav called Matilda, continue to serve every weekend a full and delicious three-course Sunday lunch for my older cousin Peter and me and any other member of the family who happened to be in town. Many a family story was told around that table.

On one such visit toward the end, Matilda led me straight to my grandfather's bedroom in a state of considerable alarm. There he lay amid the familiar furnishings: the eighteenth-century prints of the frescoes then being unearthed in Pompeii; the narrow bed of solid mahogany, with bugles and drums molded in gilt at the head and the foot —a cot that Napoleon might have used on campaign, I always fancied. He was staring up at the ceiling and mumbling what sounded to Matilda like nonsense. But it was not nonsense; the old man was passing the time, and doubtless comforting himself, by reciting his favorite poem, "Horatius at the Bridge," the most famous of Macaulay's *Lays of Ancient Rome*. He had given me an antique copy, beautifully bound in leather, for my birthday the previous year.

That was the last time I saw my grandfather. It seems singularly appropriate to me that this farewell should be wedded in my mind with such a literal picture of the misty past flowing into the murky present. He had been born in 1876. Never mind that he had been a prestigious publisher (of Isak Dinesen, among others); to me, in fog-bound '50s London, that date meant Custer's Last Stand (a less successful last stand than Horatius's) and linked me to the wide-open spaces along the Little Bighorn. To children a generation removed, grandparents approach the past and its inherent mysteries much as a priest would a shrine, or a medium the spirit world; my grandparents' intercession with those mysteries awakened my curiosity about the past.

My mother's influence also ensured that I was early on marked as a history buff as well as a naturalist. When I was five she hand-printed for me, on a sheet of poster paper, "the chart" (as it became known), which traced the threads of European civilization from prehistory to the present. It was complete with crossed swords for battles, turrets for fortresses and all sorts of other historiographical icons, beautifully inscribed, and it was my proudest possession for years until it fell apart beyond all mending. Years later, she toyed off and on with the idea of writing a history for children, and it is a great pity that she never accomplished it. She had a rare gift for capturing the imagination, had she only accepted it. In a sympathetic paragraph about her in his memoirs, Alan Pryce-Jones wrote, "She died before she became old, partly because she was acutely aware of potentialities lying fallow, so that she could impose no coherent pattern on her life."[21]

21 Alan Pryce Jones, *The Bonus of Laughter*.

Although my mother was an American citizen, she had been born and bred in England and had never set foot in the United States until we moved there as a family.[22] Her parents lived in London as American expatriates. My father's background was British, so the family had Anglo-American roots from the beginning, and when we emigrated to the United States shortly after the war's end—I was still a baby—we became transatlantic as well. New York was home to me and my two siblings until I went to boarding school in London.

Every other summer when we went to England, we stayed in Amberly, where my mother's parents had a country house. As well as fossils and birds, my major preoccupation at Amberley was archeology. A number of Roman sites were to be found in the surrounding countryside, and they were from time to time the object of family excursions, especially the Roman villa at Bignor in whose second-century mosaics dolphins sport around a striking head of Medusa. Ford Madox Ford described it as "a small collection of thatched huts, like a cowlick on an Anglo-Saxon skull, on the skyline of a spur of the Southdowns."[23]

The top of Amberley Mount was crowned by a dew-pond, a man-made pool lined with clay to catch and hold the rain.[24] It was like a circular mirror to the sky. Its unique vegetation and aquatic life were a source of endless fascination, but even more so was the thought that it had existed since time out of mind. It was like the entrance to a time machine where one could still imagine Masefield's woad-covered men "Crying to the gods of the downs till their brains were turning / And the gods came." Every walk along the Downs yielded pockets full of evidence of their presence in the form of worked flints, their natural gray-blue

---

22 To her dying day, my mother spoke with a very English accent. She hated to hear her voice recorded because she said it made her sound just like the Queen. But her voice didn't stop her vigorously campaigning for the Democratic candidate during every presidential race throughout my childhood. On being introduced to Adlai Stevenson, years after his run for the presidency, she told him she had canvassed for him, to which he replied jokingly, "You did? With *that* accent?"

23 Ford Madox Ford, *Provence*.

24 Dew-ponds are found on chalk hills all over England. These relics are something of a mystery, although nowadays they are considered not necessarily to be the work of the ancients.

bleached white by the ages. They were all over the place, mostly crude Paleolithic scrapers, but occasionally I got lucky with a far more polished Neolithic tool. Ancient shards, too, were aplenty if you knew where to look. My cousin Peter taught me to distinguish coarser Iron Age pottery from smoother Roman bits by the chips of grit contained in the clay, and I became quite expert at identifying the various fragments. My prize find was a precious piece of imported Samian ware, once adorned with a dec-orative relief that had long since worn away to leave a ghost of the orig-inal pattern in exposed natural clay against the bright red glaze.

Somewhat further afield, there was Stonehenge and, in Dorset, the great prehistoric citadel of Maiden Castle. Considered impregnable in its day, Maiden Castle was eventually captured by the Romans who advanced behind a smoke screen of burning gorse. Every year, we had a ritual picnic with my uncle's family at one of these sites. We had the great slopes and ditches of the Iron Age fort or the standing stones of Stonehenge all to ourselves, and the day would culminate in a glorious game of Romans and Britons (our version of Capture the Flag) that was played over rolling empty downland and involved every member of both families.

It was my interest in Roman Britain that inspired my grandparents to take me—I can't have been more than ten—to have lunch with their old friend, the Duke of Wellington. The Duke was in the process of unearthing the Roman city of Silchester, which lay within his domain, and they thought that I would be interested to see it. I was in high hopes as we drove up the avenue of majestic *Wellingtonias* (the English name for the imported giant redwood) to Stratfield Saye, the stately home built by a grateful nation for his forebear, the hero of Waterloo. But when we vis-ited the excavations after lunch, I had to hide my disappointment po-litely. I remember an overgrown wall, a wheelbarrow and doubtless pits and markers. Somehow, I had been expecting more from a Roman city: swords half hidden in the dirt, the broken wheel of a chariot or a stash of coins bearing the laurel-crowned profile of an emperor.

But no English boy could have failed to be impressed by the martial trophies and memorabilia of the Iron Duke that filled every room of the house or, in the grounds outside, to be touched by the gravestone of

Copenhagen, the horse he rode all day at Waterloo. At lunch I learned the fascinating fact that the Dukes of Wellington held from their sovereign the unique, hereditary right to hunt swan. It wasn't on the menu that day, but my grandparents joked that upon hearing the Duke take an honored guest aside and promise him a "special" culinary treat, his son and heir would protest, "Not swan, *again*, father." My grandmother, who always loved the underdog, insisted that the Duke allow me to hold in my hands the Royal George, which somehow had come into the possession of the Wellesley family. It was the decoration that, on the scaffold before he was beheaded, Charles I took from his breast and handed to the Bishop of London with the single enigmatic word "Remember."

My grandmother was the patron saint of lost causes. Her family was from the American South and had owned a plantation in Kentucky at the time of the Civil War. Long before I read or saw *Gone with the Wind*, her stories from that time had imbued me with sympathy for the hopeless chivalry of the Confederacy. These romantic notions received a severe blow one day when she dug out, from a cupboard full of family souvenirs, the Plantation Book. It was a record of the daily income and expense of running the estate and included the journal entries that noted the pitifully slow progress each slave made toward purchasing his or her freedom. The veil of historic distance could not conceal or soften such a wrong. Another reminder of this was waiting for me back in New York when I tried to buy some Confederate tin soldiers at our friendly neighborhood toy store; the proprietor said he didn't carry them because memories of the Civil War (almost a century old) were still too near the bone.

On a heavy Elizabethan table in the hallway at Amberley House stood a signed photograph of Robert E. Lee. It was given to my grandmother by her "old Uncle Smediloe," J. G. Smedley, one of Lee's officers. Smedley's handwritten inscription to her, dated Christmas 1900, recalls a meeting "at which many strangely interesting memories of the dreadful American Civil War were touched upon; and when your interest in General Robert E. Lee was, I suspect, first awakened." It goes on, "And please also to remember that, on the 11th of June, 1864—a few days after the battle of Cold Harbor, at which I was present—when the news was hastily brought to General, at Headquarters, that General Grant was, *at that moment*, crossing the James River, there were but two individuals present with him in his tent and who heard him exclaim with great vehemence '*At last, then, they have found the key to Richmond.*' — and that I was privileged to be one of the two who heard those now historical words."

Many of my grandmother's stories were handed down from her mother, who was a small child at the end of the Civil War. According to one, she was on her father's shoulders watching the Union gunboats sailing down the Ohio and shelling as they came, when she cried out in fright, "Papa, Papa, is we for Jeff Davis now? Not *now*, Papa." Another told of the war's aftermath: all the family's slaves had gone, save for one old retainer. Each day he would go out to range the countryside for food on their only mule, not coming back until evening. If they heard his cry from far away, "The Lord will provide for old missus," the family knew he had found nothing for them to eat, and they would go hungry that night. Many years later, in Amberley, my great-grandmother read Margaret Mitchell's recently published best-seller. When she came to the part where Scarlett and her family are starving in the ruins of Tara, tears streamed down her cheeks as she relived her own experiences.

This story, told by my grandmother, has left me with two very clear mental images that mirror each other across the divide of time, place and fortune: the old man on the mule silhouetted against a Kentucky twilight among the shattered ruins of the estate; and my great-grandmother, whom I never met, at Amberley sitting before the fireplace in the big room that looked out over a lawn with great trees toward a balustrade with a view of the Wild Brooks.

It was high up in one of those trees that I one day lost my kite. I appealed to my grandmother, who was lame and walked with a stick, to do something. Pointing her walking stick aloft, she cried out, "St. Anthony, a shilling for your poor!" The kite duly fell from the branch it had been stuck on. My grandmother had great faith in St. Anthony, the patron saint of lost objects, and she kept a running account with him to help her find anything, from her glasses, to pillowcases, to our toys. Several days later she took me to the local Catholic cathedral to pay her debt. As we walked down the gloomy aisle, she pointed out, one by one, the Stations of the Cross, whispering in my ear with each thrust of her stick, "Pain! Pain!" Her faith in the Saint did not extend to Catholic dogma.

My grandfather was a stern presence, not unkind but intimidating, and unyielding in the manner that I now realize is the classic trait of the New Englander. When at the age of eighty-five he broke his hip, he assured the surgeon with great seriousness that he did not want to be a bother and would condescend to allow himself to be given a general anaesthetic. He was one of five brothers and grew up in western Massachusetts along the Connecticut Valley. Coincidentally, the family's coat of arms is five wings on an azure field, and their sister Catharine, the youngest, always identified them with her five brothers.[25] My grandfather delighted in the kind of domestic catastrophe—such as the electricity going off—that brought back the skills he had learned as a country boy: "I wasn't brought up in Ashfield, Mass, for nothing," he would say with satisfaction, Ashfield being the town of which his father was the rector. But it was Aunt Catharine (as she was known by everyone, regardless of generation except her own, to whom she was Cousin Catharine) from whom we learned most about our New England ancestors starting with the Pilgrims.

The actress Diana Rigg once starred in an American television series as a nubile British transplant struggling to make the grade in 1970s New York. It didn't last long, but the show did have one good line. When her would-be mother-in-law boasted that her ancestor had come over on the *Mayflower*, Diana quipped, "And it was doubtless mine that sent him." Almost as good a pinprick to the pride of Colonial Dames is the tale of our ancestor who came over on the *Mayflower*, took one look at Plymouth Rock and went back to England. It was not until ten years later, when perhaps he felt that the bugs in the new colony would have been sorted out, that he returned on the *Mary and John*.

---

25 According to one of them, Great Uncle Jimmy, who was responsible for preserving the house, this was bought in about 1800 from an itinerant vendor of such perquisites. In his monograph on the history of the house, he wrote, "This coat of arms purports to display five wings of the English merlin with the bird itself as its crest. But the painter, not having a merlin to copy, used the American sparrow hawk instead, a smaller hawk and more colorful." James Huntington, *Forty Acres*.

The family eventually settled in Hadley. Here the Connecticut River seems to hesitate before its assault on the basalt ridge that links Mounts Tom and Holyoke. As if to fill the geological pause, the river makes a loop around a fertile plain, and here the house, Forty Acres, was built in 1752. It still stands — as a museum now — and has always been a powerful presence in family lore.

For one thing, the place was said to be haunted. My great-uncle, who saved the house and turned it into a museum, regularly heard steps climbing the stairs, doors being opened and closed, unseen beings leaving a room. On occasion the imprint of a body was said to form mysteriously on a certain bed, and it has been alleged that he was not above ensuring that it did so for visitors every now and then. The one time my parents stayed there, my father lay awake all night, his imagination a prey to every creak or groan the old house made. Having declared with her customary sangfroid that they were her family's ghosts and so she had nothing to fear, my mother slept like a log.

The most often recorded Hadley ghost was "the kindly old lady in brown," which was how Aunt Catharine described her. On a visit to Hadley as a young girl, she had woken up one night to find someone leaning over her, as a mother might lean over a child. Reassured, she drifted back to sleep. On inquiring next morning who the nice old lady was, it transpired that her midnight visitor was no guest, but well-known to those who lived at Forty Acres nonetheless. She was the widow of an army captain who had built the house and was killed in the French and Indian War at the Battle of the Morning Scout. After the skirmish, a friendly Indian appeared at the window and passed his sword, its hilt broken off to indicate that the captain was dead, through the opening. According to family legend, the captain was captured and killed so dreadfully by the Indians that only one member of the family in each generation could know the details of his fate. To the best of my knowledge, my grandfather, who claimed to know, never passed the awful secret on but took it with him to the grave. This story made an enormous impression on me, and I used it as the subject of a poem for an English class assignment at Westminster. It began:

He went away in uniform
Among the homespun men:
He went to fight the Frenchman,
To save Great Britain's gem.

The town of Hadley was replete with other legendary figures to spark a child's imagination. "The Angel of Hadley" was not a ghost, but his sudden appearance must have seemed almost supernatural to the settlers one fall Sunday in 1675 at the height of King Philip's War. While everyone in the village was at church, a tribe of hostile Indians surrounded Hadley and were preparing to attack. Just in time, a commanding presence, unknown to the people and dressed all in gray, appeared at the church door and warned them. He rallied the men, and with a professional soldier's skill he led them into battle, routing the Indians. As soon as it was over, he disappeared again, to be known ever after as the Angel of Hadley who had miraculously appeared to help the town in its hour of need. The Angel was, in fact, one General Goffe, an officer in Cromwell's Roundhead army in the English Civil War and one of the signers of the death warrant of Charles I. After the collapse of the Protectorate and the return of the monarchy, as a regicide, he was a marked man. He went to ground in Hadley, where he lived, like Anne Frank, in a secret room in the parson's house, daring to venture forth only on Sundays when the settlers were sure to be in church. Thus he was the only one to see the natives massing for the attack.

Aunt Catharine used to tell another, more charming, Hadley tale. Shortly after the end of the War of Independence, the family was gathered at Forty Acres for Christmas. As she told it, a party of the young people went wandering in the woods that still surrounded the family fields—perhaps escaping from the boredom of an endless meal dominated by their elders' conversation. Coming upon an opening in the woods, they found an old man cooking a modest but festive meal for himself over a fire. On finding himself observed, he beckoned to the children, mainly with gestures because he spoke little English. His tattered clothing was all that remained of the uniform of a Hessian regiment. The children gathered that he was a German who had been a soldier in the pay of King George. At some point during the war, perhaps at Saratoga,[26] he had been captured, and after his release, he had decided to stay in the New World, where he appeared to be eking out a living. He then pointed triumphantly to his masterpiece: a young evergreen growing at the edge of the clearing, which he had hung in the tradition of his homeland, with ribbons and decorations made from pinecones or cut from paper and tinsel. Aunt Catharine always claimed that this was the first Christmas tree in New England.

For Aunt Catharine, her ancestors were the guardians of the obligations to which her heritage bound her. In her memoir, *The Little Locksmith*, Katharine Butler Hathaway remembers her as a student at Radcliffe regaling her with tales about her family history.

. . . all the people in her stories had one distinguishing quality in common, which made them, either by blood or marriage, Huntingtons — a romantic race of people different from other people. As she told me her stories, she spoke in a minor key yet always with a kind of exquisite flourish and toss which showed me that although they, the Huntingtons, appeared to be required to endure more than the ordinary amount of personal tragedy, their spirit had never been defeated. . . . Still, her dominant mood was one of twilight melancholy, and she nearly always brought her nightly stories to an end with a Huntingtonian flourish, composed of a murmur and a sigh, and with her eyes downcast in sad meditation, she would shake her head slowly in the midst of its cloud of beautifully brushed hair, and fall into silence, forgetting me, and I would go wandering away to my own bedroom under the same kind of delicious spell as if I had just heard read aloud another chapter in the most fascinating novel I had ever found.

Her description describes perfectly my own memories of Aunt Catharine. I can see her sixty years later sitting in the little garden of wild plants and wildflowers she created behind her house on Boston's Beacon Hill, discussing the issues that absorbed her — civil rights, the war in

---

26 According to Alice Morehouse Walker's book *Historic Hadley*, Hessian prisoners taken at Saratoga did pass through the village, and General Burgoyne himself recuperated there.

Vietnam. Putting down her teacup, she would conclude a smoldering observation with the same "murmur and sigh" and the same inward shake of her head.

The defining event in a long and active life was her arrest for protesting what she considered the judicial murder by the Commonwealth of Massachusetts of two Italian immigrants, Sacco and Vanzetti, in 1927. To her dying day, she believed them innocent with all her heart. On the day of the execution, she demonstrated in front of the State House in Boston, along with Edna St. Vincent Millay and Margaret Hatfield Chase, and was arrested and charged with "sauntering and loitering." When she was brought before the court, the authorities advised the defendants to plead guilty to these "technical charges brought against them, pay the small fine and the incident would be considered closed." She refused. "I feel," she said, "it is time someone should protest against this legal subterfuge and make clear the exact status and the exact significance of the act for which I and others are here today." She went on, "I am an American citizen by inheritance. The name of my family appears on the Declaration of Independence. When the liberties which my ancestors established are endangered as they have been in Boston these recent horrible weeks, I consider it peculiarly my duty to protest." And she ended with this: "I don't believe that this is the sort of country which my ancestors tried to make—and that is why I walked in front of the State House yesterday." As I write this—on the seventy-fifth anniversary of Sacco and Vanzetti's death—I have on my desk a photograph of the three women, very erect and dignified, taken in front of the State House that day, and in the background, a man is jeering at them. I wonder if he would have kept laughing had he heard my great-aunt's testimony from the dock the next morning. Though she never forgave the state—she regarded Governor Fuller as a common murderer—or city that in all other respects she loved and whose spirit she embodied, she went on to achieve prominence in the world of the arts in Boston. On her 100th birthday, shortly before she died, the mayor of Boston proclaimed it Catharine Huntington Day.

A historian who had studied the family papers (all ninety-two linear feet of them) told the descendants gathered together for the 250th anniversary of Forty Acres, "Yours is a family that never saw a cause it could not embrace—or argue about!" Public involvement was also something of a family trait on my father's side of the family, and a Scottish tradition made it equally colorful. Urquhart Castle, dominating one end of Loch Ness, is *the* romantic ruin par excellence (it is the second most photographed castle in Scotland, after Glamis), and the Monster has made Urquhart Cove its home. My grandfather was said to have had frequent social intercourse with it, and I have always liked to attribute my dedication to protecting endangered species to this familial connection: Nessie is my kinsman.

Scarcely less improbable than the monster was my seventeenth-century namesake, Sir Thomas Urquhart, the translator of Rabelais. Alas, I cannot claim him as an ancestor in any direct sense as he had no acknowledged heirs.[27] This is too bad, since for his part, he traced his lineage back to Adam and Eve by way of, among others, the princess who found Moses in the bullrushes. This arcane piece of research includes numerous etymological observations on the origins of our name, the pronunciation of which baffles most people anywhere in the world other than Inverness, Scotland, where it is like Smith.[28]

Sir Thomas Urquhart was a true and wonderful product of an extravagant age. In translating Rabelais's bawdy tale of Gargantua and Pantagruel, his imagination proved a worthy equal to the Frenchman's, especially in the matter of lists, a popular field for virtuoso competition in those days. So, for example, while in the original, Gargantua's governesses have thirteen descriptive epithets with which to honor their young charge's penis, Sir Thomas gives them thirty-seven, bettering his

---

27 However, on a signet ring given to me by my father, I have his coat of arms: "demi otter goules on a wreath sable crowned with an antique crown."

28 Nowadays I tell acquaintances who want to pronounce Urquhart to imagine it spelled Erkutt, but I have been resigned since I was a child to the many forms of phonetic butchery of my surname—Yogourt and Workhard were but some of the more creative. I vividly recall the day in my first-grade class when I learned to spell it out loud: "U-R-Q-U-H-A-R-T. That's what my mother says every time she talks on the telephone!" I exclaimed. Living in New England, I now quite frequently come across the name Orcutt, which is another derivation of our name.

author both in quantity and quality of invention.[29] In addition to trans-lating Rabelais, he invented a Universal Language; unfortunately for the universe, this masterpiece became a spoil—literally—of the English Civil War. It was lost after the battle of Worcester, in which Sir Thomas fought on the royal, and losing, side. The future King escaped and fled to France, hiding in oak trees and stopping the night at a number of pubs along the way (including the George and Dragon just a mile from our house in Amberley). But Sir Thomas was captured. Even in this extrem-ity, however, his penchant for lists did not fail him. In his memoirs, he is explicit—and ruefully witty—about the extent of his loss: a "manu-script in folio, to the quantity of six score and eight quires and a half, divided into six hundred and fourty and two quinternions and upwards, the quinternion consisting of five sheets, and the quire of five and twenty." These were used by Cromwell's soldiers "for packeting up of raisins, figs, dates, almonds, caraway, and other such like dry confections and other ware as was requisite; who doing the same themselves did together with others kindle pipes of tobacco with a great part thereof, and threw out all the remainder upon the streets, save so much as they deemed necessary for inferiour employments and posteriour uses."

After being confined briefly in the Tower, he went to France where he joined the Stuart court in exile. (Judging from his writings, he must have been impossible, and one can imagine his jailers breathing a sigh of relief at seeing the last of him.) When the King was restored to the throne of England as Charles II, Sir Thomas stayed in France, where he is said to have died of laughing. According to some, the laughter was inspired by

---

29 "*L'une la nommoit ma petite dille, l'autre ma pine, l'autre ma branche de coural, l'autre mon bondon, mon bouchon, mon vibrequin, mon possouer, ma teriere, ma pendiloche, mon rude esbat roide et bas, mon dressouoir, ma petite andouille vermeille, ma petite couille bredouille.*" (*Gargan-tua and Pantagruel*, Rabelais)

"One of them would call it her pillicock, her fiddle-diddle, her staff of love, her tickle-giz-zard, her gentle-titler. Another, her sugar-plum, her kingo, her old rowley, her touch-trap, her flap dowdle. Another again, her branch of coral, her placket-racket, her Cyprian scep-tre, her tit-bit, her bob-lady. And some of the other women would give these names, my Roger, my cockatoo, my nimble-wimble, bush-beater, claw-buttock, eves-dropper, pick-lock, pioneer, bully-ruffin, smell-smock, trouble-gusset, my lusty live sausage, my crimson chitter-lin, rump-splitter, shove-devil, down right to it, stiff and stout, in and to, at her again, my coney-borrow-ferret, wily-beguiley, my pretty rogue." (Urquhart's translation)

pure joy at the Restoration, but a family tradition holds to a more mordant explanation of the circumstances. When he first arrived back in
England at Dover, King Charles was welcomed by the mayor of that city
who presented him with a copy of the Bible. Every English schoolboy
knows that the King received this gift with the noble avowal that "on my
travels this Book was ever closest to my heart." A page who was present
at this moving scene and knew a number of things in France that had
been a good deal closer to the King's heart hotfooted it back to tell Sir
Thomas, who always liked a good joke. He is said to have died laughing
at this one.

Our more traceable ancestor survived the Battle of Culloden, where
the Highland army was brutally destroyed by the English general, the
Duke of Cumberland. Having escaped with his life, he headed for London on the sensible grounds that the heart of the enemy's kingdom
would be the last place anyone would think to look for him. After things
had calmed down, he got a job as factor for the English owner of a Scottish estate in the Lowlands and so returned to Scotland. My paternal
grandfather, Murray Urquhart—who communed with the Loch Ness
monster—was his descendant. Beyond a few very formal occasions when
we were presented as grandchildren, my memories of him are limited to
one or two meetings when I was at University; he was an artist and very
kindly sent me a couple of his paintings with which to decorate my
rooms. His watercolors especially are very good, but his is hardly a household name in the art world.[30]

My grandmother's forebears came from Dorset, where they owned a
rope-making business on the sea. At the beginning of his memoirs, my
father refined the essence of my grandmother into a single word: "My
mother's favorite word was 'worthwhile.' It was a moral criterion . . .
[that] weighed pleasure against moral worth, and invariably came down

---

30 Except, apparently and for unknown reasons, in Lebanon: my father, who spent a good
deal of time in the Middle East for the U.N., tells of how, many years after his father's death,
he braved an artillery barrage at the height of the Lebanese civil war to attend a reception
in a Beirut bunker at the insistence of a Lebanese businessman whose sole purpose was to be
introduced to the son of "one of the greatest painters in the world."

on the side of moral worth. It expressed perfectly the ethos of the nonconformist, provincial, intelligent middle class from which my mother came."[31] She taught at Badminton, a girls' boarding school in Bristol founded and run by my great aunt Lucy and her companion for life. As well as being academically excellent, Badminton, under their leadership, was bastion of intellectual stimulation and tolerance. Indira Gandhi was a student there while her father was a political prisoner, and as the 1930s wound on, the school rolls included increasing numbers of Jewish refugees. Summer visits to see my grandmother always included a sumptuous tea with Aunt Lucy and Miss Baker beside the stone goldfish pond in their garden on the school grounds.

We would also go to Bridport, where my father was born, and neighboring Lyme Regis, where I spent as much time as possible searching the cliffs for fossils. At my grandmother's house there was a little round table, the top of which was decorated with an inlay of polished fossil ammonites and belemnites. She also had a glass-fronted cabinet that was full of strange and wonderful treasures collected over a long life, any of which she might occasionally bestow on one if she thought it was appreciated. One year, she gave me a hoard of Roman coins, and I spent many happy hours trying to identify each one from a catalogue, letting my wishful imagination fill in where the book was lacking. She lived to be a hundred, and on my last visit just before her death, she recited "The Pied Piper of Hamlin" to me, complete from memory.

The Coronation in 1953 was the perfect excuse for all sorts of retrospectives on England's past, and the British diplomatic corps in New York decided to celebrate the event by putting on a very idiosyncratic play. *The Pageant*, as it was called, covered the history of the Sceptred Isle in a series of humorous historical vignettes. The script was written by my father and another friend. For weeks, our house was turned into a the-

31 Brian Urquhart, *A Life in Peace and War.*

atrical workshop with my mother tirelessly painting flats to evoke the Bayeux Tapestry, making props such as the Stone of Scone or the bejeweled top for the Royal Coach and attending to a hundred other details. She also wrote the lyrics for some of the songs ("As the Queen rides by England's history escorts her. May she never ride alone") in appropriately celebratory, four-square mood.

The Pageant took place on a steamy summer Saturday in the auditorium of Sarah Lawrence College. Future ambassadors played James II throwing the Royal Seal into the Thames (in this case a large inflatable rubber seal as used by young children learning to swim) or George III taking the waters at Brighton and gloomily picking up a teabag washed up on the beach from Boston. Covered in blue paint (woad) and dressed in a bearskin, my father played the part of an ancient Briton, a sort of chorus who wandered in and out of the audience as the centuries rolled by, commenting (as I recall in a heavy West Country accent) bemusedly on the great events that were being enacted on the stage. I had a number of walk-on parts — I enjoyed being a page to the First Elizabeth — but my big role was as the young Winston Churchill practicing his "On the beaches" speech in front of Mr. Marconi's new wireless apparatus before an adoring young Emily Pankhurst. Wearing a sailor suit topped off with the straw gondolier's hat my parents had brought back from Venice, I squeaked away in my unbroken voice. "We will fight them on the beaches, on the landing grounds — what's a landing ground, nurse?" As I finished my speech with an impassioned "We will never surrender," Emily gushed, "Oh, Winny, I'll vote for you." To which I replied, "Don't be silly, Emily. Women can't vote."

The Coronation provided one further somewhat dubious vignette. My American grandparents had a Hungarian parlor maid whose name was Elizabeth. Their democratic heritage notwithstanding, my grandfather told her, in the kindest and most reasonable terms, that it would be quite impossible to have a servant with the same name as the Sovereign. From then on she was known as Erszi, the Hungarian form of Eliza.

Quite apart from family stories and whimsical excursions into the more distant past, the historical event that hung most immediately in the air was the Second World War. I was actually born in London six months before VE Day, during the V1 and V2 raids. According to Bill Maxwell—an old friend of the family with a fertile imagination—my mother, accompanied by Nanny, walked to the hospital across a blacked-out Hyde Park in the middle of an air raid. In his memoirs, my father, who was in the army in Europe at the time, described his side of the story "I had made elaborate plans to get news of this event. . . . The codeword was—God knows why—'Mauser' for a boy and 'Ratter' for a girl. . . . [The] Telex message read: 'Mauser dropped safely at 0425 hours . . .' This was intercepted by the Intelligence Branch, and I had some difficulty in explaining the prosaic truth." In grade school, on being given an assignment to write an autobiography, I began mine in melodramatic style: "A rocket came down and I was born." When VE Day came, my mother wanted me to stay up to see the celebration bonfire in Amberley, but Nanny said I would never remember it and whisked me off to bed. In the attic in Amberley among many more familiar treasures, there was a crate full of bunting and banners from that day, and they always seemed mysteriously beyond my experience.

The first summers of home leave in England that I remember, there were reminders of the war almost everywhere. Some items were still rationed, such as orange juice that came in a narrow glass bottle. The Cunard liners in which we sailed across the Atlantic every other year had not so long before been used as troop transports; on both the *Queens*, the wooden railings were scarred with the initials of the GIs on their way to the invasion of Europe.[32] The docks in Southampton were still heavily bomb-damaged. On one return trip aboard the *Queen Mary*, the ship struck a submarine cable in Cherbourg, and we had to return to Southampton for several days where we watched from the deck as divers in helmets and weighted suits went over the side to repair the damage.

The barns and storerooms of Amberley were full of relics from both world wars. We converted yards of blackout material put away in a trunk into cloaks or curtains for our rather halfhearted theatricals. In the attic,

---

32 On one of these voyages, my parents took me up to the first-class lounge to stare at, from a distance, the Duke and Duchess of Windsor. He reminded me irresistibly of Tenniel's drawing of the Red Queen in *Alice in Wonderland*.

we found my father's military paraphernalia, such as his tin helmet and his tent and sheaves of aerial reconnaisance photos. In the toolshed, a bayonet and an entrenching tool (but no bits of skin and hair as were to be found on Uncle Mathew's in Nancy Mitford's *The Pursuit of Love*) hung from the beams, and old gas masks lay under cobwebs and gunny-sacks in the corner. Except for the gas masks, which we found creepy, we appropriated everything we could use to play at being soldiers. However, when we found a German flag with the swastika and nailed it to the flag-pole, the gardener's wife told us off in no uncertain manner, much to our embarrassment.

Most of the older men in the village had fought in the First World War, many of them in the Royal Navy as the anchors tattooed on their arms attested. They mostly drank gin and so frequented the village pub that served spirits. Two of them clipped our hedges and did other odd jobs for my grandparents. They were dour old men, always dressed in black save for a white collarless shirt. My grandmother called them the two gloom birds. But our gardener always had a twinkle in his eye and frequently a pint of bitter in his hand. I can see him now in his tweed cap, sitting at the table of the farmer's pub, enjoying a hand-rolled ciga-rette and a jaw with the other farmers. "First today, sir," he'd say, raising his glass, if he saw us come in. He had served as a stoker on a battleship at the Battle of Jutland. When he came on deck after the engagement, which he had spent at his post in the bowels of the ship, he said he had never seen so many dead fish in his life.

The vicar, a retired bishop, had been on the *Lusitania* when it was tor-pedoed by a German submarine. He had in his collection of memorabilia a medal struck by the Germans that showed Death, a skeleton, in a Cunard Line cap selling tickets for the fatal voyage. But I remember best the village blacksmith, who had seen action in the Sinai and at Galli-poli, where he was one of only five men in his unit to survive that ordeal. However, his composure remained totally unrattled by his experiences in one of the First World War's biggest military disasters. My grandmother called him "the good, the true and the beautiful," and he was a saintly man, always ready to use his old skills to mend our soapbox go-carts or to make us pins out of his leftover horseshoe nails. He was one of the finest men I have ever known; talking to him was like being in touch with the earth.

The fatal bungling of the Anglo-French landing at Gallipoli was one of my grandmother's bêtes noires. She would line us three children up and drill us on its enormities by posing leading questions and making us answer, one after the other, in triplicate. "Why did the British officers stop during their assault on the beach?" "For their tea," "their tea," "their tea." With her walking stick she would point at each of us in turn, like a conductor bringing in a soloist. "What was the French admiral's name?" "DeRobeck," "DeRobeck," "DeRobeck." She also recalled telling a joke from the campaign to the British leader of the expedition, Sir Ian Hamilton. The men had a bet on which smelled worse, a goat or a Turkish prisoner. A burly sergeant-major was assigned the role of judge, and the first contestant, the goat, was led in, whereupon he fainted. Then the Turkish prisoner was led in, and the goat fainted. Sir Ian Hamilton was not amused, because, my grandmother told us, the British do not make fun of their enemies.

Amberley held another treasure trove, this one from between the wars: a collection of 78s from my mother's childhood and her old hand-cranked gramophone. For hours on end we listened to Frank Crummit sing "Abdul Abulbul Amir," Gene Autry croon "South of the Border" and Paul Robeson boom out "Ol' Man River." Best of all was his song "Ballad of the Americans," a stirring labor-oriented history of the United States that began, "In '76 the sky was red." At the end of one summer in the early 1950s when it came time to return to New York, it was inconceivable that we could survive a whole year without all these favorites, and we asked to take them with us. We got Crummit and Autry and "Ol' Man River," but my parents would not let us take "Ballad of the Americans" because of its political baggage. "But America is a free country," I protested to my grandmother in frustrated disbelief. "Not while Senator McCarthy is around," she replied. I did not realize that some of my father's closest friends and colleagues at the United Nations were being actively persecuted during the Red Scare.[33]

---

33 Some twenty years later, while I was working for the Boston Symphony Orchestra, this came back to me during a Boston Pops concert for the Harvard Twenty-fifth Reunion. Every year it was *the* event of the summer season at Symphony Hall, with Arthur Fiedler sporting

A shattering "end of innocence" came with a single event. A U.S. Air Force officer came to a school assembly and showed us three films, documentaries of the bombing of Pearl Harbor, the dropping of the atom bomb and the tests of the hydrogen bomb at Eniwetok Atoll. He followed the films with an explanation of the need for the Distant Early Warning system then being built, and ended by demonstrating a simulated hit by a Nike missile on an attacking Russian bomber. Somewhere in the course of his talk, he showed us a map of Manhattan marked with the rings of various levels of destruction from an atomic strike. Ground Zero, as chance would have it, appeared to be our house on East 70th Street. From then on, current events, even the sound of the news on the radio, made my blood run cold. History—any era but the present—suddenly acquired a new escapist value.

The terror of atomic war did not go away for years. And when it did, it was an overriding faith in nature that finally exorcised it. In my last year at boarding school, I wrote a story for our magazine in which I combined my rescue of a small fish left behind in a tide pool with a verse from a poem by John Donne that we had studied. It amounted to a renewed conviction that the world would be spared "for the sake of that fish." My adjustment of the vowel in the poem's "sonne" seemed entirely appropriate.

I have a sinne of feare, that when I have spunne
My last thred, I shall perish on the shore;
Sweare by thy selfe, that at my death thy sunne
Shall shine as he shines now, and heretofore;
And, having done that, Thou haste done,
I feare no more.

•

a crimson Harvard blazer from the podium. On this occasion, it was announced that the first piece after the intermission, Sibelius's *Karelia Suite,* would be conducted not by Maestro Fiedler but by a member of the Harvard class of '48, David Schine. Schine was one of McCarthy's most prominent hatchet men. On stage, some of the musicians put down their instruments and refused to play. Many patrons just happened to linger too long over their drinks in the bar and missed the performance. After the concert, I went out for a drink with one of the second violins. "That man ruined my father's life," he said bitterly. "No way was I going to play for him." One wonders through what organizational lacuna Harvard allowed such a preposterous piece of programming to slip.

In addition to belonging to a family that relished the past, I have been enriched by sharing the perspectives of two cultures—both linked by the historical cat's cradle that binds the New and Old Worlds together.[34] Nowhere do I feel this largesse more viscerally than when I find myself in the middle of their respective countrysides once again after long absence. As different as the granite ridges of New England are from the chalk hills of Sussex, both lands reflect the imprint of my ancestors and have in turn imprinted themselves on me.

The British fantasy writer Susan Cooper has described the effect of growing up with a long history all around you. "If you are English, Scottish, Welsh or Irish—or like most of us, a mongrel mixture—if you are born and brought up on this long-occupied land, you acquire by a kind of osmosis a sense of the continuum of place and time." This continuum is ingrained in us from evidence we collect, subconsciously but all the time, from the buildings and environment around us. The "old country" is rooted in an uninterrupted written history that dates back nearly a thousand years to the Domesday Book and can be traced fairly continuously a further millennium before that to the Romans. Considering the discovery of a battlefield in the gamekeeper's park, Richard Jefferies[35] wrote,

It is strange to think of, yet it is true enough, that beautiful as the country is, with its green meadows and graceful trees, its streams and forests and peaceful homesteads, it would be difficult to find an acre of ground that has not been

---

34 My American grandmother liked to poke fun at the manners on both sides of the Atlantic with the story of how the King of Naples and the Pope were rescued from Garibaldi's advance up the Italian peninsula in 1860. A British and an American naval squadron were dispatched to take the pair off the promontory of Gaeta, just north of Naples. While the British captain was immersed in aristocratic courtesies and diplomatic persiflage, and losing precious time into the bargain, the American cut to the chase and snapped, "You take the King, I'll take the Pope. Come on, Pope." I have never found this story in a history book, but whether apocryphal or not, it makes an amusing parable of Anglo-American stylistic differences.

35 *The Gamekeeper at Home.*

stained with blood. A melancholy reflection this, that carries the mind back-
wards, while the thrush sings on the bough, through the nameless skirmishes of
the Civil War, the cruel assassinations of the rival Roses, down to the axes of
the Saxons and the ghastly wounds they made. Everywhere under the flowers
are the dead.

The New England version of history is a much truncated one, a mere
four hundred years. When my house in Maine, one of the oldest in town,
was built in 1798, part of our home in Amberley was already 500 years
old.

Cooper goes on to speak of this sense of the continuum as "a treasure
which most of us don't know we possess. Like love, it is most apparent
through the size of the aching gap left when it is gone." Born but only
partially brought up in the "long-occupied land," I have spent roughly
equal time on either side of the "Pond." Adjusting from one to the other
is something I can do more or less without thinking. It took seeing
England through the eyes of my American wife when we lived there for
a spell to appreciate again the distinctive differences between the two. In
doing so, I realized how unconsciously I had been staking my dual heritage on a game of Double or Nothing: despite considerable insights into
the two countries, in many ways I was a stranger in both.

In one of the most poignant poems I know, the Greek poet C. P.
Cavafy tells of a people who have lost their "continuum" and forgotten
their roots. He prefaced his poem with an extract from an ancient source
that describes how the descendants of a Greek community, cut off and
left behind in a foreign land, had given up the customs and speech of
their ancestors save for one festival each year; "during this they gather
together and call up from memory their ancient names and customs, and
then, lamenting loudly to each other and weeping, they go away."

> *The only thing ancestral that remained to them*
> *was a Greek festival, with beautiful rites,*
> *with lyres and flutes, contests and crowns.*
> *And it was their habit towards the festival's end*
> *to tell each other about their ancient customs*

and once again to speak the Greek words
that hardly any of them still understood.

The poem rings in my ears like a warning. All around us, the continuum is breaking down as we daily sacrifice our sense of place to the pressing demands of the world we live in. Ironically, it is neither foreign threat nor material poverty like the hardscrabble grind of Fabre's childhood but economic success that contributes to "the nest . . . no longer [being] recognized." Our sense of cultural identity is being undermined by unprecedented mobility at the same time it is trivialized by the imperative to consume. Disoriented by our wandering ways and anaesthetized by feel-good messages that are as shallow as they are cynical, we are losing our roots, to the detriment of how we live and the places we used to love and call home. It is happening on both sides of the Atlantic. However, our colonial ancestors having deliberately wiped out one "continuum of place and time"—that of the Native American culture they found[36]—America has had less time to put on the weight of the past and has less with which to resist these trends.

As we trade away a sense of belonging to one place for the benefits of mobility, family stories become more important than ever. The tales I heard from my grandparents are part of my treasure, to use Cooper's word, and I am very conscious of how they identify—and belong to—me. If they are passed on, they at least bear witness to "the aching gap" and perhaps can help to close it. On Thanksgiving, when the sky is leaden (and I think of the wolves in the Natural History Museum), we should feel the cold wind blowing as the breath of our persevering ancestors who worked for a future that is our present. Hardly exceptional in themselves, they were a few strands pinched out of the millions of threads from which the tapestry of our civilization is woven. We all have our own cluster, positioning each one of us at our own unique angle to the larger context. By tugging on our threads, teasing them out, twitch-

---

36 When a much younger sedimentary deposit covers an eroded rock formation, geologists call the break in the record a dysjuncture. It is a good word to describe the same process in history.

ing at them, we begin to unravel our own bit of a saga of which, however fleetingly, we are as much the center as the spider in its web. Pull on that little knot over there, and I find you and your story at the end of it, ready to join the cavalcade at least for a while with me. Over here, this tangle must wait for someone else to come along to help unravel it; and somewhere there is probably a mare's nest so far unnoticed that someone, someday, by their own tugging and teasing, will help twitch into the clear. We still have much to learn that is "comforting too and pious" from all our pasts.

Even when they appear less than comforting or pious, it would be as well to have come to terms with them. The past is the endowment we carry into the future, and viewing it in the light of our ancestors' deeds can be a salutary experience. When they were on "the wrong side," we are inclined at least to attempt some accommodation or reconciliation where we might otherwise find only fault and blame, because they are, like it or not, our forebears. When as a child I realized that only a couple of greats ago my ancestors owned slaves, it shocked me deeply. But however abhorrent, there is no reason to suppose that in the same place and time I would have been any different. Which raises the question: Why are we different now and what changed us? To find the real answer, we need humility enough to refrain from applying to earlier eras the standards of social conduct we have just learned, or are still learning, today. I have no doubt that my descendants will find plenty to blush at in my late-twentieth-century liberal beliefs. I do wonder which ones they will find most obnoxious and hope that they will be forgiving.

Our scattered stories are pieces of a jigsaw puzzle. Picked up randomly enough at first blush, we start connecting them, and a pattern emerges. Sir Thomas loses his manuscripts at Worcester, while the King spends the night at the George and Dragon just outside Amberley on his flight to France; a death by laughter at the news of the Restoration, while General Goffe retires to his priest hole in Hadley. Scarcely noticeable flecks on a pointillist canvas (some perhaps rather questionable) in themselves, they add immeasurably to the richness of the picture. Or perhaps they are more like a skillfully carved detail high in the vault of a Gothic cathedral: a labor of love by an unknown artisan, unseen but present, that when added to all of the other anonymously executed capitals gives a particular character to the nave. They are what makes history come alive, what gives us the sense of the expanse, and above all the depth, of time. It is important that we know they are there so that each of us can say, with my great-aunt, that it is "peculiarly my duty" to honor the past and heed its lessons for the present. This obligation starts with the land in the contours of which we may meet the shades of the past dancing through time. For me that place is Amberley.

Landscape, with Man

The Author of the following letters, takes the liberty, with all proper deference, of laying before the public his idea of parochial history, which, he thinks, ought to consist of natural productions and occurrences as well as antiquities.[37]
—Gilbert White, *The Natural History of Selborne*

T HE TRAIN FROM LONDON still stops at Amberley every hour. Just after pulling out of the station at Pulborough, my heart always quickens to the clatter as the rails cross the Arun River and we start the last part of the journey, across the Wild Brooks. Through the compartment window, the passenger picks out a relic from the heyday of English canals, a length of the Arun-Wey. At Hardham, the railway cuts through a chalk outcrop, bypassing the tunnel down which bargees, lying on their backs, once propelled themselves along its wall with their feet. But as the train emerges from the deafening reverberation of that narrow defile, one is blessed with one of the most serene views in the world. Water meadows and fields dotted with venerable oak trees reach all the way to the flank of the South Downs, the ridge of chalk hills that stretches eastward from Amberley Mount until they meet the English Channel and become the cliffs called the Seven Sisters. Ten miles distant stands what's left of Chanctonbury Ring, a folly of beeches planted on top of the ridge by a nineteenth-century clergyman. Once a landmark for miles around, it was decimated (along with much of southeast England's woodlands) by the hurricane of 1987. As the train rattles

---

37 Selborne is not far away from Amberley; one of the tributaries of the Arun rises there. In both, nature and history have converged around a village of less than a thousand people and produced a similarly cherished landscape.

on, the cottages of Amberley appear on a rise halfway up between the Wild Brooks and the Downs. At one end of the village, the gray walls of Amberley Castle seemingly grow out of the water meadows themselves.

Rootedness is having a special place where one's life hopes and fears are hidden. Mine is this little hamlet in West Sussex, midway between the water and the sky. Although after my first year, I never lived there a full twelve-month round, my roots are and will always be in Amberley. It is a haven to return to, and its presence across the Atlantic combines the bolstering comfort of an old friend, the reassurance of a beacon and the ever-present pang of yearning that Sir Walter Scott put into verse.

> Breathes there the man, with soul so dead,
> Who never to himself hath said,
> This is my own, my native land!
> Whose heart hath ne'er within him burned,
> As home his footsteps he hath turned
> From wandering on a foreign strand.

Once past the castle, the train starts to slow down as it approaches the station through cultivated fields. The chalk pit comes into view, a monument to nineteenth-century industry. Here the men of the village toiled until the 1950s quarrying lime for cement and paid for their efforts with lungs full of chalk dust. In the process, a white cliff was carved out of the rolling green hills, and the contrast turned Amberley into a haven much enjoyed by London's artists at the turn of the century. The village was a favorite spot to paint for one Royal Academician much admired by my American great-grandfather, a would-be artist himself. He sought out this gentleman with a view to taking lessons from him. Rebuffed, he achieved his aim nevertheless by setting up his easel next to the great man. At the same time, he established a home for his family by buying all the cottages at the end of the village nearest the church. We had, until it was stolen in a break-in one night, a single painting of my great-grandfather's, a view across the Wild Brooks to the chalk pit, and of its genre it was lovely. The canvas has gone, but the view has hardly changed since he painted it.

There are two ways to cover the mile from the station to the village. The most direct one is by road, but on foot that is a hazardous business. It is full of blind curves and fast cars, and there is little margin for error. One used to be able to avoid some of this by following a public footpath past the impressive medieval gateway of the castle. But the chatelaine had it closed, and the castle is now a very fancy hotel that hardly encourages hikers. Instead, a footpath runs along the river and wanders across the Amberley Wild Brooks, and although longer it is infinitely preferable, a meditative walk that puts one in the "Amberley" frame of mind.

On a day full of the fickle promise of early spring, the water meadows are all movement. The wind whips ragged cloud shadows across the path, lightening and darkening the landscape as if by remote control. Lapwings fly helter-skelter from field to field, making their strange liquid cries, like interference on a radio tuner, as they perform their rollercoaster antics against the sky. Cutting through this flat familiar world, green lanes of sedge mark the course of brimming ditches. A gray silhouette, a heron, stock-still, materializes for a moment before coming majestically to life and flapping away, low across the fields, to settle again just out of sight. From a copse of oak trees over the meadow, a yaffle—what they call a green woodpecker in Sussex—laughs. Along the path to the village, the hedges will produce a fine crop of sloes to be gathered for sloe gin come autumn. A hundred such encounters over the years fill my memory's scrapbook: a moorhen, startled from her nest in the reeds, staring at me apprehensively, her head just breaking the pond-weed on the surface of the water; the dive of a drumming snipe over a field of marsh grass and the unforgettable thrill of the throbbing sound—made by its feathers—heard for the first time; the powerful musculature of a hare highlighted in the red rays of a setting sun as it races across the rosy fields.

Over to the west on the other side of the Arun, the pointed steeple of Bury church stands out against the hills. You can cross over on a footbridge now, but when I was very young, anyone wishing to go to Bury from Amberley had to hail the ferryman over the water, and he would punt you across. Change has come just upstream of the village, too. The Withy Bed, once a dense thicket of willows on a bend in the river, has been drained and cut. All that is left are a few bare trees in which wood pigeons roost, and one can take a boat through its central channel to the river itself with ease. I remember when it was an impenetrable jungle. A reed-bed in the middle used to buzz with every kind of bird and insect. And beyond, on slow summer afternoons, when the air was heavy with the smell of new-mown hay, the lazy green-brown Arun washed my boyhood fantasies down to the sea.

Further down the track and across a stile, the cause of the Withy Bed's demise becomes apparent; the meander of the river has been curbed by a vast flood-bank, which casts a shadow like a black band across the green fields in the late afternoon sun. For centuries these fields were managed as water meadows. In the old days, they would have been underwater at this time of year, and sometimes even in summer. But in the 1960s, men who could describe the immemorial waters in "cusecs" and turn them into a "design flow" came with heavy equipment to scour out the riverbed. They built these flood banks like a straightjacket that follows the river up to Pulborough. Now the Wild Brooks don't flood as they did. The Arun no longer fertilizes them, and its waters cannot protect them from cultivation. They are not as "wild," and the Withy Bed is gone.

The village of Amberley consists of a single street with a loop that follows the contour of a ridge above the water meadows and gives farmers and ramblers access to their fields. The houses are made of chalk and flint, with diamond-paned windows trimmed in brick. When I was a child, almost all their roofs were made of thatch, and the ones that still survive are now preserved by order, as is proper for one of the most picturesque villages in England. Dutch elm disease, however, was beyond the county council's control, and the magnificent trees that once shaded the village street as it approached the church are gone, their only memorial some tall stumps up which a captain of industry has trained his climbing roses.

However, the graveyard of St. Michael's, the Norman church at the end of the main street, has still enough yews to put one in mind of Gray's *Elegy*.

Beneath those rugged elms, that yew-tree's shade,
Where heaves the turf in many a mould'ring heap,
Each in his narrow cell for ever laid,
The rude Forefathers of the hamlet sleep.

Inside, a fine Romanesque dogtooth arch reflects the curve of Amberley Mount, a green dome rising above the village and bisected by a white longitudinal stripe, the chalk track that runs to its top. Beyond the church, the castle guards the gap in the Downs through which the River Arun flows. A thirteenth-century Bishop of Chichester built it at a time of peasant unrest, but for all the splendor of its walls perched above the marshes, its defensive situation was never called upon.

The village pub was called The Thatched House, although it has had a tiled roof since before I can remember. The joke used to be that it was the only *un*thatched house in the village. It was licensed to sell beer only, and the farmer who owned it would come in from milking in his great Wellington boots and tramp across the slate slabs to draw pints of bitter from kegs kept cool in the taproom (sometimes, he would overlook a beer and ginger beer shandy for us children). Then, with my parents, we would take our refreshment across the farmyard to the old pigsty that looked out across the Wild Brooks. With the lush green pastures of the water meadows, the water along the dikes reflecting back to the sky a knifelike blue and the little chalk track meandering into the distance, it was a view of pastoral peace worthy of Constable; my parents used to say there was just one bend too many in the path for it to be real rather than a picture.

The village looks out to the Wild Brooks and up to Amberley Mount and the Downs. It is on these Downs and the fields that slope from them southward to the sea that the story of Sussex, and much of England, starts. Kipling loved Sussex and wrote many a paean to the country thereabouts and its history. I like none better than "Puck's Song," the last stanza of which T. H. White took as the dedication of his *The Once and Future King*:

She is not any common Earth,
Water or wood or air,
But Merlin's isle of Gramarye
Where you and I will fare.

Kipling's poem speaks of the soul of Sussex, the passage of time and its folk along the flanks of the Downs. Each stanza is an inventory of the land.

And see you marks that show and fade,
Like shadows on the downs?
O they are the lines the Flint Men made,
To guard their wondrous towns.

As you look across the rolling hills, Kipling's "lines" are all around you. A walk up the chalk path that leads to Amberley Mount will produce from the earth turned over by moles small chips of flint, bleached white by the ages. On the surface of some, a convex or concave marking, the "bulb of percussion," testifies to the stroke of man. Some are crude flint scrapers left by Paleolithic peoples as they roamed these hills for game before the Ice Age. Keep walking east along the ridge, or along its sides where sheep and cattle have grazed for eons, giving the turf its characteristic spring. Beyond the dew-pond the lines and angles of a redoubt materialize in the distance, commanding the track that still runs the length of the South Downs. These fortifications date from the Iron Age, but long before, just after the ice sheets had withdrawn, a Neolithic tribe might well have built a defensive stronghold here, a reminder that war first came to England at about this time. When the need for stone tools and weapons could no longer be satisfied by finds on the surface, the Flint Men sunk mines into the hills. Across a valley from the encampment, they found a flint seam below the chalk, which they worked with picks fashioned from deer antlers. And all over, like miniature Downs themselves, tumuli mark the burial sites of the ancient chiefs.

And see you, after rain, the trace
Of mound and ditch and wall?

O that was a legion's camping-place,
When Caesar sailed from Gaul.

By the time the Romans invaded, the Arun Valley around Amberley was part of a kingdom ruled by Cogidumnus. In exchange for collaborating with the Romans, he was confirmed as *"rex et legatus Augusti in Britannia"* and added Tiberius Claudius to his name for good measure. His palace, an impressive example of Romano-British architecture with magnificent mosaics, was discovered in the 1960s just ten miles away, at Fishbourne, near Chichester, and has been partially excavated (well over half lies under a council house development). One happy find was the fragment of a bust of a boy's head, which may well be the only clue we have as to the looks of the *"rex et legatus"* since whoever it was must have been important enough to warrant a portrait thus, the King's son, heir to the wily Cogidumnus.

Looking north across the floodplain of the Arun, one can still see bits of Stane Street, the road from Londinium (London) to Novio Magus (Chichester), running northeast–southwest with characteristic Roman straightness. Along the route, the Roman overlords took for themselves the richest agricultural lands, forcing the British natives to work the more marginal Downs. To this day, the outlines of their fields — "mound and ditch and wall" — show up like watermarks across the hillsides, and the ground is full of pottery shards, both Iron Age and Roman.

South towards the sea lie fertile fields, now as then, and the marauding Saxons found them easy and profitable pickings after the Romans withdrew and the Empire crumbled. Instead of the Roman road, their preference for transportation was the river, and for the first time, the Wild Brooks on either side of the Arun were turned to agricultural account, thanks to the heavy double-yoked, ox-pulled Saxon plough.

See you our pastures wide and lone,
Where the red oxen browse?
O there was a City thronged and known,
Ere London boasted a house.

Villages had long ago sprung up on either slope of the Downs, where springs gush from the base of the chalk escarpment and the sites are dry and sandy. The Saxons organized these communities into parishes, and the names of the villages one looks down on from the ridgeline have the immemorial thud of the Saxon suffix: Greatham, Rackham, Parham, Cootham, Clapham. Each one consisted of a narrow strip of land running up and down the slope—from the chalk of the downland to the clay of the water meadows—to ensure fair distribution of the different-quality lands.

> See you the windy levels spread
> About the gates of Rye?
> O that was where the Northmen fled,
> When Alfred's ships came by.

A gentle hike from Amberley Mount down a dry glacial valley and up over land now plowed with wheat takes one to another of those parishes, Burpham, where there is an excellent pub for lunch after one's walk. Built on a steep-sloped chalk spur that hangs like an appendix into the floodplain, it is now on an oxbow of the Arun. But in ninth-century Saxon England, with the river on one side and a stream on the other, Burpham was strategically located enough for King Alfred the Great, who drove the Danes from English shores, to establish a garrison against their raids. Then came the Normans.

> See you our stilly woods of oak,
> And the dread ditch beside?
> O that was where the Saxons broke
> On the day that Harold died.

Although the Normans landed further east, King Harold's last-ditch reinforcements at the Battle of Hastings came from Sussex, and the lands belonging to these knights were confiscated after his defeat. William ("the Norman King who loved the tall deer as if he were their father— in the words of his contemporary—and set store by the hares that they too should go free"—Richard Jefferies in *The Gamekeeper at Home*) gave the land around Amberley to one of his strongest adherents, an indication of its importance. Sussex was the region closest to Normandy, the mother state, and after the Conquest the Arun Valley became a vital route to France. When the river cut off the meander at Burpham and formed the oxbow, the settlement lost much of its strategic importance. Besides, the burgeoning trade across the Channel required a bigger port. Arundel, to the south, offered better access to the rich fields of the coastal plain and an even more impressive command of the Arun gap. The Normans established their new center at Arundel. Of the Norman building, little remains but the Keep, but Constable painted the later turrets of Arundel Castle silhouetted against the skyline of the Downs, and it remains a view worthy of England's greatest landscape painter.

> Trackway and Camp and City lost,
> Salt Marsh where now is corn —
> Old Wars, old Peace, old Arts that cease,
> And so was England born!

Ever since I can remember, "Puck's Song" has been a talisman that provided an intimate key to my own feelings for Sussex and Amberley, love for its beauty and pride in its historical importance, including history that mercifully never happened. My father, who was an intelligence officer in World War II, brought back from the war a thick Wehrmacht document including detailed maps and pictures (mostly from tourist postcards) of the south coast of England. Even in the twentieth century, the natural features of the Arun Valley made it a favored invasion route, this time for the Germans.

✦

A British geographer from the turn of the last century, Sir Halford Mackinder, hypothesized that history was the product of geography. His theory was part of the geography course when I was at University. Like Keats dipping into Chapman's Homer, I felt like some watcher of the

skies when a new planet swims into his ken. Applying his theory to the
Old World, which is what mattered in his day, Mackinder saw the development of social democracy as something that could only have happened in a land sheltered from the threat of the Tartar hordes. Over the
centuries, the flat Central Asian plain had allowed these aggressive
horsemen to roar across the continent of Asia and break, wave upon
wave, over western Europe. Here the increasingly fractured geography of
the land absorbed and dissipated the impetus of their assaults, much as a
rocky headland absorbs the fury of a breaker. According to his theory,
the land most effectively sheltered from the terror from the east was
England, insulated from events in Europe by the English Channel. Thus
protected, it could become the cradle of democracy.

This may have the ring of Edwardian complacency, but in 1904 his
interest in geopolitics led Mackinder to promulgate his famous dictum:
"Who rules central Europe rules the heartland, who rules the heartland
rules the world island; who rules the world island rules the world." By
the World Island, he meant the Eurasian continent. Some years later,
the person who found this prescription for ruling the world really interesting was Adolf Hitler, since Mackinder's "heartland" was Prussia and
eastern Europe where the great expanse of the steppe meets the first ripples of geologically contorted Europe.

Mackinder is not much heard of these days.[38] When I was at University, one of the obvious criticisms leveled at his work was that the revolution in communications since the beginning of the century had
rendered his worldview obsolete. (Essay question: Compare and contrast
the railroad and the aeroplane with the Mongol horse. Discuss with ref-

---

38 Several years after I went down from University, I picked up a copy of his *Social Democracy* at Goodspeed's, the secondhand bookshop in Boston. I happened to be on my way to
pay a farewell call on a gentleman, a perfect relic of the Edwardian age and an old friend of
my father's, who was leaving Boston to spend the rest of his days in Ouchy, on the Lake of
Geneva. At one point during a lull in the conversation, I happened to mention my lucky
find. "Who wrote it?" he asked. "I don't think you would have heard of him," I replied, not
from any conceitedness on my part, but because I thought the prospect of anyone sharing my
recherché interest remote in the extreme. But he pressed me, and so I told him it was a geographer called Mackinder. "Sir Halford?" he cried delightedly. "He nearly married my
mother." It turned out that my book had come from the same library of which he was divest-
ing himself before his departure.

erence to Mackinder.) Even as a perspective on the past, Mackinder's, like any theory, has limits; geography cannot explain everything. But as a lens through which to contemplate history, its logic continues to have a powerful appeal for me. The same sensibility that responded so enthusiastically to Sir Halford Mackinder is what drives me as a conservationist. When in the early 1990s even the CIA began to redefine national security in terms of the world's natural resources and how they are distributed, I couldn't help feeling that Sir Halford would be smiling. And on a more local scale, my favorite landscapes are those in which one can read the intertwined forces of their natural geography and the history that made them.

In the restrained style of an algebraic formula, let $L = N + H$: Landscape equals Nature plus the effects of History. Like any good equation, one can shuffle it around so that History (as it can be read in the land) equals Landscape minus Nature. For virgin wilderness, where Landscape and Nature are the same, H would equal zero: History as the neutral passage of time unaffected by human interference. If one were looking for an avenue to pursue in order to give back to an overexploited Nature, then N might equal L minus H: a restoration project that would undo some of our impacts on the land.

This could usefully be applied to the Wild Brooks and the Downs around Amberley. During my lifetime, both have lost the bloom of centuries of care. More than half a century ago, my grandmother used to deplore the rows of council houses that were appearing around the marshes. Later the dredging stopped the river's annual floods that had kept them wild. On the top of the Downs, the land was plowed up with government subsidies. The velvet turf on Amberley Mount where we once collected field mushrooms in the late summer now has the look of threadbare corduroy, its flanks overgrazed so that in places the chalky soil shows through. In one dell just above the village the rounded contour of the hillside has been gouged by the tracks of motorbikes doing wheelies and doughnuts. When the Nature Conservancy Council, the quasi-governmental body charged with protecting British nature, established some experimental reserves to protect Environmentally Sensitive Areas along the South Downs, Amberley Mount was deemed too far gone, even though it is one of the remaining holdouts of the endangered downland blue butterfly.

However, public efforts have started to tip the balance in nature's favor again. In the mid-seventies, the Amberley Wild Brooks were the site of a singular environmental victory. When another "improvement" project was proposed to pump the Wild Brooks completely dry, there was an overwhelming public outcry, perhaps the largest since the locals had protested the billeting and food levies of Cromwell's army in 1645. But unlike that revolt, which was ruthlessly suppressed, this time the protest was successful. In a landmark case, the natural ecosystem was held up as irreplaceable, and for the first time in England, the powerful drainage boards were defeated. The Nature Conservancy Council stated: "This is a test case. . . . If it became known that we sacrificed this outstanding wetland for the sake of a minute increase in national food production, Britain would lose credibility among the nations who rightly expect us to take the lead in the matter of rational use of natural resources."

Not only was a damaging project stopped, but since 1989, the Royal Society for the Protection of Birds has been managing the Pulborough Wild Brooks (smaller but adjacent to Amberley's) in more environmentally favorable ways, with controlled summer grazing of cows and sheep and limited mowing for hay. Seasonal flooding, along with these more traditional uses of the land, has already significantly improved the habitat for wintering wildfowl and breeding shorebirds with impressive increases in their populations.

And efforts to restore the Downs are slowly gaining momentum. A button proclaiming "South Downs, our next national park" gives me hope that government subsidies may one day be used to undo the mischief they did to these hills in the fifties. And the National Trust recently launched a bid to save the great crested newt in a number of dew-ponds in the area. Perhaps there is hope for the dew-pond on Amberley Mount. Not without a struggle, the last twenty years have seen the beginnings of salvation for this beautiful part of England—as well as the world. We are beginning to grapple with the impending loss of our most treasured landscapes.

❧§❧

The fields in which humans and nature have played together over a long period of time are the landscapes that set our souls to singing. The hedgerows of England, the woodlots and fields of New England, even the marshes and ponds of so "wild" an area as the Camargue in France: all have been shaped by centuries of human use. We need to focus as much energy on saving them as we do the rainforests. Our souls may crave places where we can escape the stress of modern life, but we cannot live like anchorites on some deserted crag amid the unadulterated grandeur of nature. Just as, in the end, it is the quality of the job that is more important to our sense of worth than the place we take our vacation, it is the countryside in which we live each day that we need to maintain and that should be lovingly husbanded, not taken for granted, as our constant source of refreshment. We need such places as never before, but they are increasingly hard to find; and each time we do, we must airbrush from our retinas one more eyesore that would otherwise spoil them.

Finding balance (it will not do to say the "right" balance, because everyone's is likely to be different) between artifact and nature is an age-old conflict inherited from the first cave-dweller who decided to build his own hut and inadvertently replaced the gods of the land with the gods of the hearth. It is a Promethean struggle that reaches down to the very core of our being: between reverence for nature and the need to conquer it, between gratitude for its blessings and an insatiable appetite for more, between a wish to protect and a desire to exploit. Our connection to the land may start with what it offers us materially—its potential to meet our basic needs of food and shelter—but its capacity to nurture soon transforms itself into an emotional and spiritual relationship.

Seven hundred years ago, the anonymous writer of *Njal's Saga* turned the spiritual pull exerted by the tended landscape into the pivotal moment of his story. One of the saga's central characters, Gunnar, having been banished, is on his way to take ship to leave Iceland forever. In Sir George DaSent's translation: "They ride down along Markfleet, and just then Gunnar's horse tripped and threw him off. He turned with his face up towards the Lithe and the homestead at Lithend, and said, 'Fair is the Lithe; so fair that it has never seemed to me so fair; the corn fields are white to harvest and the home mead is mown; and now I will ride back home, and not fare abroad at all.'"

As humans have worked on the land, the land has worked on their minds in a symbiosis that has produced a sublime mutual sustenance, not least because it was substantial and enduring, while men, ephemeral on such a time scale, came and went. Old Mr. O'Hara's voice comes echoing down the years at the end of *Gone with the Wind*. "Land is the only thing in the world that amounts to anything, Katie Scarlett O'Hara. 'Tis the only thing that lasts." Once more the rolling fields of Tara fill the screen with the elegant antebellum mansion in the distance. Scarlett knows that the old man is right, and the swelling violins of the movie's score affirm our longing for the strength that springs from the land. But it is no longer so simple. As we have liberated ourselves from the natural cycles that power the landscape as a living thing, we have forgotten the spirit of giving as well as taking that made agricultural land productive and aesthetically refreshing for centuries. We consider the land from the comfort of "a room with a view," reveling in the blessings it provides while steering clear of its demands. Ever better career opportunities have made us mobile beyond our grandparents' dreams, but our geographical roots continually erode until home is no longer an unqualified place. When offered professional advancement at the price of pulling up stakes, very few of us have had Gunnar's fortitude to decide to "not fare abroad at all." We have let the treasure of rootedness slip through our fingers.

Since we are always moving across the land, why worry if a place we leave becomes degraded from destruction or neglect? At a conference on the dry but critical topic of sustainable development in Maine, I heard a Penobscot Indian woman describe how her community had reacted when "in the early 1960's, the skidders came, driven by people who spoke only English. We observed these machines and their drivers, and said, 'Well geez, they must be acting this way because this isn't their home. That's why they're acting so sloppy and rough.'" She went on, "None of us is acting like we are in our home. We act like we're not at home, that our mothers won't see what we do, that we won't get told on by sisters and brothers, because we're not at home, somehow."[39] Up to that point the conference's presentations, mostly by economists, had been pretty doctrinal, but there wasn't a dry eye in the house when she finished.

The lands "in which a long struggle of adaptation between man and his environment has brought out the best qualities in both" that appealed so much to T. S. Eliot are as endangered as wilderness. What will replace the stubbornness of old Gerald O'Hara when the taproots of personal connection to the land have been severed? Where will something like the elegiac imagination of Rudyard Kipling or Richard Jefferies spring from? Bates College's Carl Straub pinpoints the only place salvation can spring from. He calls it "the cultural loam, built from a rich, complex deposit of myths, theories, collective memories, and obsessions which nourishes us as human animals and which enables us, all the time, to make worlds of meaning out of the raw vitalities of arid deserts and river canyons, of starry nights and the tiniest shreds of microscopic life." But cultural just like natural loam must be constantly produced and tended. If either source of its richness — nature or culture — becomes degraded, then the other begins to waste away. "The wiping out of landscapes, all of which have histories and embody memories, wipes out those histories and memories," says Professor Straub.

A desire to be rooted in a landscape made familiar through the ages by the efforts of our forebears is fundamental to our nature. The fields in which our ancestors toiled, as much as the graves where they lie buried, are the threads that have held generation after generation together. In our different ways, we struggle to hold on to the comfort of the past through things that remind us of this. Piero Camporesi, an expert on Italian food and folklore, writes: "The Sunday drive outside the city becomes a voyage in time in search of roots, of irremediably lost origins, an attempt to recuperate through the mediation of the dinner table (talisman and magic object) slices of the past by techniques of cooking that are impossible in the city; to recuperate with the magic help of soups and stews by now mythical in urban households, a universe of lost smells and flavors that restores — in an illusory fashion, as with all drugged liturgies

39 Claire Bolduc, from *Toward a Sustainabale Maine*.

inevitably destined to alter the relationship of time and space—the ghost of a lost culture."[40]

Happily the memory remains. We still recognize the wisdom in Gerald O'Hara's voice, "Land is the only thing that lasts." But we have yet to internalize our recent discovery that the earth is fragile and finite. Although our ancestors understood how to live in nature far better than we do, they had not discovered this important fact. It was as irrelevant a piece of information as it was inconceivable. The scale of the disconnect between how we have conceived of the earth in cultural memory and just how much we need it now to support our species for the future is beginning to sink in. It is a chasm we must cross before we are pushed over the edge by the demons we have unleashed in our wake. The cables of the bridge to the other side are our ties to the land; we need them to feed our spirits no less than our bodies and to tell us who we are.

On one visit to Amberley, after an especially protracted absence, I rediscovered stored in a dusty barn my old anthology of English poetry from school. I took the book with me on my flight back to America and spent the whole trip thumbing through it at random, lost in a world of past associations, until suddenly we were on the final approach to Boston's Logan Airport. One poem particularly I read over and over again: "The Soldier," Rupert Brooke's premonition of death at the beginning of the First World War. And especially this verse:

> A dust whom England bore, shaped, made aware,
> Gave, once, her flowers to love, her ways to roam,
> A body of England's, breathing English air,
> Washed by the rivers, blest by suns of home.

Each phrase brought with it a split-second mental image—glimpses felt but just out of reach as in a dream—welling up from the past. Most

40 Quoted by Mary Taylor Simeti in her book *On Persephone's Island.*

of all, it was "her ways to roam," country lanes that I remember lined with hedgerows of hawthorn and a crossroads, its corners shaded by four towering chestnut trees. As the 747 banked over Sister Corita's gas tank to make its final turn, my eyes were brimming with tears of pure and delightful sentiment.

Who knows at what point in our individual development our imagination gets filled with such stuff? I know that although I have spent quite as many pleasant years in New England, my heart, fed by a jumble of half-remembered sights and sounds and smells as chaotic as a kaleidoscope, has always been lightest in England. In early spring, the intimate picture painted by Browning still strikes home with the sting of an arrow:

O to be in England
Now that April's there,
And whoever wakes in England
Sees, some morning unaware,
That the lowest boughs and the brushwood sheaf
Round the elm-tree bole are in tiny leaf,
While the chaffinch sings in the orchard bough
In England — now!

Even though the feeling of exile that I carried for many years has eventually been overcome by the sheer force of Maine's scenic beauty, I can never quite stifle a twinge of envy at the line "whoever wakes in England" at those times when it isn't me.

And every time I return to England, I feel a corresponding unfathomable excitement as the plane makes the last hour or so of its flight to Heathrow airport. The longer the period of absence, the stronger the feeling. That wonderful writer of wonder, Susan Cooper, describes the experience this way. "You look down from the airplane, flying over Britain, and—if you are lucky, and there is no cloud or fog—you see a patchwork, a map of the past. It is the story of a people, written upon the land: a long dialogue between people and place. In one form or another, men have lived here continuously for more than a million years. They have not molded the country as the glaciers did, grinding down the peaks and carving out the lakes, but they have scribbled on the land." Just as we have "scribbled on the land" and buried our history in it, the land itself has imprinted its image on our psyches and carved it in our hearts. The Arun, the Wild Brooks and the Downs are that part of England that, in Rupert Brooke's words, "bore, shaped, made [me] aware." In the churchyard in Amberley lie my great-grandparents, my grandparents and my mother, and I hope that when the day comes I will join them there.

> And think, this heart, all evil shed away,
>   A pulse in the eternal mind, no less
>   Gives somewhere back the thoughts by England given;
> Her sights and sounds; dreams happy as her day;
>   And laughter, learnt of friends; and gentleness,
>   In hearts at peace, under an English heaven.[41]

41 Rupert Brooke, "The Soldier."

If Music Be the Spice of Life

If music be the food of love, play on!
Give me excess of it, that, surfeiting,
The appetite may sicken, and so die.
That strain again! It had a dying fall.
O, it came o'er my ear like the sweet sound
That breathes upon a bank of violets,
Stealing and giving odour. Enough! No more!
—William Shakespeare, *Twelfth Night*

EVER SINCE IT BECAME clear that a seat in the recording booth was not likely to be a part of my career, I have fantasized about what it would be like to be a classical music disc jockey. I got my chance to find out thanks to the winning bid at a fund-raising auction when I was head of the Maine Audubon Society. My program was an eclectic one. The variety of directions from which music and nature can summon each other, as well as the variety of styles that can be employed in the summoning, is an endless source of fascination to me. As befitted a naturalist making his radio debut, the pieces I chose all had to do with the outdoors, but there the unity ended.

To emphasize that nature can be enjoyed from the balcony of the Grand Hotel as well as from a forest path, I introduced the show with a snippet from Noël Coward's "World Weary"—"I want to get right back to nature and relax"—before plunging into the rugged world of Sibelius's tone poem *Tapiola*. If Coward's urbane, sophisticated accent suggests white tie and tails, Sibelius's music evokes the wolf-skin cloak. *Tapiola* pays homage to the raw forces of nature symbolized by Tapio, the brooding spirit of the Finnish forest primeval. A simple repetitive dirge, ominously calm, opens the piece, but before the composer is done, he has whipped it into a gale that sets the forest trees to groaning.

My next selection used nature as a metaphor to illuminate the human condition. In the three Ritual Dances from his opera *The Midsummer Marriage*, Michael Tippett uses the hunt as archetype. In music that is powerful and graphic, each piece combines one of the elements with a season: the Earth in Autumn, the Waters in Winter, the Air in Spring. With each dance, the prey comes closer to its end. The hound pursues a hare who escapes in the nick of time by doubling back on his tracks; an otter chases a salmon, which escapes, too, but wrenches itself as it squeezes through a gap between two rocks; and finally a stooping falcon takes a little bird as it hops about a plowed field.

As an invocation of a natural object for a supernatural purpose, I chose the famous aria "Casta Diva" from Bellini's opera *Norma*. The moon is the Mother Goddess who looks down on the sacred grove and guides the Druids while her priestess incites them to rebellion against the Romans. I wound up the show with two Laurie Anderson songs: "Big Science," as a sort of warning against the alienation of nature:

> *Golden cities. Golden towns.*
> *And long cars in long lines and great big signs.*
> *And they all say: Hallelujah. Yodellayheehoo.*
> *Every man for himself.*

And a final choice, "Sharkey's Day," which contains an extraordinary image of nature at our command: "You know? They're growing mechanical trees. They grow to their full height. And then they chop themselves down."

In my allotted hour, I could only scratch the surface, nature having inspired composers since the lyre and before. Music cannot capture the colors of a Turner or a Monet, nor the metaphysical flights of fancy of a Wordsworth, nor even the homely insights of Frost's natural metaphors. But as a prism for gazing at nature it can capture physical and emotional weight — the sheer mass of a mountain or the restlessness of the waters — and interpret them in a way that brings the elements into a personal

relationship with the listener to an extent impossible in any other medium. Sometimes this emulation is conscious — the surge of the ocean at
the end of Rimsky-Korsakoff's *Scheherazade* — but it can equally be a natural affinity with musical form. The way in which tonalities struggle in a
Bruckner symphony inevitably results in an experience that must be
described in terms we commonly use for mountains: tectonic, spacious,
towering. No wonder that as often as not the picture on the record jacket
is of a mighty Alp.[42] There are certain moments in music when the effect
of tempo, notes and scoring can only be described in the vocabulary of
the living elements.

Just as they are endowed with a sense of wonder that only nature can
cultivate or charm, most children are also endowed with some level of
innate musicality. At an early age, they go through a phase of enhancing
their every action with a running soundtrack. It is stretching the point to
call it singing — its defining quality is that it is incessant, its mood deaf-
eningly recognizable to any bystander — but it is based on a rudimentary
awareness of the tonal system. Beyond that, in my experience at least,
musical ability expects to be developed rather more assiduously and must
overcome innumerable psychological hurdles however inadvertently
they have been placed in the way. We are made self-conscious about our
natural instrument, our voice: it is too loud, off-key or sings the wrong
sort of music. And we are made to learn an instrument for reasons that
are quite unclear, not to say dubious: it will bring you enjoyment one
day, or you'll regret it if you don't learn. I said the same to my daughter;
I can see her now aged seven or eight practicing a beginner's arrangement of Beethoven's "Ode to Joy" with tears of rage and frustration running down her face, quite oblivious to the irony.

In much the same way that Roger Tory Peterson's field guide started to
introduce the world to bird-watching in 1934, *Peter and the Wolf* has
been the introduction to music for generations of children ever since it

---

42 The composer Robert Simpson finishes his appraisal of Bruckner's works, which is otherwise almost entirely musicological, as if he can no longer resist the elemental simile: "The
frothing tide that often threatened his work and his sanity has long drained into crevices in
the soft earth, but the hard and jagged rock of his life's achievement is still there. It has survived all seeming odds. The cracks in the stone are honourable scars on its mighty face."

was written, two years later. More than twenty years before Rachel Carson coined her famous phrase, Prokofiev instinctively tapped into the sense of wonder surrounding animals and nature. It inspired him, one of the most cosmopolitan of composers, to fashion brilliant musical portraits with a naturalist's eye. Only with the kettle drums that mimic the hunters' guns does he resort to onomatopoeia in the score. The discipline of his musical invention triggers our imagination and, more than any literal sound effects, allows us to see the various animals as they appear.

The flute, whose arabesques depict the bird, emulates the freedom of its flight quite as much as its twittering. By choosing the clarinet for the cat, Prokofiev lets us hear the feel of its velvet paws, while the tune's furtive phrases conjure up its stealthy passage through the long grass. In the same way, the oboe turns into a duck paddling around a pond, the bassoon into a grandfather remonstrating. Alone among the single melodic lines of the other animals, and my personal favorite, French horns in harmony depict the rapacious eyes and temper of the wolf. The organizing principle of the work, Peter's youthful, devil-may-care energy, belongs to the string section of the orchestra, and the way Prokofiev plays out his themes, combining and recombining them to tell the story, is as musically satisfying as it is literarily precise.

The version I grew up with came as an album of 78s with Basil Rathbone as the narrator. On the cover, the picture of Peter and the animals in the story had been simplified into colored, geometrical shapes, mostly squares and circles, which my young literal mind found perplexing. Thirty years later during my stint at the Massachusetts Audubon Society, I enlisted Robert J. Lurtsema, the dean of all classical disc jockeys, to narrate a performance of *Peter and the Wolf* at Audubon's Night at the Boston Pops. There was a pet wolf in Lincoln at the time whose owner used to exercise him over the Mass Audubon sanctuary, and Robert J. agreed to pose with the animal for some press shots. He was to perch in a tree and dangle a lasso over the wolf's head. When the appointed hour came, the celebrity, sure of his capacity as an animal whisperer, greeted the wolf as an old friend, only to leap quickly out of range as it made a grab at his outstretched arm.

Peter and the Wolf tells a good story, and the music makes the character and behavior of the animals that inhabit it come alive. But the associations are self-conscious, if not outright anthropomorphic. The piece is an artifice, the meticulous work of an artist, like an intricately chiseled caryatid. To continue the lapidary analogy, other music is instead like the perfectly smoothed and shaped stone one finds on a beach. Writing of the evolution of folk song, Ralph Vaughan Williams quoted Allingham's *Ballad Book* to describe "the countless riddlings, siftings, shiftings, omissions, and additions of innumerable reciters. The lucky changes hold, the stupid ones fall aside. Thus . . . the ballad glides from generation to generation and fits itself more and more to the brain and ear of its proper audience." Added the composer, "Nor can we say how old it is; in one sense any particular tune is as old as the beginnings of music, in another sense it is born afresh with the singer of today who sang it." It was Vaughan Williams's arrangement of an old French folk tune that we sang at Christmas as "The Holly and the Ivy," its minor key seeming to suggest a wilder wood for "the running of the deer." The Hungarian composer Béla Bartók, who also based much of his music on traditional songs and dances, said that they were "as much a natural phenomenon . . . as the various manifestations of Nature in fauna and flora." Such music resonates deep down in highly personal ways that I can only describe as *ur-feelings*.

Vaughan Williams believed that the "essence of a good folk tune is that it does not show its full quality till it has been repeated several times." The most initially attractive tune may pall after repeated hearing, whereas the real McCoy thrives on the "riddlings, siftings" that Allingham spoke of. I think of the "Ashokan Lament" that accompanied Ken Burns's *Civil War* on PBS, immensely effective and popular in the series but without staying power, to my ears at least.[43] However, there are tunes that seem to have sprung fully rounded from the composer's brain, as if it were a gem tumbler. Thomas Mann could have been thinking of

---

43 According to the composer, Jay Ungar, "Ashokan Farewell is written in the style of a Scottish lament or Irish Air. I sometimes introduce it as, 'a Scottish lament written by a Jewish guy from the Bronx.'"

Robert Schumann's "Sonntags am Rhein" when he described German lieder as "products of an intellectual art, [that] at the same time sprang from all that was profoundest and most reverent in the feeling and genius of a people."

> *Des Sonntags in der Morgenstund'*,
> *Wie wandert's sich so schön*
> *Am Rhein, wenn rings in weiter Rund'*
> *Die Morgenglocken geh'n!*[44]

A climactic vision of the landscape shimmering in the sun "contemplated by beloved God" crowns the song's visceral impression of idealized woods and fields, hills and streams, and time.

In fact, Mann was discussing the songs of Schubert, singling out "Der Lindenbaum" in particular to describe the wellspring of feelings certain songs arouse. It is the key to the sensibility of the main character in *The Magic Mountain*. "To him the song meant a whole world, a world which he must have loved, else he could not have so desperately loved that which it represented and symbolized to him." "Der Lindenbaum" was one of the songs my father used to sing with a Spanish colleague from the U.N. Gustavo Duran had been a professional musician and composer in his youth and played the piano with tremendous élan. They would start off playing duets for piano and oboe together. My father was an accomplished oboist who might have had a professional career.[45] Often it was music by Bach, originally written for the violin. But after dinner, they would turn to a book of Schubert lieder. The more plaintive songs of *Winterreise* were favorites, including "Der Lindenbaum," but it was "Die Post" that we loved especially and would join in the singing with abandon. In the accompaniment, Gustavo's fingers made the impatience of

---

44 On Sundays in the morning hours, / how pleasant it is to wander / along the Rhine, when all around / the morning bells are chiming! (Text by Robert Reinick [1805–1852], translated by Emily Ezust.)

45 During my childhood, my father would often play in the evening. However, in the course of being kidnapped on a U.N. mission in the Congo, he had his nose and hand broken, and after that, playing the oboe became too difficult.

the horses of the mail coach a tangible presence hovering over the piano, while my father's light baritone voice singing *"Mein Herz"* on the sustained notes at the end of each verse carried in it all the wistfulness of the world.

As long ago as I can remember, my parents taught us folk songs, most of them from the British Isles at least originally. The ballads were full of good stories, and they also brought nearer a place-based past. From my father came the songs from his own childhood, such as "Widdecombe Fair," "Rafferty's Pig" and "The Bonnie Earl o' Murray," which he would sing in the appropriate accent, West Country, Irish or Scottish as the case might be. Whenever we went any distance in the car, we would go through the whole repertoire. Some of the minor melodies, like "The Oak and the Ash," or the modal cadences of "O come, O come Emanuel" at Christmastime, seem to spring from the earth itself straight to the heart. Cowboy songs like "I Ride an Old Paint" and "The Lone Prairie" held the additional glamour of the landscape of the West. Listening to Roy Rogers singing "Cool Clear Water" and "Tumbling Tumbleweed" was to open up a world full of cottonwood trees and arroyos, as vivid as it was imaginary. I felt I knew those wide-open spaces, and I yearned for them although I had never been further west than New Jersey.

When a new song that touched a wishful nerve came within reach, I needed to possess it, listening to it over and over until I had memorized the words of every verse and made it mine. Over the years, being able to sing all the verses of so many songs from memory has served me in good stead on many a long road trip with my own children. One never knows when it will come in handy, for instance at a conference on endangered species in Finland, in the midst of Tapio's domain a stone's throw from the Russian border. It included governmental representatives from Eastern (then communist) Europe, and the atmosphere was pretty stiff to start with. But our Finnish hosts had two secret weapons to break the ice. The first was the sauna; after seeing the Soviet delegate in the buff, it was harder to feel intimidated during the working sessions. The second was music. Every night after dinner all the delegates got together and sang from a collection of songs prepared by the conference organizers — most of them I had sung all my life.

A couple of years before I went off to boarding school, my parents bought a television, and the regular programs opened up a new source of songs and tunes. From time to time one of them pops back into my life, and it is like greeting a long-lost friend. Or rather what the French call a *faux ami*, a term that is similar in two languages but has a dangerously different meaning in each. Thus it was a surprise to find out, the first time I went to Gounod's *Faust*, that the title tune from *Lassie*, so redolent of the fields over which she bounded on one mission of mercy after another, was really *"Avant de quitter ces lieux,"* Valentin's prayer in which he begs God's protection for his sister. And on radio, the theme song for *Sergeant Preston*, which seemed exclusively to summon up the snowy wastes of the wild North West over which he and his sled dog, Yukon King, fought for law and order, turned out, at a Boston Pops concert years later, to be the overture to von Suppé's *Donna Deanna*, a far cry from the Yukon.[46] And I would never have expected that the music I associated with the credits of *Million Dollar Movie* and its image of a Hollywood clapper would one day evoke the splendor of Tara in *Gone with the Wind*.

The most sacred of all the songs from television was "The White Buffalo," from an episode on *Rin Tin Tin* in which the boy and his dog search for a miraculous White Buffalo. My best friend (with whom I roamed the Natural History Museum) and I first saw it one evening when I was staying at his house, and it became an instant charm for us. Although we would hardly have used the term then, we felt instinctively that the quest for the White Buffalo was an archetypal symbol for making peace. In good cowboy fashion, the legend had a ballad to go with it, a line of which urged people to "treat all men as brothers, no matter what they do." When they heard me singing that, my parents scoffed at the sentimentality of the words, but they seemed wonderful to me, and after all, Beethoven had the same idea in the choral symphony.

Another theme song that had an immediate mysterious appeal was

46 My parents had a friend called Preston, and he would bring me *Sergeant Preston* comic books when he came to dinner. I never really suspected that he was the Mountie, but it was a good game, and he had in fact been a sergeant during the war. In fact, he was the inspiration for "the Loot," the American soldier socialite in Evelyn Waugh's *Sword of Honor* trilogy.

the music from the Orson Welles film *The Third Man*. Certainly the sound of the zither was unlike anything I had ever heard, but the tune itself was bewitching. It was among the 78s at Amberley (along with Frank Crummit and Paul Robeson) and was one of my grandmother's favorites. She was notoriously unmusical, but there were one or two marked exceptions, and this was one of them. I have a very clear memory of her listening to the "Harry Lime Theme," swaying her cane in time to the jazzy rhythm with the merest suggestion of a shift of the shoulders and the racy raising of an eyebrow. The music itself—as is the movie—is a classic effort to evoke a sense of place and time, in this case postwar Vienna.[47]

The other exceptions were on two 12-inch 78s that my grandmother kept carefully apart from the 10-inch records that we played all the time. On special occasions, mysteriously unpredictable to us, she would pull them out of their place of honor in the cupboard of an enormous oak Elizabethan dresser, and play them with a newly sharpened steel needle on the wind-up gramophone. One was a duet, *"Niemand liebt dich so we ich,"* which I later discovered came from an operetta by Lehar, *Paganini*. Shaking her head she would close her eyes as if inwardly speaking the words to a lover. Doubtless my fondness for Viennese *schmalz* can be traced to this syrupy but ecstatic song. The other was the Russian folk song "Dark Eyes" sung by the great Russian bass Chaliapin. The drama in the voice made a deep enough impression on us, but it was also often accompanied by a still more riveting sight: my cousin Peter, who claimed half his ancestry from Russia, proving the fact by doing a Cossack dance, with a lampshade on his head in place of the traditional Russian bearskin.

If not the music, it was certainly the emotion of all three pieces that affected my grandmother so deeply. The last week she was ever to spend

---

47 It was a great favorite, and it never occurred to me that it might be controversial until one evening on a skiing holiday in St. Anton. A zither player was part of the après-ski ambience in a restaurant where we were eating, and I begged my father to ask him to play "The Third Man," the only tune I had ever heard played on the instrument. To my surprise, my father said he couldn't and explained that Graham Greene's tale of postwar corruption in Vienna was still too close to the bone in 1950s Austria.

at Amberley, I was on holiday from school. By this time, the hand-cranked gramophone had given way to a new, electric record player. On its lid was a label on which she had written: "From the French *Madame Solario*." She had bought it for us with the French royalties of her best-selling anonymous novel, a Jamesian story set on Lake Como in the early 1900s that involved incest. One day when I was playing the old records in the big sitting room, she sent my grandfather in to beg me to turn off the gramophone, as she found the old favorites too distressing. Within a month, it was apparent that she had known she had not much time left, and as she prepared herself to say good-bye, the memories brought back by all those songs must have been unbearable.

At Westminster the Church of England Hymnal proved to be another source of what our music master used to call "rattling good tunes." Every day of the school term we attended a short morning service in West-minster Abbey, and precious few of the hymns we sang did not make this compulsory activity worth it. I found "Holy, Holy, Holy" a bit four-square and repetitive. But the English countryside blossomed in the soaring vaults above our Gothic pews with hymns such as "Jerusalem" ("And did those feet in ancient time walk upon England's pastures green") and the lovely "As pants the hart for cooling streams." Hymns "for missions over-seas" conjured up foreign lands: "From Greenland's icy mountains to India's coral strand" (even if we usually sang it as "The Church's one foundation is Jesus Christ our Lord," I could keep the more evocative words under my breath), "Bread of Heaven" (as sung by Katharine Hep-burn at the beginning of *The African Queen*). And always "Eternal father strong to save, / Whose arm has bound the restless wave," the Royal Navy's hymn that I had heard night after night watching Noël Coward's *In Which We Serve* on *Million Dollar Movie*. If we sang a particular favorite at morning prayers, the day was sure to be a red-letter one.

A short walk from Westminster lived a former English teacher, John Burn, who had retired early to devote himself to composing. John was guide, teacher and friend to a select group of students and provided infinitely valuable advice of the kind one would now get from the school guidance counselor. With a face like a carved Austrian pipe, he looked much older than he was as he greeted one at his study door through a haze of Erinmore tobacco smoke. He was particularly partial to the Impressionists, to which style his own music added a Stravinskian edge, and one day as I approached his door, I heard lovely liquid phrases coming from his piano. He was, by coincidence, playing John Ireland's "Amberley Wild Brooks." He had a prodigious collection of records from which we could pick and choose, and it was he who introduced me to the music of Gustav Mahler. For most of the other great composers, I at least knew their names and even had some idea of the kind of music they had written. But here was a composer I had absolutely never heard of before. Not all of the symphonies were available on record and some only on obscure labels. But Mahler's day was coming. In the wake of the celebrations, in 1960, of the hundredth anniversary of his birth the public started to hear his music again and clamored for more. Within five years, most major recording companies were at work on the complete symphonic canon with top conductors and orchestras.

From the moment I heard his music, Mahler obsessed me in about equal parts for his inspiration from nature and for his neurotic *Sturm und Drang*. The highly strung and prophetic Sixth Symphony with which I started suited to perfection an introspective teenager with a love for the out-of-doors. The relentless march that sweeps up the listener as the first movement opens, the A major–A minor motto that scatters heartbreak throughout the work, the crushing hammer blows of fate at the end: all belonged to a universe that was totally new and unexpected. And the cowbells. The response of the composer to a beloved landscape, the alpine pastures where he composed many of his symphonies, was soon my strongest bond with Mahler. Mahler said of himself that he was thrice homeless: "as a native of Bohemia in Austria, as an Austrian among Germans, and as a Jew throughout all the World."[48] One is tempted to look to the first part of this declaration for his affinity for nature. The woods and brooks of Bohemia seem to murmur and bubble throughout the

48 Alma Mahler, *Gustav Mahler, Memories and Letters*.

music of Czech composers even when they have not specifically indicated the source of their inspiration as in Dvořák's symphonies, to say nothing of Smetana's *Moldau* or Janáček's *The Cunning Little Vixen*.

I devoured Mahler's works as, one by one, I got my hands on them. If ever there was a hymn to the nature gods, it is the Third Symphony. That summer was an unusually fine one for England, but if clouds threatened the morning at Amberley, they would be driven away by its great opening, "Summer Marches In," blasted fortissimo out the open windows. The Third is recognizably a symphony, albeit one that is straining at the leash. But within its symphonic structure, Mahler tells us quite explicitly and beautifully about nature and the feelings nature arouses and in the end intuitively links the natural world with the profoundest of all feelings. After nearly an hour of music that starts with the Great God Pan and goes on to probe "What the animals tell me," "What the flowers tell me," "What night tells me," "What the children tell me," Mahler gives us "What love tells me." This love is faith, and the movement is one of the most exalted adagios ever written. When listening to the adagio from the Third Symphony, I think of a remark made by a Japanese Shinto priest to a Unitarian minister friend of mine. "It is too bad you have only one God; for us there is a god in a stone or a tree, in everything. You don't know what you are missing."

If his naturalistic pantheism found its most unadulterated form in the Third Symphony, the palpable presence of nature underscores all of Mahler's orchestral scores and many of his songs. The morning beckoning of the sleepyhead by the outdoors has rarely been so delicately depicted as in "Frühlingsmorgen" (Spring Morning) with a phrase in the piano accompaniment, incidentally, that to my ears is straight Janáček, attesting to his Bohemian heritage. And the song from the *Lieder eines fahrenden Gesellen* (*Songs of a Wayfarer*), "Ging heut' morgen übers Feld" (Going over the Field This Morning), the tune of which he incorporated in the First Symphony as well, is one that I would have expected Peter to sing after he got the wolf, when he became a teenager and was disappointed in love for the first time. While *Das Lied von der Erde* has certainly more to do with human *weltschmerz*, the Chinese poems Mahler used as a text are heavily dependent on their authors' awareness of the seasons and natural phenomena. The very last lines were written by the composer himself and appended to the end of the Chinese poem which he called "Der Abschied":

Die liebe Erde allüberall blüht auf im Lenz und grünt aufs neu!
Allueberall und ewig blauen Licht die Fernen!
Ewig. . . . ewig. . . .[49]

It is the closest I can come to imagining the eternity I believe in. In the end the only balm is nature.

From Mahler, it was but a small step to Wagner. Since first hearing *Götterdämmerung*, I have often pondered on the overwhelming aspect of Wagner's music and what the depth of my personal response to it means. I cannot deny that it traffics in the dark as well as the light side of the unconscious, and to a degree that would be unhealthy in a lesser work. Instead, it is cathartic. There is a nobility in the whole that heals, and an honesty that exorcises the individual devils it has summoned up. Wagner's greatness is that, for all that they are gods and demigods, his characters are all lurking somewhere in our psyches. The least attractive have their sympathetic side; the grandest are riven with deep-seated flaws. *The Ring* is arguably the most heroic attempt in all of art to portray the conflict of our material desires and our ultimate dependence on nature, our cosmic kicking against the pricks and all the complexities it produces. Whether one sees it as mythic struggle, as an allegory for the industrial revolution or as psychological metaphor, the forces that engage each other throughout all four operas are man and nature. The music takes nature's part, leaving the poem to man.

The starker visions of his grandsons, Wieland and Wolfgang, notwithstanding, Wagner wanted nature — rivers, mountains, clouds, rainbows, horses, goats and, of course, dragons[50] — portrayed on the stage to match his score. The illustrations of Arthur Rackham would surely have appealed

---

49 The lovely earth everywhere blooms forth in spring and grows green anew! / Everywhere and forever shines the blue horizon! / Forever . . . Forever . . . (Translation by Alfred E. Meyer)

50 Wagner wanted the most realistic sets that could be made at the time, which were not

to him. But for us today, they carry the freight of their late nineteenth-century style—part pre-Raphaelite, part Art Nouveau—which although pleasing intervenes by its period trappings. Wagner's music bypasses all that and is timeless. It taps right into the subconscious, and the subconscious pushes us into an archetypal relationship with mountains and rivers and forests. From the moment the first horn call in Das Rheingold cuts through the watery arpeggios—as the rising sun penetrates the river's depths and lights up the gold itself—to the climactic orchestral tutti—as the Rhine overflows its banks extinguishing and redeeming the burning earth—at the end of Götterdämmerung, the orchestra summons up the natural world in all its ancient splendor. The result is prodigious.

The early opera Der fliegende Holländer is a simpler version of love and redemption, but its evocation of the forces of wind and wave—and their sinister association with the supernatural—are none-the-less electrifying. By his own account, Wagner first "heard" the opening strains of the overture in the wind that lashed the rigging of a storm-tossed ship in which he was escaping across the Baltic in the wake of the disturbances of 1848 and, as usual, his creditors. In the 1990s, an old Russian rust-bucket of a factory ship used to anchor off the coast of Maine each summer, where it took on incredible quantities of pogies, a very oily and smelly fish, to be processed onboard. Against the brilliant aquamarine of the waters of Penobscot Bay, it stood in stark contrast to the expensive and elegant schooners cruising by, its ship-bound sailors dangling ropes over the side to trade trinkets with the little pleasure boats that came out of the harbor to ogle it. To the west, the hazy Camden Hills trailed off into the hinterland and the woods of the deer hunters. Here, I realized,

---

always good enough. G. B. Shaw commented, "As usual, people are complaining of the dragon as a mistake on Wagner's part, as if he were the man to have omitted a vital scene in his drama merely because our stage machinists are such duffers as to be unable, with all their resources, to make as good a dragon as I could improvise with two old umbrellas, a mackintosh, a clothes-horse, and a couple of towels." Wagner was especially unlucky with his dragon. In what must be one of the earliest major postal screw-ups in history, the original dragon found itself shipped inadvertently to Beirut, instead of Bayreuth, the site of Wagner's new opera house. I always hoped that my father would turn up a bit of it in the bazaar on one of his many peacekeeping journeys to Lebanon: a bit of articulated tail or a fang, perhaps.

was the perfect setting for a modern *Flying Dutchman*, with costumes out of the sporting goods department of L.L. Bean. I am still working on it.

Within the symphonic repertoire, it is an accepted practice to disparage "program music." Mahler himself could never quite decide; he wrote programs for his early symphonies, then discarded them. Certainly, compared with a work such as Strauss's *Alpen Symphonie* with its precise notes on the nature of a hike up a mountain, musical logic has a more profound presence in a Mahler symphony. "My music arrives at a program as its last clarification," he wrote, "whereas in the case of Strauss the program already exists as a given task."[51] But there is no denying that within those strictures, his music mirrors fairly accurately the profound feelings that nature stirred in him. Alma Mahler tells a touching story of Mahler and Brahms taking a walk together in the countryside. "They came to a bridge and stood silently gazing at the foaming mountain stream. A moment before they had been heatedly debating the future of music. . . . Now they stood fascinated by the sight of the water breaking in foam time after time over the stones. Mahler looked upstream and pointed to the endless procession of swirling eddies. 'Which is the last?' he asked with a smile."[52]

I am immediately biased in favor of the many other composers who have been inspired by nature and am always curious to listen to how they approach it. Certain onomatopoeic temptations—the cuckoo, for instance—aside, music, like poetry, can avail itself of powerful intuitive associations that we all recognize: rhythms to capture the surge of the sea, tonal leaps to suggest lightning, arpeggios for moonlight on the water. A railway engine is a far cry from a vista at dawn or a sunset over the mountains, but the comments of the Swiss composer Arthur Honegger about his tone poem *Pacific 231* could apply to both. "I have aimed not to imitate the noise of an engine, but rather to express in terms of music a visual impression and a physical sensation." In that spirit, never have we felt the sun rise so magnificently, nor with such cosmic pregnancy, as in the opening of Richard Strauss's *Also Sprach Zarathustra*, a phrase that

---

51 Quoted in Neville Cardus, *Gustav Mahler: A Centenary Celebration.*

52 Alma Mahler, *Gustav Mahler, Memories and Letters.*

perhaps represents the acme of musical attempts to express the inexpressible (and certainly the best known, thanks to the movie 2001).

The reflection of human aspiration in the grandeur of nature is what
makes pieces like *Zarathustra* so satisfying. We require more than a backdrop for historical drama or a pretty postcard picture, such as Respighi's
Pines of Rome, no matter how brilliant or original its orchestration. More
than a simple imitation of nature, music, perhaps better than any of the
arts, can plumb the depths of the personal response to its wonder. In order
to capture that successfully, strong emotion needs to be harnessed by
musical form. Roger Sessions, the American composer noted for his rigorous approach to musical logic, and a distant cousin, once told me how
he and his teacher Ernst Bloch had each written a fugue for the other. His
teacher congratulated him on the purity of his counterpoint, and the rich
clashes it produced. For his part Roger praised Bloch on the liberties he
took with strict form in order to produce a more euphonious result.

Since I am no music scholar, whether or not the music sticks to the
letter of the law is for me immaterial, but I like to sense the struggle. If
inspiration is a spirited horse that stamps its feet and shakes its mane
until one is conscious of its beautiful body, form is the bridle and harness.
Not necessarily obvious and sometimes almost invisible, it keeps its subject going in the right direction and gives one the satisfaction of seeing
it arrive at its destination. Like T. S. Eliot's ideal of the "struggle of adaptation between man and his environment," inspiration and form bring
out "the best qualities in both."

This is particularly critical in music that purports to be based on nature,
which has a tendency to meander. (Think Delius!) In *Die Meistersinger
von Nürnberg*, Wagner has his hero Walther von Stolzing describe his
two masters in the art of singing: a book of poems by the long-dead min-
nesinger Walther von der Vogelweide, read by the hearth during snow-
bound winter, and the music of outdoors in the woods in spring.

> *Wann dann die Flur vom Frost befreit,*
> *und wiederkehrt die Sommerszeit,*
> *was einst in länger Winternacht*
> *das alte Buch mir kund gemacht,*

das schallte laut in Waldespracht,
das hört' ich hell erklingen:
im Wald dort auf der Vogelweid',
da lernt' ich auch das Singen.[53]

This earns a sarcastic comment from his nemesis, the grouchy Beck-messer: *"Oho! Von Finken und Meisen lerntet Ihr Meister-weisen? Das mag denn wohl auch darnach sein!"*[54] The next four hours of *Die Meistersinger* prove Beckmesser wrong because Walther has the creative genius to bend the teachings of the finches and tits to his artistic purpose.

However, in real life, I share a good deal of Beckmesser's suspicion, especially when it comes to the contribution that unadulterated natural sounds can make to a composition. There is something mindless about the way New Age music incorporates singing whales, howling wolves or yodeling loons. Plastering natural sounds over classical music — juxta-posing a Bach fugue with the calls of a pod of whales, for instance — tells us nothing new and amplifies our appreciation of neither. With its pseudo artistry and self-indulgent tonal wallowing, it undervalues both nature and music. As with so much of their Native American mystique, New Agers end up prostituting the real thing. They make me yearn for Des Esseintes, the ultimate aesthete, who seeks to experience everything but wherever possible from the privacy of his darkened, scented room in J. K. Huysman's decadent book *À Rebours*. "Nature has had her day; she has finally and totally exhausted the patience of all sensitive minds by the loathsome monotony of her landscapes and skies." The book, usually translated as *Against the Grain*, celebrates the antithesis of nature and natural laws.

Part of the problem is that this kind of music is as much about advo-cacy as it is about notes, and it lacks the edge of a Kurt Weill. The pres-

---

53 And when the fields the frost defied, / and summer shone in radiant pride; / what during winter's dreary spell / that ancient book had told so well, / that song I heard o'er moor and fell, / through field and forest ringing: / from birds' song on the Vogelweid, / 'twas there I learned my singing.

54 Oho! The finches and titmice taught you our Mastersinging? What manner of teaching was theirs!

ence of an eagle's cry alone carries the message; it does not need to be worked into any musical logic. It is also about "celebration," a word often used to describe these concerts. But I hear nothing more than a feel-good miasma of sounds, albeit pleasing. Celebration should be about striving and have more muscle. I would as soon listen to the novelty record we had when we were children of a flock of canaries singing "Come Back to Sorrento." At least it had a point, namely to encourage our canary to sing.

Some serious composers have tried to use natural sounds more creatively. The prolific composer Alan Hovhaness, inspired by Roger Payne's recordings of the songs of the humpback whale, incorporated them in *And God Created Great Whales*. I heard it premiered at a New York Philharmonic Promenade concert in 1970, and it is a pleasant if facile piece, heavily pentatonic, "sound[ing] openness of wide ocean sky," according to the composer's commentary in the program notes. "Song of whale emerges like giant mythical sea bird. Man does not exist, has not yet been born in the solemn oneness of nature." The sounds whales make are extraordinary, and it is not mere anthropomorphism to call them songs. Spectrographic analysis shows sequences of sounds, lasting up to half an hour, repeated with little variation and without pause, so that "the songs are, in fact, circular, joined at the ends: we cannot say whether they have a strict beginning and end."[55] "We who live on land," concludes Dr. Payne, "deal with our world largely through vision, but in the sea, where sound is carried far better than light, hearing is more useful than vision. Thus it is perhaps not so surprising that some of the most beautiful sounds of the wild world come from the sea." Nonetheless, to my ears, George Crumb's *Voice of the Whale*—a work inspired by whale songs but realized entirely on orchestral instruments—has far greater musical interest and is ultimately a more fulfilling response to the majesty of the great creatures.

The most convincing piece of music incorporating natural sounds that I know is Finnish composer Einojuhani Rautavaara's *Cantus Arcticus*, which he subtitles "Concerto for Birds and Orchestra." Perhaps it is

---

55 "The Music of Whales," Roger S. Payne in the Promenades program.

because he made the tapes himself in the marshes above the Arctic Circle — so that the creative process started in the out-of-doors with the air thick with mosquitoes — that I am prepared to cut him some slack. The tapes are used in the manner of *musique concrète*, and the skill with which they are integrated into the orchestra makes up for the fact that I am left wondering how a musical depiction of the "voice and mood of a person walking in the wilds" might sound using instruments alone. In this case, the human part of the bargain — the composer's work and inspiration, to say nothing of creative talent — is the equal of his wild collaborators.

By contrast, one composer, Olivier Messiaen, has created virtually a new musical language out of the rigorous deployment of exact musical transcriptions of birdsong, whose "melodies alone are interpreters of thought." He was the contemporary focus, besides the great baroque composer, of the Oxford Bach Festival one summer in the mid-sixties. I sat behind the composer during a performance of his monumental *Turangalîla* Symphony in the Oxford Town Hall. The hall is not a large one, and the enormous orchestra filled the stage to bursting. The sound, augmented by the ethereal strains of the *ondes martinot*, was stupendous in so confined a space. In some passages it pinned one's ears back until one felt rather than heard the music. When it was over, the person sitting next to Messiaen asked him about the acoustics. He pronounced them perfect. The force in the music of *Turangalîla* has its roots in humanity's awe in the presence of creation; it has a strangely pagan element for this most Catholic of composers personified by a wild and wooly theme from a choir of trombones that recurs throughout the piece.

After a work of such architectonic grandeur, Messiaen's next piece, *Réveil des Oiseaux*, is a musical fantasy based on a very precise depiction of the dawn chorus in a French countryside in May from midnight to noon. (Twelve hours, however, is telescoped into just over twenty minutes.) Nearly forty different species of bird are involved. There are musical favorites such as the cuckoo, lark and nightingale, but also, in what must be their debut appearances, Cetti's warbler (E-flat clarinet), little owl (violin) and chaffinch (also violin). The major instrument around which the birds sing is the piano, which itself portrays wryneck, robin and blackcap among others. Messiaen called it "a completely truthful work"; it is also one of great complexity and compositional skill. His biographer Paul Griffiths says of Messiaen that "he is far more conscientious an ornithologist than any earlier musician, and far more musical an observer than any other ornithologist."[56] I have heard but never seen his opera *St. Francis of Assisi*, but a friend described the immensely long second act. After a full hour comes the sermon to the birds, forty-five minutes of contemplation. Some of Messiaen's most light-flooded bird music[57] alternates with the tortuous string writing that underscores the saint's struggle for perfection. "I don't know why," recalled my friend, "but at the end I found myself in tears."

While it can hardly be compared to the overpowering nature of operas like *The Ring* or *St. Francis*, film music offers its composers a very particular opportunity to evoke the landscape we are seeing on the screen. And as accompaniment to a narrative, the most successful scores conjure up human emotions and bind them indissolubly to the natural scenery. Vaughan Williams's music for *Scott of the Antarctic*, from which he crafted the *Sinfonia Antarctica*, portrays the frozen wastes—"frigid sounds on the lower strings and a cold-steel effect of single, unconnected xylophone notes"[58]—while a thrusting theme on the strings illuminates the indomitable spirit of the gallant explorers.

The American composer Virgil Thomson wrote a number of film scores, of which *Louisiana Story* is a particularly good illustration of the symbiosis of music and film in creating atmosphere. When I was at University, I heard a concert version at the Royal Albert Hall in a box with the composer. I had brought a young woman whom I hoped to impress, and after the concert she and I went out to dinner before I put her in a cab to go home. When I returned home, quite late, Virgil was there—he

---

56 Paul Griffiths, *Olivier Messiaen and the Music of Time*.

57 As well as the turtle dove, robin and blackcap, several Antipodean birds participate. "*Je n'ai jamais entendu ces oiseaux dans notre Ombrie*," a brother tells St. Francis. "*Moi non plus*," replies the Saint, "*ils chantaient dans mon rêve*." ("I never heard these birds in our Umbria." "Nor I, they sang in my dream.")

58 Roger Manvell and John Huntley, *The Technique of Film Music*.

and my mother shared a passion for cooking, on one occasion filling the bathtub with live terrapins prior to turning them into some exotic meal. My girlfriend's father had just called asking where we were, and the composer's eyes were twinkling at the thought that I would be horsewhipped on the steps of the father's club.

An analysis of the opening of *Louisiana Story* is an exercise in how music can express man and nature on film, incidentally using local folk songs.

In the first scene, the score is the binding agent that gives continuity to the atmosphere which surrounds lotus-leaves, birds, snakes and the boy in his pirogue. Music follows the camera, though not mechanically. Its motion sublimates the motion of photography. . . . The composer's tunes are of such versatility and are handled with such ingenuity of orchestration that they accompany with perfect propriety shots of beautiful flowers, weird alligators and the terrifying machine of the marsh buggy. The treatment of the [Cajun] folk songs is equally deft.[59]

The "binding" relationship of camera and score reaches its ultimate when script and story are dispensed with, as in *Koyaanisqatsi*, a collaboration by composer Philip Glass and director Godfrey Reggio. The title is a Hopi word meaning "life out of balance" or "a state of life that calls for another way of living," and the film is an environmental indictment. I witnessed how powerfully it succeeds in the faces of Maine Audubon's members when I arranged for the composer to show it in Portland. Glass's repetitive rhythms and arpeggios—sometimes calm but more often frenetic—drive a cinematic exploration of the way we treat our Earth. It stretches from the southwestern desert to space, and it shifts from the extraordinary beauty of our planet to the ugliness of what we have done to it and the hopelessness we have left in our wake. The last sequence shows the burning wreckage of a rocket tumbling through space, seemingly forever, while the chorus chants a Hopi prophecy: "A

59 Frederick Sternfield, *Film Music Notes*, quoted in *The Technique of Film Music*.

container of ashes might one day be thrown from the sky, which would burn the land and boil the oceans."

At the opposite end of the spectrum, a film can also be made to superimpose itself retroactively on a "found" piece of music. The standard was set in the use of the slow movement from Mozart's Piano Concerto No. 21 in the Swedish film *Elvira Madigan*. While the lonely sound of the piano pointed up the hopelessness of the doomed lovers, the orchestra's melancholy accompaniment seemed to reflect exquisitely their wanderings into the woods and waters of southern Sweden. Every now and then, I will hear a piece of music whose orchestral color or lilting tune seems evocative enough to be the theme of a film. The phrases are usually concise, with a simple beat, and the ability to sustain a couple of recognizable variations of mood. And they contain within them all the musical answers.

I discovered just such a piece—an obscure seventeenth-century composition on a connoisseur's label—for the soundtrack of a twenty-minute film I made as a student. The film featured dreamy sequences of a man wandering about gardens and woods from the past, and in one of its incarnations, the music was colored by a cascade of notes on the harpsichord that perfectly matched a scene by a little waterfall. It was called simply Canon in D Major. The year was 1972, and few people had ever heard of it. But as Pachelbel's Canon it burst into public consciousness some years later when it appeared on the soundtrack of the 1980 film *Ordinary People*. It has been on the Hit Parade ever since.

❖

My grandmother had a favorite quote that she used to give guests to act out when a weekend house party was playing Charades (or The Game, as we called it) after dinner in the big sitting room at Amberley: "If music be the spice of life, play on." It was a misquote of the Duke of Illyria's opening speech in Shakespeare's *Twelfth Night*. To the Duke, music is "the food of love." But as far as The Game was concerned, my grandmother's version was just as good, and a certain subversive tradition encouraged variations like this as adding zest to the game as well as confusing the guests.

As far as I am concerned, if music be the food of love, it also adds immeasurable spice to life. Keats wrote to his love, Fanny, "Give me books, fruit, french wine and fine weather and a little music out of doors, played by somebody I do not know." Like bird-watching, which can make almost any location more interesting, music can enhance almost everything, adding pleasure to contentment and taking the edge of anxiety off pain or fear. One of the songs my father used to sing was Schubert's "An die Musik." *"Du holde Kunst"* ("You lovely art") the voice begins, in comforting C major from which it never really departs. Just the sound of the German words of the second verse particularly moved me.

> *Oft hat ein Seufzer, deiner Harf' entflossen,*
> *Ein süsser, heiliger Akkord von dir*
> *Den Himmel bess'rer Zeiten mir erschlossen.*
> *Du holde Kunst, ich danke dir dafür.*[60]

But long before I understood them, the tune had captivated me with its simple appeal. The crowning line is one of those rare heart-stopping phrases that can only be called "perfect." Flirting with the relative minor over a sustained chromatic rise in the left hand of the piano, it makes a restrained crescendo before being repeated in an echo that dies away to its quiet beginning.

In some compartment of my brain, there is a private jukebox that is automatically activated to select a tune appropriate to almost any circumstance. These musical clues turn quite mundane experiences into something fun, rather like a Buddhist's *gatha*. Stacking a cord of firewood, I hear the giants stacking their hoard in *Das Rheingold,* and as the pile gets higher, the sensuous leitmotif as Fasolt glimpses Freia, Goddess of Youth, behind the gold, when I catch a crack of daylight between two logs. Following a path into the grove of white pines near my house calls up the delicate "Eintritt" from Schumann's set of piano pieces, *Waldszenen*. Going into the garden to pick roses, I find myself humming

---

60 Often a sigh has escaped from your harp, / A sweet, sacred harmony of yours / Has opened up the heavens to better times for me. / You lovely art, I thank you for that.

Schubert's endearing "Heidenröslein" (Hedge-roses); if by the time I prick my finger I haven't already got to the part where the rose stabs the boy— *"Röslein wehrte sich und stach"* (The rose armed itself and stabbed) —the words immediately come to my mind, as an oath comes to my lips. On occasions like these, the association is at a fairly conscious, literary level. However, sometimes it works in reverse, and it is the tune going through my brain that hints at things turning over just below the surface of my thoughts. In either case, a collection of music, ready to be called into use by some outside association, adds a private depth to any occasion, a kind of movable musical feast.[61]

In that spirit, I can conceive an entirely auditory trip into nature through the medium of music. In some pieces, she might have the upper hand, in others it might be a human reflection that counts. In still others, the landscape might hum along inside a classical musical form, unbidden but present, as in a Dvorák symphony. One could go to sea, climb a mountain or cross a desert; there are a huge number of alternatives. Rather than face these extremes, I prefer to enjoy a brief saunter through an imaginary landscape of the most appealing kind, the countryside. I am dedicating this concert to the aesthete Des Esseintes so that he can enjoy without ever leaving the hall the "visual impression and physical sensation," in Honegger's words, of an excursion into nature. Des Esseintes once saved himself the effort of traveling to London, experiencing the complete visit in his imagination through his observations of the clientele in a tavern en route to the Paris railway station. He might have experienced the train ride, too, through *Pacific 231*, although I suspect it would have been too noisy for his highly strung senses. As a result of my concert, perhaps his sensitive mind will come to think better of nature's "loathsome monotony."

Our hike starts in a meadow with another work by Honegger, but very different. Written in 1920, *Pastorale d'été* captures the perfect peace of a

---

61 As for the store of memorized lyrics, my ability to produce a line for any occasion serves no real purpose in life and is unappreciated, especially by my wife. She eventually invented a parlor game that requires players to be given a word and then find a song lyric that incorporates it. I always win.

field in the summer sun as does no other work I know. As dreamy and lyrical as *Pacific 231* is strident and discordant, it is almost a lullaby. Like *Tapiola*, it starts with a rhythmic figure out of which the whole landscape grows and to which it ultimately returns. Picture yourself lying in a field, half dozing, drunk on the scent of newly cut grass, the warmth of the earth and the hum of nature. There is a change in the wind, which brings out a vision of wood nymphs dancing; you look up to watch, but laziness and contentment soon reclaim you. The opening figure returns, and the scene quietly evaporates, like a genie going back into its bottle.

But there is more to life than a daydream. The Good Friday music from the last act of Wagner's *Parsifal* infuses the inherent tranquillity of the meadow with the pain it is necessary to experience before redemption. So, too, has the pasture been carved out of the wilderness. The aged Gurnemanz uses water from a brook to baptize Parsifal, and suddenly the woods and fields glow with tranquillity and beauty.

> *Das merkt nun Halm und Blume auf den Auen,*
> *dass heut des Menschen Fuss sie nicht zertritt,*
> *doch wohl, wie Gott mit himmlischer Geduld*
> *sich sein erbarmt' und für ihn litt,*
> *der Mensch auch heut in frommer Huld*
> *sie schont mit sanftem Schritt.*
> *Das dankt dann alle Kreatur,*
> *was all da blüht und bald erstirbt,*
> *da die entsündigte Natur*
> *heut ihren Unschuldstag erwirbt.*[62]

It is very different from the exotic beauty of the Flower Maidens whose charms Parsifal overcame in Klingsor's garden. These are the simple

---

62 Now grasses and flowers in the meadow know / that today the foot of man will not tread them down, / but that, as God with divine patience / pitied him and suffered for him, / so man today in devout grace / will spare them with soft tread. / Thus all creation gives thanks, / all that here blooms and soon fades, / now that nature, absolved from sin, / today gains its day of innocence. (Translation by Lionel Salter)

fields of home that we yearn to return to. But however cheerful they look, the dew on the grass is made of tears. The line *"Das merkt nun Halm und Blume auf den Auen"* strikes me with the same mysterious intensity that Hans Castorp felt for "Der Lindenbaum," which meant "a whole world, a world which he must have loved, else he could not have so desperately loved that which it represented and symbolized to him."

Following Gurnemanz's brook as it flows out of the meadow, we have little choice but to give the orchestra a break and summon a piano with either a string quartet or a singer. In either case, the composer would be Schubert. I can't hear the sound of a mountain stream running into pools or over rocks without the accompaniment of the "Trout" quintet in my head. The piano part with its runs and trills would summon a trout from the deepest pool to frolic in the rivulets. While the "Trout" takes one on a pleasant stroll along the banks of the brook, perhaps contemplating sadly the need of the fisherman to catch the fish, *Die Schöne Müllerin* takes one straight into the heart of a young man of almost Mahlerian neuroticism. The brook tries to keep him company, but in the end even nature cannot stop his heart from breaking. Meanwhile, Schubert treats us to some musical sketches of life along the miller's stream. The way nature and the young man reflect each other's moods makes these lieder the musical equivalent of Caspar David Friedrich's paintings of mountains and forests.

Let's keep the pianist for a short encore: Schumann's "Vogel als Prophet" from the *Waldszenen*. The bird is up there in the branches flitting from twig to twig on a web of 32nd notes; it might be a warbler gleaning the leaves for insects up and down the tree, if only we could get a good look at him. His carefree twittering changes to a more solemn tone reminiscent of a chorale—he is a prophet, perhaps warning us of the loss of his winter quarters in the rainforest—before he returns to his more mundane business.

It must be about noon, and the brook has led us deep into the woods, but there is a sunny glade to rest in. As we sit quietly, the orchestra has returned to the stage, and we start to hear the forest murmurs from the second act of *Siegfried*. Its beauty stands out all the more in an opera that lacks charm, however splendid the music is in many other respects. In his

Jungian interpretation of *Der Ring des Nibelungen (Wagner's "Ring" and Its Symbols)*, the psychoanalyst Robert Donington explains this passage as a pregnant pause in the action in which Wagner totally immerses Siegfried in nature. For a moment we feel again the pristine purity we have not encountered since the very beginning of *Das Rheingold*, at the bottom of the River Rhine. In his analysis, Donington gets to the root not only of Wagner's music, but to the very pull upon us of nature itself.

. . . the birds, the forest murmurs, the forest itself are all talking to him about his mother. In the intuitive language of symbols, all nature recalls to us our deepest memories of mother and behind these our innate knowledge of the mother archetype. Our love of nature is nothing so vague and colourless as mere aesthetic appreciation. Her fecundity is the very image of motherhood. Her swelling downs and her secret valleys evoke the very outline of woman. Her clear streams are invitations to rebirth visions. Her groves and forests are patterns of feminine reassurance and feminine mystery. We cannot love nature without secreting fantasies which in their forgotten origins are mother fantasies.[63]

No wonder this concert would be so successful.

A storm is brewing, which will put an end to our excursion. We have quite a choice. It might be all "sound and fury signifying nothing" as in a Rossini storm, which is usually no more than a device to ensure that the lovers are reconciled by finding themselves together, though presumably dripping wet. Or it could be cataclysmic, embodying all the forces of the world, also designed to bring the lovers together, but at a supernatural level, in which case we resort to Wagner again and the prelude to Act I of *Die Walküre*. For sheer graphic depiction of a thunderstorm, but in this case the lover has lost all hope, try Berlioz's *Symphonie fantastique*. The lonely shepherd forlornly playing his pipe as the thunder approaches is the ultimate romantic image of despair. However, Berlioz is so literal (and literary) and his musical descriptions so precise that only

63 Robert Donington, *Wagner's "Ring" and Its Symbols*.

a real shepherd who had had a similar experience could really appreciate his musical rendering.

And then there is the storm from Beethoven's Sixth Symphony, the *Pastoral*. At the end of the day, we could have experienced almost the whole of our walk in this one work. And the wonder of it is that save for a very few special effects—a cuckoo, thunder and lightning—it is almost entirely done through intuition. It is not the landscape that is painted, but the composer's response to it. I find it practically impossible to get up in the morning, the first day of a weekend in the country, with-out hearing the opening theme—Beethoven subtitled it "cheerful impressions awakened by arrival in the country"—seeping into my head. And after the storm, we have not found our lover, nor have we given up hope. We are glad. I was once caught in a monumental thunderstorm in one of the flattest places on earth, the Horto-Bágy National Park in Hungary. A friend and I were looking for great bustards, and when the clouds welled up over the horizon, we were lucky to find at least some shelter from the rain in a shepherd's hut made out of straw. The storm passed directly over us, so that thunder and lightning were simultaneous as we huddled under the hay bales, which were our best protection from the deluge. And then the late afternoon sun came out. The grass was coated with raindrops that glistened in its horizontal rays, while to the east the sky was the color of ink. That's when you hear Beethoven's peas-ants and their song of thanksgiving.

In "An die Musik" the poet blesses the art that kindles love when life is dark.

> *Du holde Kunst, in wieviel grauen Stunden,*
> *Wo mich des Lebens wilder Kreis umstrickt,*
> *Hast du mein Herz zu warmer Lieb' entzunden,*
> *Hast mich in ein bess're Welt entrückt!*[64]

---

64 O blessed art, how often in dark hours, / When the savage ring of life tightens round me, / Have you kindled warm love in my heart, / Have transported me to a better world!

I had a piano teacher once, a great bear of a man with rheumy eyes, who said that listening to the end of the *Jupiter* Symphony in which Mozart finally brings all the major themes of the movement together in the culminating fugue was like being touched by the Almighty. It's as good a description of nature. Like music, nature transports one to a better world. Both are about hope. So I would close my concert with a piece that looks to a time of peace, albeit far in the future. Like all his music, Leoš Janáček's tone poem *The Ballad of Blanik Hill* is bathed in the landscape of Bohemia. It tells the story of a young man who finds the Knights of St. Wenceslas deep inside the rocks of Blanik Hill, armed and awaiting the call to liberate their country. He swoons and when he awakes, the knights' swords have been beaten into ploughshares. But as he leaves the hill and hastens to his village, he catches sight of his reflection in a stream. He has become an old man, and in his village no one recognizes him. A peaceful world will take a long time, but the lark singing over the countryside in the closing bars leaves us with hope.

Abroad

Birding Through the Renaissance

When from our lofty perch we looked down on the structures
man had raised for his protection and his pleasure, to store
his food or to contain his gods, the centuries fused before our
eyes into a single span. And, as if the graves had opened,
the dead rose up invisibly. They are always near to us when
we look upon a land we love, in which an ancient culture has
its roots; and just as their heritage lives on in stone and
tillage, their ancient spirit rules over meadow and field.
—Ernst Jünger, *On the Marble Cliffs*

I
T IS HARD TO IMAGINE a city where nature has less of a chance
than Siena. Even theatrical Venice cannot deny the presence of
the waters of the lagoon that flow in and out twice a day and whose
fingers pry into and corrupt her most artificial corners. But in Siena, not
a tree grows around the Campo, the piazza that is the heart of the city;
no blades of grass penetrate its cobbles. There are animals, it is true—a
dolphin, a leopard, a porcupine, even a snail—but they have been
twisted into the heraldic shapes that adorn the brightly colored silk
scarves fluttering from every street corner, the symbol of that particular
quarter or *contrada*. These colors are taken by the jockeys who ride for
the glory of their neighbors in the annual Palio, a breakneck bareback
race around the Campo. Perversely, this bit of medieval pageantry brings
to mind the lines of the Chorus, spoken in the prologue to Shakespeare's
Henry V: "Think, when we talk of horses, that you see them printing
their proud hooves i' th' receiving earth." The sand brought in to cover
the iron-hard, polished stone of the Campo's pavement for the Palio is
no "receiving earth," and the thought of those hooves making a tight
turn around a corner is as painful as that of fingernails on a blackboard.

And yet, leading tours to Italy for the members of the Maine Audubon Society, I have twice included a visit to Siena. There are in the town hall two monumental pictorial allegories, called *Good Government* and *Bad Government*, and their symbolism is as relevant today as it must have been in the first half of the fourteenth century when they were painted by Ambrogio Lorenzetti. The lush and fruitful plains of the first are contrasted with the blasted heaths and devastated landscapes of the second; happy and industrious farmers and townspeople revel amid the one, whereas they are hunted down and put to fire and the sword all over the other. The message of these pictures could hardly be clearer: our natural systems are at once source, symbol and symptom of our quality of life; their wise stewardship must be the standard by which any government is judged.

This artistic testament to environmental concern is why we went to Siena. It is evidence not only that environmentalism is not a new idea, but that its timeless message needs the support of the public. If a picture is worth a thousand words today, it must have been priceless at a time when most of the populace could not read. Standing in front of these works of art, I felt with a *frisson* the presence of six and a half centuries of citizens whispering in my ear, "Why do you insist that environmental concern started with Earth Day?" Still, Lorenzetti must have been ahead of his time. With their secular message, the Good and Bad Government frescoes stand out as unique among the other religious paintings of the period that fill the council chambers.

However, on the walls of the Pinacoteca across the Campo, I noticed two intersecting developments that seemed to be more than a coincidence. As Madonna and saints moved from the unapproachable hauteur of the icons that typified the early Sienese style to a more empathic humanity, they also began to inhabit nature rather than a celestial void. Lorenzetti (or possibly Sassetta; art historians disagree) even painted two little landscapes in their own right. Doubtless this reflects in part evolving artistic skills, but I couldn't help wondering if something else was going on. I sensed a subliminal equation between the expressiveness of the saints and the welcoming countryside. Could the ability to capture human feelings in a painting and to place them in familiar scenery have prompted a deeper contemplation of our relationship to the land? Were these the qualities about the Good and Bad Government allegories that drew public attention from the start? As early as 1425, Siena's home-grown saint, St. Bernardino, used them in his sermons, saying, "When I am outside of Siena, I have preached of the peace and war that you have painted, and which, besides, is a very beautiful invention."

St. Bernardino preached some of those sermons in the Piazza del Campo itself, in the shadow of the Campanile, a shadow that makes its daily progress across the square like the hand of a clock, driven by what Leonardo da Vinci called "that venerable snail the sun." Called the Torre de Mangia after a medieval bell ringer, its silhouette rises above the city, slender and sheer, until it swells into a crenellated parapet like the bud on an amaryllis made of Legos. I was determined to make it to the top, despite a dreadful fear of heights.

The bell tower is over 250 feet above the Campo, and the twisting staircase up to it took its toll. As I stepped out onto the open parapet, I felt light-headed, and my hands involuntarily reached out for the com-fort of the wall. But my efforts were rewarded with a panoramic view of the terra-cotta city below stretching out into the Tuscan countryside as far as the eye could reach. At the same instant, directly above my head, the great bronze bell (which Leonardo himself once drew) sounded the twelve strokes of noon.

I was once at a Buddhist retreat for environmentalists just outside Los Angeles. It was led by the Zen master Thich Nhat Hanh, and the activ-ities of the day were periodically punctuated by the gentle chime of a bell. Interrupting whatever it was we were doing or thinking, we tuned the following *gatha* to our breathing: "Listen, listen. This wonderful sound brings me back to my true self." It returned us to the present moment, which thus became "a wonderful moment." But such a sum-mons to the present need not always be gentle. When the sudden wail of a police car interrupted our meditation, Hanh commented that that, too, was a mindfulness bell; it was only a few weeks before that Rodney King had been beaten senseless by Los Angeles cops. At the top of the Torre de Mangia, the colossal din of the great bell in my ears was likewise a mo-ment of awareness, bringing me back to the present across the centuries stretched out below me and inviting me to ponder further on what brought me here as an environmentalist.

More than one environmental puritan challenged my choice of a tour destination such as Italy as being more the province of a museum or cultural institution than an organization devoted to the conservation of nature. Undeniably, there are better places in Europe to visit than Italy if your principal goal is to see an above-average number of bird species or wildlife. (The excesses of Italian hunters are well-known, and having worked on bird conservation campaigns in the Mediterranean at Birdlife International, I have seen firsthand their impact on wild birds.) Furthermore, the sort of love of the outdoors generally associated with the first steps toward an environmental consciousness is not what springs to mind when one thinks of Italy. Traveling through Italy on a night train, I have more than once made myself the cause of endless skirmishes by opening the compartment window even a crack for some fresh air; the horrified cries of *"Fa male! Fa male!"* from fellow passengers still ring in my ears. At home, too, shutters must be tightly bolted against the mysterious vapors of the night.

Nor is nature, as a realm to be penetrated for itself, readily apparent as one beholds a piece of Italian art. Sandro Botticelli's *Spring,* which might be expected to have some bearing on nature, is instead a classical idyll that not only paints nature in anthropomorphic terms, but is really only interested in what spring means to people. The same is true of Italian music. Botticelli's painting might easily have been inspired by Francesco Landini's *ballata* "Ecco la primavera" written about a hundred years earlier. "Spring has come and it makes the heart joyful; now is the time to fall in love and be happy. We see the air and fine weather which also call us to be happy. In this sweet time, everything is beautiful. Flowers and fresh green grass cover the meadows and the trees too are in blossom." Two centuries after Botticelli, Vivaldi continued in the same vein in *The Four Seasons,* which is about shepherds and farmers, hunters and skaters, more than nature. I can never hear the largo from the fourth concerto, "Winter," without being once again in the Villa Foscari, otherwise known as the Malcontenta and one of the masterpieces of the great architect Andrea Palladio. I was with my mother, and we had admired the Giants on the walls and the simple utilitarian furniture around the rooms. Now we were sitting in a cozy parlor before a fire, while outside a raw autumn rain pattered against the windowpanes. Even though it was not actually winter, the context was pure Vivaldi, with its beautifully warm, contented violin melody over pizzicato strings like the raindrops outside. By contrast, Beethoven is always out-of-doors; his raindrops buffet a lake, and sparkle and drip off the summer wheat as the storm passes into the distance and the sun comes out.

Even in the Romantic era when nature came into its own as an artistic subject, Italian composers endowed it with very different values than, say, the Germans like Wagner or Strauss or even Weber. The musical storm that opens Verdi's *Otello* is about human conflict; in Wagner's *The Flying Dutchman*, it evokes nature as a protagonist itself. In all of Verdi, there is not a depiction of nature that is more than a colorful backdrop for the plot: the light of a seaside garden in Genoa, the beauty of the Nile, the natural murmurings of Windsor Park. In evoking dawn over the Roman countryside in the last act of *Tosca*, Puccini uses church bells and a shepherd's voice. They are sound effects, albeit of an exquisite nature.[1]

It is precisely because of these attitudes that Italy offers a challenge to the conservation-minded that is almost irresistible. The historical impact of the environment — the landscape and the climate — on different cultures, and vice versa, is a fascinating quest, however unpromising it may at first appear from the point of view of the pure environmentalist. I have not forgotten my college course on Sir Halford Mackinder and his theory of geography as the key to history. If geography as destiny is usually interpreted from a terrain's natural features, art and cultural artifacts can bear eloquent witness to it as well. Paintings and palaces, gardens and churches provide marvelous opportunities to illuminate the relationship of a people with their environment if you look for the signs.

Not that an active environmental consciousness does not exist in Italy.

---

1 Mahler described Puccini's tone picture with a touch of irony. "Magnificent tintinnabulations and a view over all Rome from a citadel. Followed by an entirely fresh onset of bell ringing," he wrote to his wife, Alma.

Whatever the Italian attitude to nature and the outdoors may be, environmental messages are everywhere in the streets. Plastic shopping bags proclaim their "greenness" with messages such as *"Rispetta anche tu la natura"*[2]
or a picture of a little elephant who says, *"Io amo la natura."*[3] Bottles urge
you not to throw them away into the environment. During the severe
floods and mudslides that plagued parts of northern Italy in the fall of
1998, the Environment Minister unhesitatingly blamed global climate
change and called publicly for a reduction in greenhouse gas emissions.
But because I was confident that we would rack up a better bird list if we
concentrated on frescoes, paintings and mosaics, I called my first tour to
the land of St. Francis of Assisi "Birding Through the Renaissance."

My appetite for combining ornithology with art history was inspired
by my first visit to St. Mark's Cathedral in Venice, which is where we
headed next. The ceiling of the atrium around the north and west walls
of the basilica tells the story of the Old Testament in mosaic, and it contains a veritable field guide to the birds of Italy. Amid the familiar religious scenes played out against the golden tesserae, the detail of the birds
portrayed would have made Peterson proud. Pride of place must go to
the pelicans, purple herons and jackdaws lining up two by two to board
Noah's Ark, right in the portico before the main entrance. But the ones
that first caught my attention were a flock of partridges in the mosaic
that describes the Israelites in the Wilderness from the Book of Exodus.
"And it came to pass, that at even the quails came up, and covered the
camp: and in the morning the dew lay round about the host." King James
may call them quail, but these are red-legged partridges (*Alectoris rufa*);
their field marks are quite distinct. In a country hardly known for environmental awareness, those thirteenth-century artisans knew their birds!

"Venice's three basic elements," wrote the photographer Ernst Haas
(1921–1986), "are light, water and stone—the immaterial, the fluid, and
the material. Whenever you walk along the canal, everything will be
reflected in the water. Reflection is the most important transformation
this city has to offer. Every view has its mirror image of a never ending

2 Respect nature also.

3 I love nature.

number of swimming abstractions." Haas's interpretations of nature and man likewise have a tendency to expand as one looks at them, like ripples in a pond, from a perfect moment to an interplay of light and color that is beyond time. The water playing with the reflection of a gondola's polished bottom is very seductive, as is the light bouncing off the pink and ochre walls that grow straight out of the canals. But corruption lurks behind the glow as if it were a mirage.

Pick your environmental issue, and you can find it in Venice, from the ravages of aerial pollution wrought on the marble statues by the nearby industrial center of Mestre to the problems inherent in a city whose major infrastructure consists of a web of open canals. There is also the precarious future of a city built on stakes in a lagoon in the Adriatic Sea. As early as 1818, reclining among the Euganean Hills overlooking the towers and steeples of Venice, Shelley mused prophetically of the day the "sun-girt city" would sink back into the ocean, adding that it was a preferable fate to the contemporary shame of Austrian occupation.

> . . . among the waves
> Wilt thou be, when the sea-mew
> Flies, as once before it flew,
> O'er thine isles depopulate,
> And all is in its ancient state,
> Save where many a palace gate
> With green sea-flowers overgrown
> Like a rock of Ocean's own,
> Topples o'er the abandoned sea
> As the tides change sullenly.

In St. Mark's, it is now very hard to grab more than a fleeting glance at the Old Testament mosaics because of the measures needed to control millions of tourists each year (an environmental disaster in itself). But in the Doges' Palace, we stood before an enormous painting of the Battle of Lepanto, in awe not so much of its artistic merit but rather of the record of a colossal naval battle in 1571 between Turks and Europeans that involved more than 500 ships. It has been calculated that the timbers

needed to build these ships involved half a million mature trees. Not surprisingly, such naval demands left the Mediterranean forests denuded,
and ship construction moved north to the Baltic soon afterwards.

There is one Venetian painter, Jacobo Tintoretto, the impact of whose
work can only be described in terms of natural forces. Not that he dwells
on nature as a subject (some of Titian's scenes, like the *Baccanale* and
Bacchus and Ariadne, are more bucolic). Not that landscape plays a more
ostentatious role on his canvases than on those of his contemporaries of
the Cinquecento. But where the prospects of Paolo Veronese — in the
Villa Barbaro at Maser for instance — seem to open a window onto a pastoral idyll, Tintoretto's compositions bring the roar of the wind right into
the room. Where Veronese is well mannered, Tintoretto is gutsy. The
energy, the vertiginous swirls that animate his paintings seem to spring
directly from the elements. One can almost hear them, and it is like the
sound that a meteor makes as it rushes to Earth.

Of this aspect of the artist's inspiration, no better example can be
found than in the Scuola di San Rocco, one of the charitable brother-
hoods that had linked the religious and social underpinnings of Venetian
life since the thirteenth century. Tintoretto won the commission to illuminate the walls and ceilings of its new headquarters with, among other
subjects, a series of paintings on the life of the Virgin. His *Annunciation*
is not only iconographically iconoclastic (the Angel Gabriel has broken
through the all-important architectural feature that usually separates
him from the Virgin, and the walls of Joseph's house show the same kind
of decay I found in some of the more interesting neighborhoods in
Palermo). The way the angel and his cohort swoop down upon the young
woman is simply as wild and unbridled as a hurricane. Two darker panels break up the biblical narrative. An otherworldly light in which lone
saints — Mary Magdalene and Mary of Egypt respectively — contemplate
a landscape transmits a foreboding that is a million miles away from the
genteel scenery of Veronese. Tintoretto's nature is unfettered by humanity and emanates from a mysterious depth. What kind of a man was he,
a dyer's son who even after he became successful continued to live near
the gates of the Ghetto where magicians and alchemists found asylum?
(After he had made his name, Veronese moved to a much smarter part

of town.) The caricature of the artist is carved in the knob of one of the choir stalls as if growing from the polished wood itself: hunched over, lurking like a leprechaun; his intentions are wholly ambiguous.

◆◆◆

Flowers and fruit from the school of Veronese—actually Giovanni Zelotti—are all over the walls of Villa Emo, built by Palladio around 1560 in Venice's hinterland, the Veneto. And a rather soulful cow—Io —makes several appearances in a cycle of frescoes around the room that traditionally belonged to the mistress of the house. My great-aunt Cora, my grandmother's sister, who lived there at the turn of the century, was haunted by Io's eyes. She had them covered with postage stamps to shield her from their gaze. When visitors were expected, so the story goes, the butler would remove the stamps one by one, and Io would stare again until the next day when he came to blind her once more with Victor Emanuel III's likeness.

The best part of a century later, over coffee in an informal sitting room in the Villa, I was telling the current resident, a cousin, of my planned trip and somewhat tactlessly explained why I intended to call it "Birding Through the Renaissance." He led me to a window, and as we looked out over his fields, he gently took me to task. With a wave of his arm that embraced the breadth of the peaceful landscape, he assured me that I was wrong about Italians and birds; and he proudly pointed across the plain to where, he said, white storks had returned in recent years.

No one can dispute, in the approach to the Villa Emo and its situation amid the farmer's fields, what refined sensitivity to light and landscape Palladio brought to his design. One also quickly recognizes the farmer's practicality, especially in the ramp (unique among Palladian villas, where broad steps are more the rule in an entrance) that is the main approach to the *piano nobile*. Palladio himself described the functionalism of the design in the catalogue of his works. "The cellars, the granaries, the stables, and the other places of the villa are on each side of the main house, and at their extremities are two dovecotes which are useful for the owner and ornament the place, and everywhere one can go under cover, which is one of the principal things looked for in a villa." The arrangement of the utilitarian buildings spreading out but connected to the elegant main house is itself recognizable as an Italian cousin of that traditional New England architectural arrangement, "big house, little house, back house, barn."

The importance of the surrounding property to the building becomes clear as soon as one reaches the portico of the main entrance. One is simultaneously drawn into the house and pulled through the foyer into the main hall, which opens towards a vista that seems to extend all the way to the foothills of the Alps on the other side. The feeling of being drawn through and out again into the out-of-doors is one that many a modern nature center has sought to emulate. Nor does the artwork on the walls leave any doubt that these people's fortunes are ruled by the earth and their response to it. The portico is dominated by a fresco of Ceres above the lintel of the front doors. Elsewhere, depictions of the seasons reinforce the message, and panels are decorated with agricultural motifs, including a startlingly early depiction of American maize. (The Emos had already put the estate to corn, instead of the traditional sorghum, less than seventy-five years after Columbus discovered America.) One room, the Salon of the Arts, is decorated with frescoes representing, among other disciplines, Astronomy, Poetry and Music, and one thinks of the farmer cultivating his mind during the long winter evenings when he cannot be cultivating his fields.

If Villa Emo speaks of farming, its Palladian sibling, the Villa Barbaro at Maser, is the second home of a successful urban family. Whereas Emo sits severely amidst its fields gazing at the mountains in the distance, but always with one eye on the sky, Maser, situated jauntily in the hills above the plain, has "the view." The jagged ensemble made by the gambrels of the dovecotes and the pitch of the main roof could be a decorative reference to the skyline of the mountains behind. Inside, the walls are graced with frescoes by Paolo Veronese himself, portraying the family in sylvan landscapes. Clearly the intent is to extend the indoors outside but to do so without crossing the threshold into anything that might soil or tear their silks and ruffles, which are also brilliantly depicted; and so the Veneto's woods and lakes and hills have been tamed by the suave urbanity of the artist.

Further south, the hills of Tuscany and Umbria are recognizably the ones in which the Holy Family appears in so many Renaissance paintings. Give or take the odd mechanic's shop and the like, the appearance of this long-cultivated landscape has not changed that much in the intervening five hundred years. The textures of the slopes have been forged by men over the centuries, but their form is ordained by natural topography. Vine, olive and cypress—the land's most obvious vegetation—were all introduced, albeit millennia ago, but how they have made themselves at home. These hills seem to celebrate an old and happy coexistence.

Was it this that inspired the thinking and teachings of St. Francis, whose gentle vision of peace and love remains extraordinary to this day? At a time when all over Europe, life was, in the memorable phrase of Thomas Hobbes, "nasty, brutish and short," St. Francis struck such a chord that Giotto and others were inspired to decorate the walls of his cathedral with pictures of him preaching to the birds. (Of course we went to Assisi to pay our respects to Audubon's patron saint. Fortunately for us, our visit took place before these frescoes were badly damaged in the earthquake of 1997.) *The Little Flowers of Saint Francis*—a compilation of stories about St. Francis passed down orally by members of his order and written down about a hundred years after his death—relates how the birds gathered round him. He told them always to praise God who "feeds you and gives you rivers and fountains for your thirst, and mountains and valleys for your shelter, and tall trees for your nests." At this, "all the birds began to open their beaks, to stretch their necks, to spread out their wings, to reverently bow their heads to earth, and to show in gesture and in song that the words of the holy father gave them great joy. And St. Francis rejoiced with them, marveling greatly at the multitude of birds, at their most beautiful diversity, and at their attention and affection, and he devoutly praised the Creator for them."[4]

---

4 Parenthetically, *The Little Flowers* tells us that St. Anthony of Padua went St. Francis one better and preached to the fish; the story is also told in *Des Knaben Wunderhorn*, an anthology of German folk poems dating back to the sixteenth century that Gustav Mahler set to music, but with an ironic twist: the fish were, in the end, unimpressed.

I pondered on this from the heights above the town one morning as I watched the sun come up over the plain, burning off the mist that floated around the pink marble façade of the great cathedral. By chance, it was the first day of the bird-hunting season, and, from all around Assisi, the shotguns blasted away. If St. Francis gave a sermon to the birds today, I wondered how many would be left to hear it. According to a recent report, Italy, with 1.6 million, has the highest density of hunters per square kilometer in Europe (5.4 compared to an average of 0.8), and, firing approximately 500 million rounds, they kill each year 150 million migratory birds. The Italian Olympic Committee considers hunting a sport, the only national committee to do so. Despite my cousin's protestations, Italian hunters are widely regarded as being irresponsible and disrespectful, shooting at anything that moves and possessing little of the mystique of communing with nature and taking sparingly of her bounty that makes hunting acceptable.[5]

As the Renaissance blossomed, a concern for nature and landscape in painting seems to diminish. Humanism, after all, was the lodestone of the times, symbolized so eloquently in Leonardo's famous drawing of human proportions. Urbino is the Renaissance town par excellence, and the main architect of the Ducal Palace was one Luciano Laurana. It was he who painted, in the mid-fifteenth century, another monument to governmental and civic perfection, The Ideal City. Unlike the Good and Bad Government paintings of the previous century in Siena, however, all reference to the surrounding countryside that must have sustained it even then has been squeezed out of the frame. And yet, in one of the great halls of the castle, the feeling of humanity yearning after nature was extraordinarily strong as we stood under ceilings that billowed like sails

---

5 At Caserta, the eighteenth-century palace of the Bourbon Kings of Naples and Italy's answer to Versailles, the smaller rooms of the palace abound with flat paintings of hunting in which the pursuit of various forms of game is conducted on the scale of a military operation: a flotilla of skiffs on a lake forms a veritable anti-aircraft barrage for waterfowl; a cavalry charge after deer; a herd of wild boar, their retreat upstream cut off by a fence, driven into a river and toward a fusillade from the royal hunting party arrayed across a bridge. King Ferdinand's bloodlust was notorious. In the account of his visit to Naples, Goethe remarked dryly, "Today the King has gone wolf-hunting; they expect to kill at least five."

until they seemed ready to lift the room out into the surrounding coun-tryside of which the many windows gave such a splendid view. And it came again, deep within the same castle's walls, in the Duke's study, pan-eled from floor to ceiling with trompe l'oeil pictures in inlaid wood. Among the trappings of wisdom, learning and war — all executed in exquisite marquetry — that befit a library, the artist imagines the world outside. Against a view of hills and fields, a squirrel crouches on a para-pet, his back to a bowl of fruit from which he has clearly just purloined a snack; and through a window left half open, an imaginary breeze forever riffles the pages of a book.

In the museum in Urbino, alongside masterpieces such as Uccello's *Profanation of the Host* and Piero della Francesca's *Flagellation of Christ* (one of the paintings, we were told, that the Italian government has identified to be spirited away in the event of a nuclear attack), a medieval miniature of a wolf and the bloody corpse of a child graphically evoked the age-old hatred between man and wolf. It made a fitting reminder that this animosity is continually revived wherever conservationists try to make amends for centuries of persecution by letting the poor beast live. As it happened, the next town we visited was Gubbio. Here St. Francis converted a fierce wolf who had done much damage and eaten many of the inhabitants. *The Little Flowers* gives another delightful description, of brother wolf repentant. He "knelt and bowed his head, and with meek ways, moving his ears and his tail, showed to the best of his ability that he wanted to observe the pact." But perhaps the larger miracle wrought by the Saint that day was on the townspeople of Gubbio, who forgave the wolf, letting him wander freely from house to house; and, says the story, when "brother wolf finally died of old age . . . the people grieved."

Pushing southward into Latium, we found in the famous water gar-dens of the Villa d'Este in Tivoli what must be the perfect example of the fusion of nature and artifice that typifies the Italian approach to nature. Confirming this suspicion, the Italian guidebook gushes over them (how-ever stilted in translation) thus: "A profusion of gorgeous art blends here with nature and forms a miraculous ensemble which is a delight to the eye and the spirit. Nature here bursts forth into a grandiose and festive revelation of green tints and trees, but an invisible hand conducts this symphony and human will guides its exuberant forces." In fact the hand is anything but invisible at anything but the most architectonic scale.

It was a cloudy day many years ago when I first saw the fountains and gardens of the Villa d'Este. From the balcony of the Villa, the hillside falls steeply away, and from every nook and cranny water tumbled down it in every conceivable form, from hanging droplets to rushing streams. In some places the view of the artfully manicured gardens below could only be seen through a curtain of water. Liquid crystal glimmered from every banister and gutter, and the whole garden tinkled with the sound of little rivulets and the patter of fountains. In its heyday in the sixteenth and seventeenth centuries, the water was made to do more than that. There was a hydraulic organ, whose notes were sounded by a powerful draft of air displaced by water falling into an enclosed basin and pumped through organ pipes. Another fountain spewed water in such a way as to crack like the detonations of a firework display. And for bird-watchers, the Fountain of the Owl once contained a veritable aviary of mechanical birds that warbled away until a mechanical owl would jump out crying harshly, at which point they would take fright and scuttle away. All these mechanical toys are things of the distant past.

And on my most recent visit I found that so, too, are the extravagant aquatic displays of the water garden. In the early 1990s, after 2,000 years of disposing of human wastes, the Roman sewage system of the town exploded, the waters turned black and the streams that fed the fountains of Cardinal Ippolito d'Este, the son of Lucretia Borgia no less, had to be turned off. Their source can never be completely cleaned, we were told. Regardless of the health hazard, the townspeople, who depend on tourism from the Villa d'Este, reacted violently to shutting the fountains down, and eventually the authorities agreed to pump water through at half strength. But only the major fountains, not the little bubbling rills that added so much to the ambience, have any water today, and they are fenced off so that no visitor risks contamination. Even with these precautions, they recommend a maximum visit of forty-five minutes, lest one breathe too much of the noxious vapors. *Fa male!*

Despite the loss of its rivulets, the garden remains a magnificent testament to an ideal of nature. Looking at the rotunda of tall cypresses, centuries old, to which the main axis of the garden leads from the Villa, one feels that nature may yet have the last word. From the guidebook bubbles another commentary: "Gripping the ground firmly with their enormous roots, svelte and inflexible cypresses, the vivid and mighty symbol of the triumph of nature, soar vertically and their pointed verdant tops seem to scratch the white clouds passing by."

Below the town of Tivoli lies the ghost of one of the most magnificent palaces ever built by man. Successive waves of pillagers have stripped it of its brilliance: ransacking emperors, needy peasants, greedy popes. A dusty path leads the contemporary visitor through the ruins of what must have been a small city. The bare bricked arches of the buildings recall the antique memory of Piranesi's engravings for good reason; it was a favorite haunt of the eighteenth-century artist. One cannot fail to be moved by the monumentality of the design, but only when one reaches the edge of an oblong artificial lake does all this mournful grandeur blossom. With its marble arches and statues, the Canopus gives an immediate idea, though still only a hint, of the elegance and artistry, not to mention mechanical genius, of which it is a reflection: the mind of the Emperor Hadrian, who created it nineteen centuries ago. The Canopus was intended to recall a sojourn in a town of the same name in the Nile Delta —a marble crocodile wallows among the caryatids that line the edge of the lake—and especially the emperor's lover, Antinous, who was drowned in the great river. To construct it, Hadrian used a little valley in his demesne that could be fed by the waters from the Tiburtine Mountains above the plain. Likewise, the major building complexes that make up the "villa" are determined by the land, which architectural historians have pointed out was a marked break with the past.

Of all the emperors, Hadrian's personality is surely the most compelling. He was a just and efficient administrator, but consumed by curiosity of the world, he spent half his reign traveling the empire. He climbed Mount Aetna to see the sun rise. As an enthusiastic hunter, he slew the Libyan lion, an enormous animal that had been terrorizing the countryside. As a strategist he built Hadrian's Wall across the north of England to keep the northern Barbarians out. He was also an artist, a poet, a philosopher and an aesthete. But it was as an architect that he built his greatest memorials: the dome of the Pantheon in Rome and the villa in the valley of the Aniene River.

Hadrian was not only an architect but a brilliant town planner. Of course, he was the most powerful man in the world, and resources in terms of money, slaves, artists and materials were no object. I kicked up a few pale tesserae in the dusty path and dislodged a stick of porphyry with my sandal. Perhaps it was dropped from the sack of some earlier pilferer. In the distance, clouds were gathering over the hills, but a sense of the aging Hadrian, filled with his memories, overseeing the building of his retreat, held me staring down the length of the lake. Here was conspicuous consumption on a scale unimaginable today in terms of quantity, but also of artistic quality. And yet the man who made all this was asking himself, "Little spirit, gentle and wandering, companion and guest of the body, in what place will you now abide, pale, stark and bare, unable as you used, to play."

> Animula vagula, blandula,
> Hospes comesque corporis,
> Quae nunc abibis in loca
> Pallidula, rigida, nudula,
> Nec, ut soles, dabis iocos.

As the storm approached, I thought of the towering cypresses in that other garden up on the hill. I thought about how the Villa Emo rests comfortably in its landscape. I thought about how the Tuscan hills still kept their olive trees and vines, and about the Good and the Bad Government. By now the sky was black. I picked up the piece of porphyry and kneaded its polished surface with my thumb. All that we had seen seemed suddenly to be but a variation of this ghost of a vision, and it all coalesced around one man, an emperor who died in A.D. 138, Hadrian. With a roar, the heavens opened in a barrage of rain and hail. There was no shelter nearby, and I was instantly drenched. Great drops washed 2,000 years of dust and earth off the purple stone in my hand. In the tradition of Lord Elgin and Sir William Hamilton, I slipped it into my pocket as a memento of the great emperor.

The Most Beautiful Country on Earth

*For a final conclusion therefore, go through the whole
earth and all the lands lying under the cope of heaven,
Italy will be found the most beautiful & goodliest region
under the sun, surpassing all other whatsoever.*
—Pliny the Elder, *Natural History* (Book XXXVII)

I T WAS THE EVENING RUSH HOUR when we arrived in Naples, and a political demonstration—an event quite frequent in the city, according to our friend Antonio—was going on. A major traffic artery had been closed off, and our tour bus found itself jammed in gridlock the likes of which I have never seen. Our plight seemed hopeless. Then, suddenly, all around us the cars started backing and filling, twisting and turning, over the sidewalk, around the bushes. Looking down from the higher vantage point of our vehicle, the little cars looked like bees bustling around their queen. As in a hive, a common knowledge seemed to have seized hold of the drivers all at once. There was no hooting, no cursing, just wiggling; in minutes, the great bus was standing alone in the street. It was an astonishing demonstration of knowing how to make things work—the ultimate in traffic control—and only possible in a city of natives. Anyone from away—like us—would have been lost.

We had driven from Rome, and the countryside we passed en route was a far cry from Pliny's conception of Italy. It had a scruffy look that we had not encountered further north. The *autostrada* carved its way through rugged hills whose dramatic scenery seemed long ago to have worn out its welcome on the people who lived there. Here a hillside had been gouged into a quarry, there one was despoiled by a rubbish dump. Even the farmers' fields looked down-at-heel and abused. Every human activity seemed to thumb its nose at the natural beauty all around it, as if deliberately to bear out the truth of the old hymn, "every prospect pleases and only man is vile."

Eventually the landscape became less populated, allowing harmony between man and nature to reassert itself. From the top of its mountain, restored Monte Cassino proclaimed once again the geopolitical influence the abbey has exerted over the boot of Italy for nearly a thousand years. And when the wild hills flattened out into the Campania, the heavily settled plain around Naples, its fields and orchards took on a more respectable look. Morning glories flowered along the sides of the highway, and a line of umbrella pines, straight as a die, marked the course of the Via Appia, the most famous of the Roman roads, connecting the capital with the port of Brindisi. The stony hills running down to the sea were covered with olive groves, their trees rigged with rolled-up nets of orange and green ready to be spread out to catch the ripe olives when the time came for them to be harvested. As we neared a town, assemblages of spars and blinds covered orchards of lemon trees, protecting them from the birds, and also the sun. In the wake of our speeding bus, all these agricultural devices left the impression of a colorful armada, Odysseus' ships, their sails furled waiting for the command to get underway.

Our itinerary took us to a number of places made famous by Odysseus' exploits. From the safety of the land, we looked past the rock of Scylla, which guards the entrance to the Straits of Messina, for our first view of Sicily. In between, we could imagine the currents that built up in this natural bottleneck and created Charybdis, the whirlpool of myth. In Sicily, at Aci Trezza, the chunks of rock that blinded Polyphemus hurled after the retreating Greek ships still picturesquely dot the bay. We did not, however, visit Cape Circeo where Circe held court. We should have, if only to ponder the assertions of archaeological explorer and sailor Ernle Bradford. According to Bradford, Circe was the priestess of a prehistoric cult that worshipped nature as a goddess. While her magic charms were powerful enough to enthrall his rank and file (metaphorically turning them into wild animals), they were not up to the rational intellect of Odysseus, which happened also to be backed up by force of arms. And so it was on her other charms that she had to fall back, and nature was once and for all conquered by man. Thus told, the meeting of Odysseus and the sorceress illuminates a critical moment in the relationship of people and nature on the Italian peninsula.

It has even been suggested that the Sirens' song the hero had to resist was in reality the beckoning of the voluptuous land around the Bay of Naples itself. After so long a voyage, exhausted by war and still so far from home, Odysseus would have found the beauty of the countryside as seductive as a mermaid and must have yearned to tarry. We know that even in the time of the ancients, this coast had the reputation of enjoying the most salubrious climate in all of Italy. But the clemency of the weather notwithstanding, there lies behind the lushness of the landscape a fatal trap: the violence of the earth itself.

Looming over everything both literally and figuratively rises the dark mass of Mount Vesuvius. A lava flow from an eighteenth-century eruption, still bare, separates the green ribbed slopes of Monte Somma, the ancient hill, from the red cinnabar flanks of the sleeping volcano. Under its menacing shadow, there is no escaping the ultimate power of nature and its capacity for destruction. It defines the character of the people as surely as the land. In *The Volcano Lover*, Susan Sontag retells a piece of local folklore, a sort of Neapolitan "Just So Story": how Naples got its fiery temperament.

Vesuvius was once a young man, who saw a nymph lovely as a diamond. She scratched his heart and his soul, he could think of nothing else. Breathing more and more heatedly, he lunged at her. The nymph, scorched by his attentions, jumped into the sea and became the island today called Capri. Seeing this, Vesuvius went mad. He loomed, his sighs of fire spread, little by little he became a mountain. And now as immobilized as his beloved, forever beyond his reach, he continues to throw fire and makes the city of Naples tremble. How the helpless city regrets that the youth did not get what he desired! Capri lies in the water, in full view of Vesuvius, and the mountain burns and burns and burns.

It is easy to wax poetic about the duality of nature here: a golden land undermined by a geological fault; the sometime dealer of death, the giver of fertile fields as well. Creation and destruction, beauty and ugliness, good and bad: all these things spring from the very nature of the Bay of Naples. Such conflicts bring the ancient gods and heroes closer here than they are in Rome. Myth provides a better explanation for a tragic flaw than religion, and before such a temper, the old gods offer, perhaps, a surer expiation. Naples is dedicated to the Siren Parthenope, not the Virgin.

Mount Vesuvius is famous for one date, August 24, A.D. 79. Before that it was a harmless hill covered with vines cultivated by the unsuspecting citizens of Pompeii and Herculaneum. When the mountain exploded that day, the great Roman naturalist and admiral, Pliny the Elder, sailed across the bay to bring help to the cities and to get a closer look at the volcanic display. He was still writing down a description of the disaster when poisonous gases overcame him, and he paid for his scientific zeal with his life. In the gray light of an autumn morning some 1,900 years later, humans, not the mountain, were the ones assailing the air and the land with poisonous gases. The spot where Pliny landed—present-day Castellammare—was lying under a blanket of smog. Smoke drifted up from fires on the hillsides above the industrial city until it was lost in the overcast sky. Fields and vineyards that came back enriched after each eruption—and provided for the villages sprouting around the mountain's slopes once more—are now being destroyed forever not by a flow of lava but by the spread of concrete and solid waste. Whatever sort of utopia the Bay of Naples has been for wanderers through the ages, the contemporary traveler must be prepared to turn a blind eye, like Nelson who fell in love with Lady Hamilton here, to the blight of environmental degradation all around.

The modern population must deal with its own impact on these hills, but the ancients found themselves locked in an uneasy struggle with a nature that was both familiar and awesome. Not far from Naples, across the Phlegrean Fields, still literally a hotbed of seismic activity, the Cumaean Sybil had her cave. Virgil describes it in The Aeneid.

> Where the huge side of Cumae's rock is carven in a den,
> Where are an hundred doors to come, an hundred mouths to go,
> Whence e'en so many awful sounds, the Sybil's answers flow.

The ancients cut a passage, shaped like a flattened arrowhead in cross section, through the honey-colored tufa rock to the Sybil's lair. Later, the Romans dug a network of underground tunnels and canals to connect Cumae with nearby Lake Averno for military purposes, among them the transportation of wood cut in the hills for the navy. The denuding of the countryside was already far advanced even before the Roman Empire. Lake Averno itself is an extinct crater filled with water. Its name is derived from the Greek *a ornis* meaning "without birds" because the igneous vapors were said to overcome any bird that flew over it. Just for the irony of it, the Audubon group did some birding overlooking its shores. We found a few gulls, ducks and a great-crested grebe on the water, and the air smelled of sulfur, as befits a place that in ancient times was reputed to be the entrance to Hades. (It was from Lake Averno that Aeneas entered the Underworld, led by the Sibyl, to meet his dead father in the Elysian Fields.)

Despite its seething foundation, Cumae was one of the most important cities of Magna Graecia. Today the village is surrounded by orchards and vineyards, the grapes of which produce a thin white wine, delicious in that ambience but like so many local specialties, disappointing when brought home. The other great Greek monument is at Paestum. Founded by refugees from Sybaris, the pleasure-loving city on the Ionian coast, after its destruction in the sixth century B.C., Paestum was dedicated to Poseidon. Once one of the most powerful colonies on the Italian peninsula, the city was later conquered by the warlike Lucanians, nomads from over the mountains to the east looking for *lebensraum*. The Greek traditions they found among the Poseidonians much impressed the newcomers, and they settled down to emulate them. Just like their descendants, they were great hunters, and their expeditions are captured with great vitality, if less refinement than the Greeks, in the paintings on the walls of their tombs. When the Romans came (Paestum is the Roman name for the city), they cut the forests on the hills above the plain to build their galleys, with, as at Cumae, inevitable environmental consequences. Soil, no longer held in place by the roots of the trees, was washed into the river. The mouth silted up and turned the area into a swampland. Next came malaria followed by depopulation as the people were forced to seek more healthy surroundings. The city with its magnificent temples was over-grown and forgotten like Sleeping Beauty's castle for a thousand years.

Not until the mid-eighteenth century were Paestum's columns and walls uncovered, and then inadvertently by engineers putting in a new road. (Its long hibernation allowed it to escape the attentions of builders and borrowers and is doubtless one reason the site is so well preserved.) In 1787, not long after its rediscovery, Goethe found it still a marshy tangle. "We crossed brooks and flooded places where we looked into the blood-red savage eyes of buffaloes. They looked like hippopotamuses." (The buffaloes, though rather more docile than Goethe's description, are still there wallowing in their muddy paddocks and producing the milk for the region's specialty, mozzarella cheese.) The great poet was quite unprepared for what he found. As usual, his observation in the field prompted wider philosophical musing on the development of artistic style through the ages. "At first sight they [the temples] excited nothing but stupefaction," he wrote.

I found myself in a world which was completely strange to me. In their evolution from austerity to charm, the centuries have simultaneously shaped and even created a different man. Our eyes and, through them, our whole sensibility have become so conditioned to a more slender style of architecture that these crowded masses of stumpy conical columns appear offensive and even terrifying. But I pulled myself together, remembered the history of art, thought of the age with which this architecture was in harmony, called up images in my mind of the austere style of sculpture — and in less than an hour I found myself reconciled to them.[6]

Today, Goethe's astonishment at Paestum's ruins provoke a longing to experience such a refreshing sense of surprise, now practically impossible to find. Another set of reflections on the passage of time is conjured up by Cavafy's "The Poseidonians," the poem quoted earlier. Despite its ironic tone, there is something unutterably sad about the predicament of

6 J. W. Goethe, *Italian Journey.*

1. The attitudes of the animals brought together in a chance encounter like the ostriches and warthogs in this diorama at the American Museum of Natural History suggest the designer had a great sense of humor

2. Top: Shooting, 1957—
The line of "guns" clad in tweed from their
hats to their plus fours

3. Above: "Concrete assassination . . .
[or] creation of beauty?"—TU with
a brace of pheasants

4. Left: First visit to Loch Ness—
TU with mother and father

5. Left: Bill & Emmy Maxwell and TU's mother playing in the dunes, Cape Cod, early 1950s—
Bill always said that when I was born my mother walked across Hyde Park in the Blitz to the hospital

6. Below: Amberley, 1958—
TU prowling around the garden in hopes of a hoopoe

7. Bottom: Camargue, 1987—
Birding with Roger Tory Peterson

8. Above: Boston, 1927—On the day Sacco and Vanzetti were executed, Aunt Catharine (middle) with Edna St. Vincent Millay and Margaret Hatfield Chase were arrested for "sauntering and loitering" in front of the State House

9. Left: Sir Thomas Urquhart (1611–1660)— A wonderful product of an extravagant age, he traced his lineage back to Adam and Eve

10. Right: Brussels, 1944—TU's father received news of his birth in code: "Mauser dropped safely at 0425 hours." File is marked "Most Secret"

11. Top: Amberley Castle seems to grow out of the water meadows themselves

12. Above: Oak Tree Cottage in Amberley-God-Knows: an artist's haven and a budding naturalist's paradise

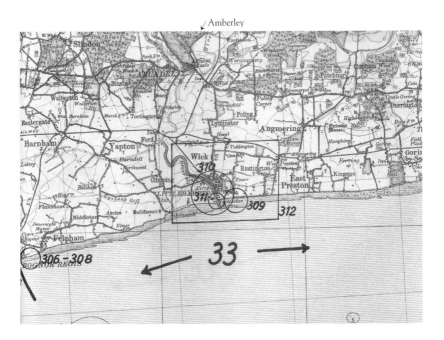

13. Top: The Arun Valley might have been a German invasion route in World War II—
Map from *Militärgeographische Angaben über England, Südküste* (Military-geographical
plans for England, South Coast)

14. Above: From the same document, bathers on the South Coast where the Arun
flows into the Channel—Marked *Nur fur Dienstgebrauch* (For Service Use Only),
most of the pictures in this Wehrmacht document came from postcards of the area

15. Peter and the Wolf—Classical music disc jockey Robert J. Lurtsema poses as Peter for the benefit of Massachusetts Audubon Society

16. Virgil Thomson—He and my mother shared a passion for cooking; she made the needlepoint pillow, the notes of which are from Thomson's opera, *Four Saints in Three Acts*: "When this you see, remember me"

17. Two monumental allegories in Siena—"The Effects of Good Government" (above) and "The Effects of Bad Government" (below) by Ambrogio Lorenzetti (ca. 1295–1348)—are as much an environmental statement as Earth Day

18. Illustration from *De Arte Venandi cum Avibus*—Holy Roman Emperor Frederic II (1194–1250) wrote this early ornithological text from personal observation

19. Piazza Armerina's mosaics (3rd–5th century) are an extraordinary testament to the wonders of the animal kingdom and the Roman passion for the chase

20. Sicilian landscape—"Many there will be who will flay their own mother and fold back her skin—The tillers of the ground." Leonardo da Vinci

21. Cathedral of Monreale (late twelfth century)—The creation of the birds

22. Dogon country, Mali—A vision of Arcady: industry that enhances rather than spoils

23. Keleya, Mali—We crammed ourselves into a wildly overloaded baché

24. Left: St. Veran and the Dragon, by Pierre Mignard (1657)

25. Below: Murals in Avignon's Palais des Papes give an impression of the natural world Petrarch would have encountered

26. Left: Camargue, 1958—
Enjoying nature rather than
cathedrals and chateaux

27. Below: *Aucassin et Nicolete*,
King-Coit Children's Theatre,
New York (1956)—TU front row,
sixth from left

28. In Wagner's *Parsifal*, the Good Friday music reconciles nature and man

29. Brunnhilde's self-sacrifice in the final moments of *The Ring* is a powerful symbol for the resolve we need; with luck, the real thing will be something less catastrophic

30. A living planet we can call beautiful:
The view of Earth that came back from space in 1969

Z.8 AMBERLEY CHURCH, SUSSEX   copyright-Bob Tracey

31. The old hymn echoes still in St. Michael's Church, Amberley—
For the Beauty of the Earth

a people who have lost their connection to the past and yet keep alive that sense of loss through increasingly meaningless rituals.

If long ago the fate of Paestum was to be deserted, the more likely end today of once splendid spots is quite the opposite. Of all Italy's sightseeing magnets, as an object lesson in the environmental perils of super-tourism Capri is hard to beat. It has been loved to death. The island has been a resort since the time of the Emperor Tiberius where, if Suetonius is to be believed, he idled away his days in cruelty and revolting depravity. He had a habit of having people pushed off the cliffs, and the very name of the island, from the Latin for "goat," commemorates the Emperor's sexual appetite. But Tiberius evidently appreciated the natural charms of Capri as well, completely abandoning Rome in favor of its solitude. He used to sit on its mountaintops contemplating the view.

Over fifty years ago, the descent on Capri of "hordes of respectable British matrons all set to have themselves a ball" prompted Noël Coward to write one of his classic songs, "The Bar on the Piccola Marina," about the exploits of the widowed Mrs. Wentworth Brewster. It is doubtless to adventurous ladies like Mrs. Brewster that we owe the inexhaustible repertoire of innuendo-ridden jokes that the local guides tell with a leer ("They're just high-spirited as all Italians are") to titillate the millions who have followed in their footsteps.[7] These days solitude and unobstructed nature are hard to come by on Capri. At the top of Anacapri, the Villa San Michele and its lovely park offer an oasis of peace and calm (there is a bird observatory there that has done important tracking of migratory birds for years), but the endless rows of shops and stalls, cheek by jowl, selling identical tourist kitsch on the way there create a poor frame of mind in which to enjoy them. The same is true for the Blue Grotto, and even the famously beautiful natural arch. If you wait your turn among the honeymooners taking pictures of each other against this natural backdrop, you can get a glimpse of a small stretch of unspoiled coastline, with perhaps a colorful fishing boat heading round

7 Times have changed. On my first visit to Italy in the early 1960s, guides were quite prudish, forbidding women and children (me) from visiting the erotic frescoes at Pompeii or Tarquinia.

the rocky point but more likely a yellow submarine on a sightseeing cruise. In any event, this untouched landscape is scarcely wider than the viewfinder of your camera. Today on Capri, nature is being pushed off a cliff, not by a cruel emperor but by a stampede of humanity all desperately seeking its solace, in vain.

Across the bay along the waterfront of Naples, life is hardly less crowded, but it is measured out in basic daily needs, in sharp contrast to the temples to consumerism and waste on Capri. An old lady brings her bag of treasures down to the seawall and opens up a couple of cans of cat food while she chirps. Suddenly the black rocks that form the breakwater become alive as from all over, cats of every size and description stalk out of their holes and converge on their benefactor. Nearby, a pair of old men, imperiously ignoring the fascinated stares of a couple of visitors, haggle over a pile of live octopuses on the sidewalk. The *polpi* look just as Browning described them over a hundred years ago: "All trembling alive with pink and gray jellies, your sea-fruit." Or, for that matter, as their pictures on plates made at Paestum in the fourth century B.C.

Further along the breakwater lies the Norman castle where the fifteen-year-old Conradin, the last of the German Hohenstaufen princes, was imprisoned before his execution in the public square of Naples in 1268.[8] His grandfather, Frederic II, stands nearby among the great kings of Sicily lined up outside the Royal Palace of the Bourbons. It is an undistinguished nineteenth-century statue, and the eagle on his helmet is faintly ludicrous. Frederic II, King of Sicily and Holy Roman Emperor, was called by his contemporaries Stupor Mundi, the "wonder of the world."[9] His reign during the first half of the thirteenth century was the

8 In Provence, on the walls of a tower in Pernes-les-Fontaines, you can see the story in a series of frescoes that invite comparison with the Bayeux Tapestry. They were painted for a contemporary who probably accompanied Charles d'Anjou on his campaign to extinguish "that race of vipers," the Hohenstaufen. According to legend, the beautiful fifteen-year-old prince, in a last defiant gesture from the scaffold, cast his glove into the crowd, where it was taken and hidden by some of the Sicilian barons as a promissory note for revenge. That revenge came fourteen years later in the uprising known as the Sicilian Vespers (1282).

9 Son of a Norman queen and the German emperor who ended the Norman dynasty in Sicily and southern Italy, Frederic was born in public (so there could be no doubt about his

last hurrah of the intellectual and artistic enlightenment that flourished in Norman Sicily the century before.

On top of his many other talents as poet, musician, diplomat, warrior, Frederic was the greatest naturalist of his age, and possibly since Pliny. Despite the luxury and refinement of his court, he was never happier than when he and his beloved younger son Manfred were out hunting with their falcons together, and he used these excursions to study natural history firsthand. Hunters were poets as well as naturalists in those days, and a poem written by Frederic's head falconer, Rinaldo of Aquino, speaks to a different attitude toward nature than, for example, Landini's "Ecco la primavera":

> Love is brought unto me
> In the scent of a flower
> And in the birds' blithe noise.
> When day begins to be
> I hear in every bower
> New verses finding voice.
> From every branch around me and above,
> A minstrel's court of love,
> The birds contend in song about love's joys.
> (English translation by D. G. Rossetti)

It is said that it was Manfred, then but a boy, who asked his father to write a book about birds. What Frederic wrote from personal observation, *De Arte Venandi cum Avibus*, or The Falcon Book, must be one of the first ornithological texts ever written. "Our work," he wrote in the prologue, "is to present things that are as they are." The original is in the Vatican Library. Frederic's biographer, Gertrude Slaughter, found the book to combine "accuracy of detail with the freshness of the out-of-

---

right to the throne) the day after Christmas in the town of Iesi. However, this triple reference to the life of Jesus could not prevent him from being excommunicated three times by succeeding popes and reviled as anti-Christ.

doors. . . . He went into every detail of the life and structure of birds as well as their habits. He discussed the action and spread of the wings,[10] the comparative weight of the feathers and the reason for their delicate gradations. He described the digestive systems, and the construction and mechanism of their eyes and feet." He illustrated the book himself with accurate drawings of all sorts of birds that could only have been the product of direct observation from his excursions into the countryside.

Frederic's reign has been likened to a preview of the Renaissance, which didn't arrive for another two centuries. As environmentalists, we have still much to learn from his vision today. Asked what was the greatest thing in the world, he replied: *"La misura."* Measure, moderation, a sense of proportion. The world, particularly the people of affluent nations, are still asking, "How much is enough?" and we seem as far away as ever from finding an answer that will save the planet.

On his way from Naples to Sicily, even so inveterate a traveler as Goethe gave Calabria a wide berth, and on most tourist itineraries it is still a land to be hastened through if not actually bypassed. Today, its mountains remain wild and rugged, and away from the coast, it is sparsely populated. Jagged peaks adjacent to older hills rounded by wind and rain attest to its long history of tectonic activity; the land has been repeatedly ravaged by earthquakes. Because of this, it is the one part of Italy whose natural beauty outweighs that of its man-made monuments.

In 1783, a particularly savage earthquake leveled more than a hundred villages in the region. Some communities rebuilt on their old sites; others took a different tack. The inhabitants of Castelmonardo moved down into the plain and built a new town, which they called Filadelfia, the city of brotherly love like its more famous American namesake. Laid out on a grid with two axes, each quarter has its own church, a square and an equal number of buildings symmetrically arranged as a mirror

10 Predating Leonardo by 250 years.

image of its pair. The *centro città* with its municipal offices and public square lies logically where the axes cross in the middle. Filadelfia is a late eighteenth-century model town that gives us a glimpse of municipal planning concepts that are as sensible today as they were then.

During the rainy season, torrential rivers descend from the mountains. In his *Book of Water,* written in left-handed mirror writing to avoid the disapproving eyes of the Church, Leonardo da Vinci argued that the power of water is the most destructive force of all. "For in a succession of raging and seething [waves], . . . growing turbid with the earth from the ploughed fields, destroying the houses therein and uprooting the tall trees, it carries these as its prey down to the sea which is its lair, . . . bearing with it the light things, and devastating and destroying those of weight, creating big landslips out of small fissures, filling up with its floods the low valleys, and rushing headlong with insistent and inexorable mass of waters." Leonardo, who described the artist as a "son of nature," was unique in his time for his attitude to nature.

What Leonardo did not mention were white goods and old FIATs and all sorts of municipal waste that now fill the dry riverbeds so that the visitor could be forgiven for thinking that it is trash, not water, that rushes down the side of the mountains every spring. Against the lofty backdrop, they are one more of the mind-boggling contradictions found every day in the Mezzogiorno. The same people responsible for these rivers of trash are the stewards of the vineyards and olive groves. And they are also the hunters who prove their masculinity with the wanton massacre of hundreds of the honey buzzards that fly low across the Straits of Messina on migration every spring. This destructive practice is as passionately defended as it is pointless. Local activists who try to halt the shooting, which is illegal, have had their offices and cars bombed.

Over a delicious plate of swordfish, freshly harpooned in the same straits and served much thinner than swordfish steaks in America, a journalist from Vibo Valencia[11] told me two stories. In a little village along the coast, the farmers bury a live cockerel up to its neck in the ground,

---

11 Rebuilt by Frederic as Monteleone in the thirteenth century, only to be changed back to its Roman name by Mussolini in the thirties.

and then, blindfolded, take turns having about it with sticks, as if it were a piñata. The one who kills the bird wins the prize. However, farmers from the same village found a bird that could not take flight. It was something they had never seen before. My journalist friend said it was a *rondone*, a swift, and by no means uncommon; in fact quite a few were soaring overhead even as we chatted. However, swifts are so designed as to be able to take wing only by dropping from a perch, such as a cliff or wall, so they are rarely seen on the ground, where they are helpless. To hold this precious "rare" bird in their hands was indeed a novelty for the villagers, and it touched them. They carefully bore it to the top of the bell tower of their church and reverently watched it fly away.

Goethe may have skipped Calabria, but he put Sicily on the map as a destination on the Grand Tour. He said that it was not possible to know Italy without going there. It must have been Sicily he was dreaming of when he wrote:

> *Kennst du das Land, wo die Zitronenblühn?*
> *Im dunkeln Laub die Gold-Orangenglühn,*
> *Ein sanfter Wind vom blauen Himmel weht,*
> *Die Myrte still und hoch der Lorbeer steht —*
> *Kennst du es wohl?*
> > *Dahin! Dahin!*
> *Möcht ich mit dir, o mein Geliebter, ziehn!*[12]

Going back to classical times, it was in Sicily that Persephone was gathering flowers when she picked an asphodel and was taken off to the Underworld by Pluto, thus creating the Earth's seasons. A more contemporary source, a friend of Sicilian extraction, recalls the many festivals, faithfully observed by her parents even in the New World, that tied the family to the land through the celebration of the seasons. Sicily has

---

12 Know you the land where the lemon-trees bloom? / In the dark foliage the gold oranges glow, / A soft wind hovers from the sky, / The myrtle is still and the laurel stands tall— / Do you know it well? / There! There! / I would go, O my beloved, with thee!

both the best and the worst of Italy, she told me, and these traditions were among the best.

Sicily surely is a contestant for the distinction of having been invaded and ruled by more foreign nations than any other piece of real estate in the world. Greeks, Romans, Byzantines, Saracens, Normans, Germans, French, Spanish have all at some time raised their standard over Sicily.[13] One glance at a map of the Mediterranean, and it is easy to see why: Sicily's importance as the crossroads of three continents invites foreign interference. And a further glance, this time at the wild topography, confirms why the conqueror would always have his hands full keeping the island pacified. Only the Normans, and of course Frederic, had the vision to make a strength out of its diversity. Domination and repression were otherwise the rule, and they have left their mark on the people and their land.

The island's earliest colonizers were attracted to Sicily for its bountiful natural resources; ancient writers describe a land of forests and rivers. But today, the island's interior, though mountainous, appears like a continuous plowed field. In his *Prophecies* Leonardo wrote: "Many there will be who will flay their own mother and fold back her skin—The tillers of the ground." Unusually for him, he was behind the times in this case: the countryside cannot have looked all that different in Roman times when Sicily was the breadbasket of the Empire. Hectare after hectare, there is not a tree in sight, except around an infrequent farmhouse, which is often just a ruin. With the summer crop harvested, the contours of the hills seem to be decked out in a herringbone pattern, relieved every now and then by chocolate brown stripes or squares where a different crop was cultivated. There are no walls or fences to break up the monotonous texture, but the empty landscape hides a mosaic of small landholdings that are defined by natural features well-known to the tillers of this land: a stream here, the brow of a hill there, a stunted tree or a rocky outcrop. Only the furrows of the plough, which suggest natural topo lines on a

---

13 In the nineteenth century, the English exerted their economic influence through the production and export of the sweet local wine from Marsala, which started as a replacement for the loss of the Madeira trade in the Napoleonic Wars.

map, give a hint that this panorama is of human origin and not a moon-scape. It is at once wild and unforgiving—and totally cultivated.

With every friable surface plowed, erosion has been a constant problem for centuries. Leonardo observed "how in violent tempests the waves [of river] . . . suck much earth into the sea, which causes the water of the sea to be turbid over a wide space." With the autumn rains, streams flow the color of terra-cotta. Off the shore where a river empties into the sea, a plume of mud stains the turquoise waters of the Mediterranean. Just as at Paestum, erosion covered another classical monument, this time with a mudslide in 1161, hiding the fabulous mosaics of the Roman Villa in Piazza Armerina for 800 years.

Lying in a wooded valley, the Villa offers a leafy retreat from the parched landscape and the broiling Sicilian sun. Archeologists debate whether it was built as a haven of contemplation for a senator or as a hunting lodge for the Emperor Maximinian. Based on the decorations, a hunting lodge seems more probable: the 1,500 animal heads that decorate the floor all around the peristyle—lions, bear, elephants, antelopes, boar, each one framed in a laurel wreath—suggest the Roman equivalent of the Scottish baronial hall with its walls lined with stags' heads.[14] In either event, Piazza Armerina is an extraordinary secular temple to the wonders of nature and the animal kingdom. Even the latrines are decorated with wild animals running free. Nowhere in Italy is natural history so exuberantly described, nor the attitude to it, going back perhaps to the moment when Odysseus took Circe, so unambiguously captured.

In one room, cupids fish from boats using nets and lines and tridents, and the fish are as varied as they are on the fishmongers' slabs in the Palermo market. (Historians believe fish was very expensive in Roman times, so one suspects this allusion of being an advertisement for conspicuous consumption.) Another room displays an encyclopedic catalogue of the hunting opportunities presumably available in the Villa's environs. Men (not cupids) on foot pursue a fox with hounds; a pair of

14 The peristyle was the covered walkway that surrounded a garden and was the heart of the Roman home.

hunters tussle with a wild boar, one dropping a rock on its head to protect his fallen comrade; horsemen chase deer whose escape is barred by a
net; a lone rider stalks a hare with a double-pointed spear; a falconer prepares to fly his hawk while his comrade catches thrushes with lime sticks
in a tree. (This last practice continues in Italy to this day in contraven-
tion of the laws of the European Union.) In the center, members of the
household and their friends recline under a canopy, their quarry already
roasting on a campfire. While one of the hunters tosses a scrap to his dog,
a servant unpacks bread and wine for the picnic. Behind, a pair of horses
tethered to a tree toss their manes, and one can almost hear them nicker.

The pièce de résistance, covering a hall more than fifty yards long, is
a paean to big game hunting throughout the Empire. Procuring exotic
wild animals from Africa and India to be slaughtered in the Colosseum
was big business. (There was no Convention on International Trade in
Endangered Species, or CITES, in those days.) A leopard is lured by a
flayed and spread-eagled goat, while another one brings down an antelope; a tiger cub is captured by the artful tactic of dropping a crystal ball
in front of the mother tiger who, seeing her own image diminished by
refraction, is confused long enough to allow another hunter to scoop up
her cub; a griffin inspects a trap that is baited by a human who peers anx-
iously out of it. Transportation of the menagerie to Rome provides
equally lively and colorful opportunities for the artists. A rhino is
dragged to the waiting boat out of a marsh; a refractory buffalo, its horns
bound, chases the slaves who are attempting to drive it; arrived in Rome,
an ostrich genteelly disembarks. Throughout the whole sequence, the
drama of men and beasts is played out against landscapes that imply distant hills, rivers and seas.

At Piazza Armerina, we met Polyphemus again, this time with not one
but three eyes, which the guide told us was an allusion to the three
craters of Mount Etna. The Cyclops supposedly lived on the slopes of the
volcano. If Polyphemus were identified with Mount Etna, the volley of
rocks he threw at the escaping Odysseus takes on a possible natural interpretation: the story in reality might describe a volcanic eruption. A local
professor gave another explanation for the myth of the one-eyed giants.
In prehistoric times elephants roamed Sicily; they probably migrated up

from Africa and down through Italy just before the land bridge at the Straits of Messina was drowned. As often happens with isolated populations, the island race got smaller and eventually died out or was killed off (we know that large game was hunted all over the prehistoric Mediterranean), leaving only their skeletons to be wondered at by the ancients. An elephant's skull has a large aperture for the trunk in the middle of its "face" that could well inspire belief in a one-eyed creature, while its massive size would make it belong to a giant.[15]

Cyclops and prehistoric elephants notwithstanding, representations of the Creation are a particularly rich quarry for the amateur art historian on the track of natural history in Italy. It reaches the pinnacle of imagination at Monreale, the Norman cathedral just outside of Palermo whose magical world of gold and colored mosaics rivals St. Mark's. In the beginning, according to Genesis, "the Spirit of God moved upon the face of the waters." Here He presides over a cauldron of waves in the center of which the face of Chaos frowns its resistance. The creation of darkness and light is largely allegorical, with light represented by the seven angels of the Revelation. But when he comes to the dividing of the waters about the firmament of heaven, the artist once again gave free rein to his intuition, portraying the event naturalistically with an elegant disc in blue-gray colors that range from almost white to almost black. As dry land appears above the waters, is it artistic coincidence that the simple plants are the first to grow at the edge of the sea, while trees grow on higher, and therefore presumably older, ground? With the creation of the animals, phylogenetic hierarchy is clearly established, with fish at the bottom of the scale. Then come the birds, which decorate the land gracefully but somewhat inanimately. The mammals, which appear on the same day as man, demonstrate their superiority by gazing at their

15 According to a musicologist friend, Handel had neither of these possibilities in mind when he wrote his opera *Acis and Galatea*, but rather a political metaphor where Acis, the shepherd who is turned into a river, becomes the symbol for all Italy (and a good nature metaphor), while Polyphemus represents the Bourbon dynasty, which was at the time (1732) attempting to swallow Italy.

Creator with great expression. His attention, however, symbolized by a beam of light, is entirely taken up with His ultimate creation.

The cathedral was built in the second half of the twelfth century when the Norman Kingdom of Sicily was at its zenith. Arab scholars flourished in Sicily under the Normans, helping to make it the scientific as well as cultural center of the world, and Muslim artistic influence is also present in Monreale. Stylized depictions of trees—the palm for life and the cypress for eternity—and stars decorate the interior, "supporting" the stories from the Bible. Around the double set of pillars that lines the cloister, the four elements are further stylized in gold and red inlay: rows of diamond shapes for earth, zigzags for water, straight lines for fire and disconnected or interrupted lines for air. Atop each pillar sits a capital, carved with an event from the life of Jesus such as the Nativity or the Passion. The builders arranged them in such a way that the sun shines on each capital at a particular time on the appropriate date for its scene.

Just as nature has been intellectualized into design abstractions on the pillars and walls of Monreale, the plants in the cloister garden have been transfigured into religious, that is to say human, concepts and values. A bay hedge, the laurels of glory, grows around the border, and the plants within it likewise have symbolic meaning. One tree grows in each corner of the garden: a fig for Genesis, a pomegranate for the Song of Songs, an olive for the Passion, and a palm for the Revelation. Each is surrounded by a low hedge of myrtle representing love. The humanizing of the countryside seems complete, and, its annual movements having been aligned to the holy events carved on the capitals, even the sun seems to have been harnessed so that its role is to highlight a Christian moment.

Early on (in Book III) of his *History of the World*, the Roman naturalist Pliny wrote of Italy,

> . . . *it is plain and evident, that in this one place there is the workmanship of Nature wherein she joyeth and taketh delight.* . . . *the whole temperature of the air, is evermore so vital, healthy and wholesome, the fields so fertile, the hills so open to the sun, the forest so harmless, the groves so cool and shady, the woods of all sorts so bounteous and fruitful, the mountains yielding so many breathing blasts of wind; the corn, the vines, the olives so plentiful* . . . *; so*

many lakes and pools, such store of rivers and springs watering it throughout;
so many seas and havens, that it is the very bosom lying open and ready to
receive the commerce of all lands from all parts.[16]

Lest there be any doubt about his opinion of his native land, he concludes his life's work (Book XXXVII), "having discoursed sufficiently of
all the works of Nature," with a chapter entitled "The Most Beautiful
Country on Earth."

His treatise starts with this statement: "She [Italy] also is the mother,
chosen by the powerful grace of the gods, to make even heaven itself
more glorious." As we wandered Monreale's precincts, this injunction to
use art to improve on nature's beauty captured in a nutshell the attitude
we found depicted all around us. Wherever we went and through whatever eras we traveled, the predominant perspective on nature, when it
was more than utilitarian, could be traced back to this sentiment. On
the rare occasions when we went in pursuit of wild birds for no other reason than to watch them, the local reaction was one of mild disbelief or
incomprehension projected as genial tolerance, amusement or suspicion.

What did we discover, "birding through the Renaissance"? Birds, animals and fishes aplenty—from the Greeks down to the present, in frescoes, mosaics and paintings—that speak of deep familiarity with
creation. Landscapes that reflect a long relationship with humanity,
although often by this time looking the worse for wear. Nature that is
sometimes gentle, sometimes unforgivingly harsh. People for whom
beauty is largely man-made and, even when it is not, is best expressed in
terms of human feelings and aspirations.

Perhaps we found the key to the Italian relationship to nature in
Hadrian's Pantheon in Rome. On the tomb of the painter Raphael, who
died in 1520, are inscribed these words: *"Ille hic est Raphael timuit quo sos-*
pite vinci rerum magna parens moriente mori." Here lies that Raphael who
living, nature feared would conquer her, and dying, would be her end.

---

16 Pliny, *Selections from The History of the World commonly called The Natural History of C.*
Plinius Secundus, Selected by Paul Turner.

Night Bus to Bamako

Tale told, tale to tell. . . .
— Will you be truthful?
— For the little ones who play at night by the light of the moon,
my tale is merely a fantastic story.
When the nights of the cool season stretch and lengthen,
at the late hour when the spinners grow weary,
my account is more: a pleasant story to listen to.
Yet for the hairy-chins and rough-heels who have traveled far,
it is a truthful story that has much to teach.
Thus I am futile, useful, instructive.
— Unfold it then, on with it. . . .

—from Kaidara *by Amadou Hampate Ba*

WE WERE BACK IN BAMAKO. Early on in the trip, I had lost my watch taking a refreshing, and in the body-parching heat much-needed, dip in a rocky pool at the foot of a cliff, but I guessed it was between three and four in the morning. It was quite dark, and for the first time since we had left Mopti ten hours before, the bus was quiet. As I had been warned, the pile of luggage on the roof would not be unloaded until it was light, for fear of its being stolen. So now everyone slept, waiting for the dawn.

My daughter, Emily, who was in the West African country of Mali as a volunteer with the Peace Corps and was the excuse for my visit, had originally opposed my plan to make the trip from Mopti by night; Peace Corps volunteers are discouraged from habitually taking the night bus because of the high accident rate in the dark on the *goudrone*, Mali's single tarred highway. However, she relented in view of the full moon that would guide the way through the flat countryside. For most of the journey, its cold light had flooded the contorted shapes of the Sahelian world whizzing by outside. As in a photographic negative, their shadows revealed lines etched with a crispness that would vanish in the harsh African day.

With this as a backdrop, I had passed the journey in an overstimulated reverie, alternately dozing, enjoying the endless richness of the pageant inside the bus and trying to make some sense of it all in my head. There was no question of reading, even had I wanted to. With the majority of the population illiterate, lights are considered unnecessary on Malian buses; instead, the beat of raucous but mesmerizing *Zairois* music —over which the passengers shouted to make their conversation heard —had filled the cabin. Now with our destination safely reached, I gave in to the desire to stop thinking. Plugging my headset into my ears for the first time, I sat back to await the dawn and enjoy a Monty Python tape borrowed from a Peace Corps volunteer for the trip. It seemed a suitably surreal conclusion to the exhilaration of the previous ten days.

It has been well said that traveling is a way of finding out who one really is. It breaks the mold of routine in one's actions and cracks open the crust of habit in one's thoughts. Some of what it produces is the stuff of fantasy, reflecting more about oneself than the way of the world. On the flip side of the coin are the surprising glimpses into the nature of things that the traveler is constantly offered, as it were on approval. In the course of several trips to Mali, I came face-to-face with many priceless intimations of this kind, but three revelations stand out. Not particularly original or earth-shattering in themselves, combined they put an indelible stamp on how I would afterwards see the world.

First was the novel idea that getting there can be at least as much fun as arriving. Like so many of us at home, I tend to think of the time it takes to get from one place to another as wasted downtime. In so doing, I now realized that I was not only consigning precious hours to the dustheap; I was also missing out on all sorts of sideshows that would otherwise enrich life with many pleasant distractions, as do the dogs and drapes and architectural flourishes that fill in the edges of a Renaissance painting and make it whole.

Then, there was the discovery of the pure pleasure of reducing one's life to essentials. Finding out that I could do without luxuries long taken for granted was part of it, but so too was the discipline of letting go of the sense that time and motion are ruled by an invisible but omnipresent stopwatch. As charity is to faith and hope, so the simplification of life is probably the greatest of my trio of revelations. It relates to both the first and the last, which was the ample demonstration that whatever else they may bring us, acquisition and consumption are hardly tickets to living happily ever after. The evidence was all around me: in the bus, in the village, in the markets; which is not to say that those mundane desires were entirely absent in my new friends. Indeed, they were ready to flare up at any time, over a glass of tea in a thatch-roofed hut, or after a successful bout of bargaining in a merchant's *magasin* or shop. Most often it took the form of a request for help in heading to the city: Abidjian in Côte d'Ivoire, and always Amerikee. It raised a profoundly ethical dilemma that bore directly on my intercourse with everyone I met in Mali and from which I could never escape: Who was I to know what was best for them; and even if I was sure that I did, how could such certainty, born from the zeal of the repentant sinner, ever survive its penetration through layers of colonial injury into a constructive point of view? Taking stock of all this made nothing of the ten-hour bus ride from Mopti to Bamako.

Independent since 1960, Mali, according to the books, is the fourth poorest nation on earth. It first aroused my interest as a child, when it was the part of French West Africa known as the French Sudan and when I was an enthusiastic young philatelist. Its stamps showed burnoose-swathed Tuaregs on camels in a variety of colors depending on the postage. But it was when I was promoting an environmental education project there for the International Council for Bird Preservation in the mid-1980s that I first really had the urge to go to Mali. Now in 1994 my daughter was in the Peace Corps, living in a village about ninety miles south of the capital, Bamako. I bought a copy of Mungo Park's journals[17] from his two expeditions to the region in 1796 and 1805 and went.

---

17 Mungo Park, *Travels into the Interior of Africa.*

Africa leaves a residual memory in the senses, indescribable but ready to erupt again in the red laterite soils that jump up towards the plane as it makes its descent towards the runway and in the equally indescribable mix of smells on the heavy air that bursts inside as the cabin door is opened. I once heard a competition on the radio to invent a new word that would describe the blending of different, pleasing smells. The example given was the scent of the sea mixed with wild rose that one sniffs on a New England beach. The invented word—"euthymy"—could just as well have been used to describe the mixture of dust, sweat, humidity, gas and who knows what else that is the wonderful smell of Africa.

On my first visit, I knew I was in for a life-changing experience the moment we stepped off the bus at Keleya, the market town nearest my daughter's village. From there, it was a five-mile bike ride to Diala over a sandy track through the bush. That our family roles were about to be abruptly reversed also became abundantly clear. My daughter took off, straight as a die, with a twenty-five-liter barrel holding our supply of drinking water strapped to the back of her bike, leaving me literally in her dust as I weaved and tottered trying to balance my American Tourister with the same ease. We were in the savanna belt, and mercifully, the landscape was absolutely flat. Here and there, fruit- or nut-bearing trees, which are protected, stood out above the scrubby acacias, and occasionally the monotonous palette was enlivened by the flaming flowers of a kapok tree. Otherwise, the colors were overwhelmingly drab and the texture of the scene flat. (It would be, I discovered later, very different just after the rainy season, when the green of the new grass provided a vivid contrast to the bright red of the wet track and the dark termite mounds that pimpled every field.) The Bamana people have no word for green or any color other than black, white and red. Everything else must be likened to something in the environment such as the new grass, or the color of the flower of the *nere* tree, a lovely spray of pale lemon.

About 800 people, predominantly Bamana, lived in Diala in mud-walled houses with thatched roofs arranged in family "concessions." They reminded me of nothing so much as the houses in Celesteville, the village in *Babar the Elephant*. Each concession was made up of as many as a dozen buildings. The women lived in round huts, while the men's dwellings were rectangular and sometimes had roofs of corrugated metal. In general, they, and their contents, were little different from the ones described by Mungo Park 200 years ago. "A circular mud wall about four feet high, upon which is placed a conical roof, composed of the bamboo cane, and thatched with grass, forms alike the palace of the king, and the hovel of the slave. Their household furniture is equally simple. A hurdle of canes placed on upright stakes about two feet from the ground, upon which is spread a mat or bullock's hide, answers the purpose of a bed; a water jar, some earthen pots for dressing their food, a few wooden bowls and calabashes, and one or two low stools, compose the rest." Between the concessions, bulls wandered freely, along with sheep, goats, donkeys, chickens and guinea fowl. All these animals were equally craven, being accustomed to being driven off with sticks and stones and blows. Even my daughter's faithful dog cringed and retreated as I greeted him in good English fashion by picking up a stick to throw for him. When I later commented on this to a member of Emily's Malian family, she remarked wryly, "I guess Malian dogs don't know that game."

Soon after sunset, one of the girls from "our" family fetched us for the evening meal, which we took in the yard of their concession. Before we ate, I was presented to the head of the household, Wongloba, a wraith-like man of indeterminate age reclining absently in his hammock. Emily took the opportunity to ask him to give me my Malian name. I had heard much about the importance of this custom and was somewhat surprised by the casual way in which it was bestowed upon me. Wongloba considered only a moment and then murmured: "Draman Bagayogo," Bagayogo being the family name. Perhaps the lack of ritual was a reminder of a Malian proverb, which the Peace Corps volunteers learn early, to the effect that the log may lie in the pond, but it will never become a crocodile. In this case, I might have a Malian name, but I would never be Malian.

Strictly speaking, I should have eaten with Wongloba and the men who sat separately from the women and children, but in view of the insuperable language barrier — Bambara was the only language spoken in Diala — custom was allowed to bend, and I ate where Emily ate. Our meal was presided over by Masaba, Wongloba's eighty-year-old mother and the most respected member of the family. After the traditional greetings and benedictions were over and we were seated on our little wooden stools, a bowl of water was passed around to rinse our hands in. That evening, I was confronted for the first time with the infamous *tò* Emily had warned me of—a stodgy porridge made out of pounded millet that is the staple diet in Mali. It appeared in a big bowl with a smaller dish of sauce, whose provenance I decided was best ignored, placed on top of it. Using the fingers of the right hand only, we each scooped up a mouthful from the part of the communal bowl closest to us and dipped it in the sauce. As a lefty, I learned to advance my right hand instinctively only after repeated jabs from my daughter's elbow, but it was an important achievement since the left hand is reserved for what my Jacobean namesake, Sir Thomas Urquhart, called "inferiour employments and posteriour purposes."

Otherwise, I quickly got very used to these meals. For all her venerable years, Masaba had a wicked sense of humor, and after I had lived in Diala a few days, she relished imitating my plummy English speech patterns. I found *tò* to be not as grim as I had been led to believe, although on the special occasions when rice was served instead, as a treat after a good market day for instance, I certainly appreciated it. And the casual courtesy of the family as we sat around the communal bowl, with the sparks of the fire floating up into the African night, induced a sense of tranquillity that I have rarely known. Occasionally the shadow of a squatting child would splash against the mud wall of one of the surrounding huts as someone with a flashlight came or left. Those evenings were something I never tired of.

After dinner, one of the children brought out a large calabash of peanuts and emptied them in a pile on the ground. Everyone set to shelling them. As in all such things, the Malians performed this task with an innate grace born of functionalism, cracking the shell of the peanut on a stone and extracting its double contents in a single dexterous movement of the right hand that ended by tossing the nuts and husks back into the calabash together. They would be separated later and the nuts taken to town to be either ground into peanut butter for cooking or sold in the market. Emily, I noticed, made a passable attempt at this technique, but I was all fingers and thumbs, and eventually Masaba sent me to bed as being too tired to work usefully.

I was awakened the next morning by the most amazing cacophony, like a dozen Woody Woodpeckers on speed. Just outside my window, a line of guinea fowls were perched on the wall of Emily's garden, and this was their energetic morning chorus. But even through my dreams, I had been aware for some time of a deeper, more insistent sound. From daybreak on, the village had resounded with the thud of women pounding millet in big wooden mortars for the evening's *tò*. Now looking beyond the guinea fowls, I saw a number of our friends from the night before at their work in the shade of a large mango tree, all dressed in the colorful wraparound dresses called *panyas*. While I watched, a rhythm developed as five or six young women started to pound alternately, calling out and clapping as they threw the heavy pestle up in the air before catching it again on the downbeat. In Bambara, to clap, *tègère fo*, is literally "to make the hands talk," a description that seemed to do better justice to the women's impulse than our monosyllabic Anglo-Saxon word. The mortars, hewn from a single tree trunk, were shaped like an hourglass, and the sound, reverberating now from every quarter of the village like stereophonic drumming, seemed eternal.

When I went over to greet them, a young woman asked me if I liked living in Mali. I said that I did, and she retorted, albeit with a smile, "You wouldn't if you had to work as hard as we women do." And it was easy to think that in Mali the women's work is never done. In the fields, they do the sowing. They go to market (mostly on foot) to buy and sell their produce, which they carry on their heads no matter how big the burden, and just about every one of them either had a small baby strapped to her back or was pregnant. The women are also the biblical "drawers of water" as I found out when I picked up a bucket from the well; as soon as she saw this, Masaba made Emily take it from me, reproving her sternly for letting me, a man, do such a thing. And as "hewers of wood," the village women provided my enduring visual impression of Africa: returning from the bush with great bundles of wood on their heads each evening, their silhouettes against the setting sun seeming to echo the hourglass shape of the mortars.

According to the WorldWatch Institute, fuelwood extraction accounts for about 95 percent of all tree cutting in Mali. To find enough wood for the open fires on which all their cooking was done, the area the women had to range over was constantly expanding as the slow-growing bush wood got consumed. Along the *goudrone*, signs appeared at regular intervals with official messages urging Malians to respect their forests: *Plantons les arbres pour nos besoins en bois*, or *Plantons et protégeons les arbres*, as well as messages of a more general conservation nature: *Environmente sain = santé sain* and *L'érosion conduit la sécheresse*.[18] Nonetheless, the men cut wood as a cash crop, and every now and then we came across stacks of firewood for sale by the roadside in surprising quantity. The forest service encourages villages to start their own tree plantations, but unfortunately for wildlife, they are mostly of exotic species like gmelina, neem or eucalyptus because they grow faster. Outside Diala, the village had established just such a plantation, fenced off with wire, under the express control of the *dougoutigi* or headman. It would not be cut until he gave the word. More magical both for people and wildlife was the sacred grove in the market town, Keleya. Here, nobody ventured because of the spirits supposed to reside there — little people who would eat you, according to my daughter — and I found its wild vegetation a paradise for birds.

It was one of the few places I found where wildlife could flourish. Another official sign from the Eaux et Forêts read: *Chassons pour vivre, non pour décimer les animaux de la brousse*.[19] Masaba remembered when there were lions and other big game animals in the area. She said they all left in the drought, but it was hard to believe that hunting had not contributed to their demise. Over half the men in the village have guns. Some of these were commercially manufactured 12-bores, but others had been made by the local blacksmith and fired plugs made out of the hide of "an animal that runs fast in the bush," which we were never able to

---

18 Let's plant trees to supply our wood; Let's plant and protect the trees; Healthy environment = good health; Erosion brings drought.

19 Let's hunt to live, not to decimate the wildlife of the bush.

identify. We would frequently meet men out hunting, mounted on their motorbikes with their shotguns slung across their backs; evidence of their success was somewhat rarer. There seemed to be very little game left, apart from the odd francolin, the local partridge, that at any approach would rocket up from the grass. In the villages, little boys carried slingshots around their necks, and any small animal they could hit, from squirrel to lizard, was fair game and got roasted. The only wild mammal I saw other than bats was a single very close relative of a gray squirrel. It was exactly midway between two villages, presumably the farthest point from human life and the safest.

Only one animal seemed to be secure: a monster lizard, probably a Nile monitor, around Keleya. It was much venerated by the people there, who believed that it would release bad spirits if it were killed. Emily told me she had nearly tripped over it on one occasion. I was determined to find it. But try as I would, I never succeeded. As a villager, amused by my efforts, told me, "You don't find it. It finds you." It was rather like *Rin Tin Tin*'s White Buffalo from my childhood—"The legend says you'll find him, if your heart is brave and true"—and a good reminder that more than half the fun of watching wildlife is the quest itself. When we look to nature for a command performance and reckon the success only in terms of what birders call a "tick," we are missing the point, as well as being in for a disappointment.

The peanuts we had been shelling the night before were to go to the market, and we offered to take them on our bikes so that eighty-year-old Masaba, who would walk the five miles to Keleya, would at least not have to carry so much. The family was hoping for a good market so that they could have some extra money for a fête to be held the next week to celebrate the sale of the cotton harvest to the government cooperative. As we made our way out of the village, calls to me of "Draman" came from all sides, together with the traditional Bamana morning greeting. Given time, a proper greeting is long and complex, but on the road it can be abbreviated:

"*I ni sogoma.*"	"You and the morning."
"*M'ba, here sira?*"	"Did you pass the night in peace?"

"Here doron."	"Peace only."
"Somogo be di?"	"How is your family?"
"Torro te."	"No problems."
"U b'ifo."	"I greet the people of your village."
"Uname."	"They will hear it."

These greetings, and the valedictory benedictions that often went on even longer, never ceased to impress me. Respect, caring and joy were equally represented in the ritual, which, however formalized a convention it might be, seemed to guarantee a higher level of courtesy and consideration, and at the same time make unseemly behavior more difficult.

I was delighted with my new persona as Draman Bagayogo. Some of the kids pronounced it "Dramany," which seemed endearing, while some of the men made of it a guttural "Drachman," which sounded almost Scottish. Since Emily had received her name, Fanta, in Bamako when she had first arrived in Mali, she had a different family name, which was an endless source of laughs and rib-digging. Her family, the Keitas, being from near the capital, are more urbane, and the name is prominent in Mali's history, both ancient and modern; the Bagayogos are bush farmers, the salt of the earth. In a less complimentary vein, I was always being told that the Bagayogos eat beans and dog or donkey meat. Ragging between one family and another is something of a national sport.

Since most of the village was going on foot, Emily and I arrived in Keleya before many of them and had time to sit and watch the world go by over a cup of Malian coffee, which consists of a teaspoon of Nescafé mixed with several tablespoons of condensed milk topped up with boiling water. Along the main drag, a couple of six-year-old boys were playing with a toy truck, ingeniously made out of wire and strips of rubber called *mana*, the equivalent of baling wire in Mali and vital to any expedition or enterprise. The path from Diala produced a constant stream of gaily chatting women, who would disappear into the bushes just before they reached the town. When they reemerged, they had changed into their resplendent market best with *panyas* and head-cloths. The vibrant colors contributed to the festive atmosphere, an atmosphere that is notably lacking in our own American supermarkets. Almost as remark-

able were some of the recycled "Western" clothes, like the lady's evening
coat trimmed with fur worn by a grizzled elder with toothless smile and
a dash that its manufacturer surely never imagined.

The first of the family to arrive was a gawky teenager called Jeneba, a
special friend of Emily's, who came running across the highway to greet
us. On the folds of her colorful *panya*, a splendid bird was repeated over
and over. It was a standard-winged nightjar, which I had seen the
evening before flying over the village. In the dusk I had not recognized
it at first, thinking it was a crow being mobbed by two much smaller
birds; it took a minute or two before I realized that the small forms
behind it were actually the "standards" streaming from the nightjar's
wings. I mentioned this to Jeneba, pointing to the birds that were all
over her, but was greeted by blank incomprehension; she had never
noticed even a bird so striking in flight. This was in fact my third
encounter that day with the local ornithologically challenged outlook.
Before leaving for the market, I had spotted a flock of exquisite bee-
eaters in a mango tree just outside the village and stopped to take a look.
We were with Masaba on the way to water her garden. When she found
out what was holding up our progress, the old woman turned to Emily
and asked in her deadpan voice, "Don't they have birds where he comes
from?"[20] And when a hawk with splendid crimson underwings flew so low
across our path that some children following me actually turned to look
at it, I had optimistically asked them what it was. "It's a bird," was the
somewhat bemused answer. Azure-colored rollers, snow-white egrets,
bearded barbets with striking red throats, bright green parrots: they were
all just birds in Diala.

At the market, there was everything you could possibly want. The sides
of the narrow lanes were lined with mats on which peppers and tomatoes
and dried fish were spread out, or piles of exotic-looking powders and
spices heaped in rows. Traditional handmade wares such as calabash

20 "He argued probably, as my guide argued: who, when he was told that I had come from a
great distance, and through many dangers, to behold the Joliba river, naturally inquired, if
there were no rivers in my own country, and whether one river was not like another."
(Mungo Park, p. 153)

bowls and utensils (I had seen the vines that produce these hard gourds trained over the walls of some of the huts in the village) were stacked cheek by jowl with Western T-shirts—Chicago Bulls was a favorite logo —and garishly enameled tin bowls and basins from China. Under a metal roof at the edge of the market sat the Peuls, the traditional cattle herders, with their dairy products. Lighter skinned and with more delicate features than the taller and much darker Bambara, the Peuls, or Fulani, came originally from the north. As the crowd milled around, the constant surge of bright finery turned the narrow lanes into a kaleidoscope of colors. Street vendors, or *tigis*, mostly young men and boys, wandered around selling fruit and other refreshments, and at strategic locations, groups of women were cooking goat or fish or rice. Doing the rounds methodically was a train of maybe half a dozen children, smartly dressed in long dark blue kilts and naked from the waist up. A white cotton napkin was folded neatly on each head, and each child was armed with a rattle. An older woman leading the parade carried a basket into which people would place gifts of vegetables and fruit. The teacher at the Koranic school, the only school in Diala, later told us that they were probably little girls, not boys, who had just been circumcised. (If they had been boys, they would have been wearing shirts.) But in either case, it was part of a ritual: the kids would drop a wallet and then hide. When an "unsuspecting" customer picked it up, they would jump from their hiding places, calling him a thief and making a commotion with their rattles. He would be obliged to return the wallet and add something extra as well.

As we returned that evening, the sky above the village was glowing. In addition to the usual cooking fires, bonfires crackled as families cleaned up their concessions. Diala was sprucing up for the fête. The walls of the huts were being relined with mud; some were being painted with stripes and other geometric designs of gray and pink, the latter made from the fine sand that lies beneath the brick-red laterite surface. As I watched the men and women raking the accumulated refuse of their everyday lives—old wooden axe handles, broken calabashes, straw detritus—into the flames, it occurred to me that with everything so easily and naturally disposed of, without any need for garbage collection, there could be no sense of litter, at least in the terms that we are used to. It was all organic, and when its useful life was finished, it could be tossed aside without any thought as to its permanence. In the village, the only synthetic trash had been brought in by us. In fact, the biggest difference between our hut and the others in Diala—aside from its cement (rather than dirt) floor, a Peace Corps health requirement—was the presence of a waste basket. And despite all our efforts at simplicity, we used it, mostly for discarded packaging from our Western imports. Elsewhere in the village, there was no plastic or paper litter. Everything was reused until it either decomposed or could be burned.

The situation was very different in the cities and towns where plastic is widely used, and the same nonchalance had left an unholy mess. Even in Keleya (population 2,000), the ground was covered with litter after the market where little boys had been peddling a bright red water-ice made from hibiscus, called *da*. It came in a polyethylene bag, which when sucked dry, was simply dropped. I found it very hard to break my litter-conscious habits and continued to clutch my wrapper long after I had finished its delicious contents, until my sticky fingers were coated with grime. For, of course, there were no trash cans to deposit in. And that was just the tip of the iceberg; in all the towns there was synthetic garbage everywhere: on the roadside, along the edges of the river, wherever wind or current or human mobility had collected or deposited it.

On the other hand, Malians know the value of conservation and could teach us a thing or two about recycling. Rather than pressing the rewind button on the ubiquitous boom boxes and using up a precious battery, they rewind cassettes by hand, using a pencil as a spindle. Wherever possible everything solid is used again and again, as I was forcibly reminded when a Peul woman in the village brought us some fresh milk in a plastic bottle labeled "Automotive Fluid." The streets of Bamako are full of stores advertising *"pièces détachées,"* the equivalent of our used parts stores. In one place, a little boy was punching out discs from a scrap of sheet metal to make cooking pans. And for those who cannot afford to have the large gold earrings worn by the Peul women, they make similar-looking ones out of car radiators, which are then gilded.

We spent our days in Diala bicycling from one village to another as part of my daughter's infant health program. Inevitably, we would be taken first to the headman, especially if this was a village where she had yet to set up a schedule. Sometimes we would start the palaver by giving the *dougoutigi* several kola nuts as a sign of respect. A particular favorite of the old men who chew it endlessly, a kola nut is about the size of a chestnut conker and contains a mild form of stimulant like caffeine. They were not grown in Mali but must always have been an important trade item because the word for "south" is literally "where kola nuts come from" (and "north" is "where salt comes from," referring to the salt trade from Timbuktoo that was the foundation of the Mali Empire in the Middle Ages). The formality of our reception varied, from a casual conversation on a straw mat under the *dougoutigi*'s hangar, or *gwa*, to what seemed like a full-fledged public meeting. In one village, Emily had to explain her project, in Bambara, to a villager she had interested in the idea, who repeated it verbatim to the *dougoutigi* seated on his mat, who then explained it to an elder, all perfectly within hearing of each other. During all this ceremony, the *dougoutigi* with extreme care removed a tick from a little boy's groin.

One chief was so enthusiastic that a man with an antelope-horn trumpet was dispatched at once to summon the women from the fields. While my daughter hooked up her baby scales to the wood strut of a *gwa* and the mothers crowded round, I was free to wander about the village. I was always fascinated by the various forms of industry, so different from anything in my own experience. Two women were getting ready to fire a couple of pots,[21] burnishing the surface with shea butter, a vegetable oil from the nut of a local tree, using a string of baobab seeds like a Brillo pad. Around the corner, an old man was husking *nere* pods,[22] rather as

---

21 "Pottery is traditionally reserved for women, since symbolically all that is hollow and is consequently a receptacle represents the feminine." T. C. McLuhan, *The Way of the Earth*.

22 Mungo Park's journals also speak of the *nere*, which he called *nitta*. Finding the inhabitants of a village collecting the fruit, he noted that they "are very numerous in this neighbourhood. The pods are long and narrow, and contain a few black seeds enveloped in the fine mealy powder before mentioned; the meal itself is of a bright yellow colour, resembling the flour of sulphur, and has a sweet mucilaginous taste; when eaten by itself it is clammy, but when mixed with milk or water it constitutes a very pleasant and nourishing article of diet." They were clearly an important dietary supplement, as he found by picking one and

one shells broad beans, except that the pods are packed with a sweet-tasting pith, bright yellow, which he laid out to dry on a cow skin. After a while, one of the women took the empty pods and boiled them up in a brew that would give the pots their glossy black finish when they came out of the fire. The firing was done by the simple if unpredictable expedient of building a bonfire around them. As soon as the flames died down, they applied the *nere* tea with a switch of leaves that sizzled at each swipe on the hot baked clay.

Behind a concession in another village, two women were attacking a haystack of sorghum plants, thrashing it with sticks seemingly endlessly. As so often in Mali, the execution of a task appeared to progress unhampered by the ticking of the clock that looms over so many of our daily chores in the name of convenience, and it seemed to make so much possible despite the meager resources. Whereas we would be constantly checking "to see if it's done yet," the women just beat and beat, or sieve and sieve, or pound and pound. The preparation of vital shea oil or butter is a good example.

The process had started just before the rainy season when the fruits ripened and were harvested, just as they had been 200 years earlier. According to Mungo Park,

The people were everywhere employed in collecting the fruit of the shea trees, from which they prepare the vegetable butter mentioned in former parts of this work. These trees grow in great abundance all over this part of Bambarra. They are not planted by the natives, but are found growing naturally in the woods; and in clearing wood land for cultivation, every tree is cut down but the shea. The tree itself very much resembles the American oak; and the fruit, from the kernel of which, being first dried in the sun, the butter is prepared by boiling the kernel in water, has somewhat the appearance of a Spanish olive.

---

exciting the ire of a local chief. "For, says he [the chief], this place has been frequently visited with famine from want of rain, and in these distressing times the fruit of the Nitta is all we have to trust to, and it may then be opened without harm; but in order to prevent the women and children from wasting this supply, a *toong* is put upon the Nittas until famine makes its appearance. The word *toong* is used to express anything sealed up by magic."

The kernel is enveloped in a sweet pulp, under a thin green rind; and the but-
ter produced from it, besides the advantage of its keeping the whole year with-
out salt, is whiter, firmer, and, to my palate, of a richer flavour than the best
butter I have ever tasted made from cow's milk.

I inwardly commended Park for his rugged courage. My arrival in
Diala had coincided with the final stages of making shea butter, and my
first impression of the village was impregnated with its peculiarly acrid
smell, rather like silage, raising considerable doubts about my hitherto
much-vaunted confidence that I could eat anything. By this time, the
women had pounded the shea nuts into a coarse paste in the same mortars they used to pound the millet. (Generally mortars are made from the
trunk of a shea tree for which the hardness of the wood makes them ide-
ally suited; otherwise, like other fruit-bearing trees, shea trees are protected as they were in Park's day.)

To get to this stage had been a lengthy process. Instead of boiling the
nuts, in Diala, to save firewood, they stored the fruit in big, deep holes in
the earth for the rainy season until the flesh had fermented and started
to rot. The smell of the oil was nothing to the odor of putrefaction that
wafted through the village as the nuts, now naked, were exhumed to dry.
Whenever I passed the roof of a hangar on which they had been spread
out, my first thought was that I was about to stumble into a sewer. And
as I walked about the village at night, it was hard not to trip in the dark
over the empty holes. Next, the rotting nuts were roasted, very slowly.
Despite the wreath of blue smoke that surrounded the mound of nuts on
top of the mud oven, it was hard to imagine that their temperature could
have been much higher than it would have been were they simply
exposed to the sun. A few sticks smoldering languidly outside the mouth
of the oven provided all the heat there was; from time to time, in an
equally desultory way, a woman would come and knock off the embers
from the sticks and sweep them under the nuts. (When I asked Emily
about this, she pointed out that however odd it might look to us, the villagers had been roasting shea nuts this way for generations, probably
with good reason based on experience.) When I arrived in Diala, the
nuts had been roasted and pulverized, and the women were kneading the

black sludge, aerating it until it gained a purplish hue. This they did by scraping the goo, ladle by ladle and using a fist-sized stone, against rocks smoothed and hollowed from years of use. With the paste finally reduced to a thick syrup, it would be boiled until the oil floated to the top and could be skimmed off. I eventually got used to the smell of shea butter, and I even managed to acquire a taste for it, which was just as well because it is an important comestible and is used in much of the cooking.[23] But I would hesitate to commend its "rich flavour" as favorably as Park did. Often, as we were going through the bush, the pungent smell of shea butter was the first sign that we were approaching a village.

After Emily finished weighing babies and advising their mothers on nutrition and care, we would be invited into one of the huts for lunch, invariably with the men (all Peace Corps volunteers, including women, have the status of honorary men in Mali). Men tend the cattle and see to the building of huts, including making the bricks out of mud. They also take care of the commercial crops, such as cotton. But they seemed to leave plenty of time for sitting or lounging under the *gwa*, drinking tea and talking while one of them might be weaving a rush mat, braiding a rope from baobab bark or tying a line of snares (this done using the toes). Wongloba, the head of Emily's family, spent most of his time in his hammock or attending prayers at the mosque. Sometimes in the evening we would see him strolling fastidiously out into the bush, a gun strapped over his shoulder and an elegant fly-whisk in one hand that seemed to belie his hunting zeal.

One afternoon when we were drinking mint tea with some men after a festive meal of rice and sauce, I became aware all at once that our friends' attention was being directed to the other side of the concession. A stranger—an African—had just entered the village on foot and had hunkered down to rest against a mud hut in the full glare of the midday sun. One of the village women was bringing him a bowl of *tò*, in accordance with hospitality. From the tone of their talk and by the way they

23 Park noted, "The growth and preparation of this commodity seem to be among the first objects of African industry in this and the neighbouring states; and it constitutes a main article of their inland commerce."

were glancing over their shoulders at the stranger, it was clear that the arrival of an unknown person in the village was by no means an everyday occurrence; their curiosity betrayed an unsettling mixture of indifference and disdain. No one made the slightest move to greet him, which was strange in this country where hellos and good-byes can go on for minutes at a time. For his part, the stranger seemed equally uninterested in his surroundings. He had a broad face framed by thick black hair growing into dreadlocks and a little goatee, and his bloodshot eyes seemed to be focused on some distant object. I gathered the stranger spoke neither Bambara nor French. Someone suggested he might understand English, so I went over to talk to him.

As I squatted down beside him, the stranger began to speak English in a runaway monotone that was almost like a chant. "The people of Africa and the people of Europe must work together to change the world." He said he came from Ghana and was walking across Africa to Europe, driven by this mission and totally alone. He had been to Moscow, and from Moscow to China, where he said his family lived. I realized then that in the strangeness of his voice might be a Chinese lilt, unexpected, to say the least, in the middle of the bush in West Africa. I did not understand a lot of what he said, all in his singsong torrent. He was oblivious to everything but his lonely mission. I felt the chill of his isolation and wondered what cataclysm had caused it: had he been brainwashed or tortured? His laserlike intensity made me want to get away. I wished him well and returned to my friends in the shade of the *gwa*. The villagers continued to regard him casually with mild amusement. It struck me how anything might happen to him on his trek across three continents with no one any the wiser. His presence was unforgettable, and yet of what use to him was the deep impression he had made on me and perhaps others along his path? I felt I might have met a prophet and had walked by on the other side. Twenty-four hours later, I wondered if he was still alive.

As we were preparing to make our way back to Diala, a young boy who had been sent scampering off by the *dougoutigi* returned with a live chicken. The *dougoutigi* took it from him, inspected it carefully and then presented it to me as a gift. I thanked him profusely, prompted in the finer points of Bamana etiquette by Emily, all the while wondering how

I was going to get the bird home on my bicycle. But the problem, and the chicken, were taken out of my hands by another young man. By the time our farewells and benedictions were over, the chicken was tied to the handlebars by its feet, and there it hung all the way home, eyeing me balefully, squawking only if I went over an exceptionally large bump.

Just before we said good-bye, four men had hit the trail ahead of us, each with a big cardboard box on his bicycle. We hadn't left the village long and were pedaling through a wood when we heard several shots coming from their direction. I had only just time to get off the narrow path before one of the bicyclists we had seen came rocketing towards us, his eyes wild with fear, leaving a large supply of cartons of cigarettes strewn in his wake. As we moved forward to investigate, a handful of soldiers fanned out, running through the trees in our direction, followed by a khaki Land Cruiser. Several soldiers had their rifles trained on the fugitive's companion who had had the bad luck to fall off his bicycle. It too was loaded with cigarettes. A friend who had accompanied us explained that they were smugglers bringing in cigarettes from Guinea, only forty-five miles away, or Côte d'Ivoire, and it was something of a game of cat and mouse with the local authorities. He said that all that would happen to the captive was that his bicycle and the contraband would be confiscated. Indeed, the soldiers or gendarmes seemed to have about the same attitude to the whole thing as the watchman, or "bulldog," in my college who, when he had just failed to apprehend us in the act of climbing in after curfew, used to say, "I'll catch you next time, sir." Our friend's sympathies were all with the smugglers; it turned out they were friends of his, but that night when we told our adventure to the family in Diala, they adopted a more conservative view in favor of the police.

Wherever we bicycled, it was surprising how many people we would meet on the way, either on foot or on bicycle or sometimes in a donkey cart. And the savanna itself, though apparently uniform, was always yielding up a memorable moment to surprise our senses. We would find it in the dense shade of a mango grove, where a breeze was blowing, beautifully cool beneath the dark green canopy. Every now and then, the indescribably sweet scent of bush flowers would waft across our path like a blessing. Once, we happened on a single magnificent flame tree in bloom out of which flew a golden oriole while a pair of glossy starlings added a metallic blue highlight to the brilliant palette. Equally striking in its own way was the rusty brown of a bare field as we pedaled up its long gradual slope past lines of small rocks that bisected it like a grid: stone rows to trap and hold what little rain or moisture might run their way. At the top we found ourselves on a blackened plateau where the villagers had burned the grass to get rid of snakes, bare except for the termite mounds that erupted like overgrown toadstools from the charred ground.

Two places had a particular magic that neither I nor my daughter ever tired of. One was a ghost town of decaying mud walls through which mango trees and baobabs now grew in abundance; Old Diala, deserted for the present site many years before for reasons not entirely clear, was now picturesquely returning to the dust from which it had arisen. The other was one of the approaches to Diala proper. Just before one reached it, the trees ahead thinned out, giving warning that a clearing lay beyond. At the edge of a ridge where the ground fell away, one looked out over cultivated fields of millet and sorghum through which the little red path wriggled its way to the village. The shadows from the trees on the upland stretched out across them, and in the last rays of the sun, green and red were wedded in a view of burnished gold. Unexpectedly, this view over an African village had the same effect as a landscape by Constable, and it reminded us both of the view from the pub over the Wild Brooks in Amberley.[24]

It was the end of the cold season, and daytime temperatures were in the 70s to 80s. However, in a matter of weeks, from March to early summer, West Africa would become one of the hottest places on earth and the rains would come. Life in Diala is dominated by the seasons, long-

---

24 Park had similar flights of homesick fancy, although his direr circumstances would have made them much more poignant. "No sooner had I shut my eyes than fancy would convey me to the streams and rivers of my native land; there, as I wandered along the verdant brink, I surveyed the clear stream with transport, and hastened to swallow the delightful draught;— but alas! Disappointment awakened me, and I found myself a lonely captive, perishing of thirst, amidst the wilds of Africa."

ingrained customs in response to them and the need to eat. Living is hard work. Although infant mortality in Mali is one of the highest in the world, I saw little evidence of malnutrition once the children had reached the age of three or four. Emily's theoretical assignment was to work in the agricultural sector, but it seemed that there was little she could do there that the villagers couldn't do better, unless it was attracting grants to install a pump, or planting a live hedge around a garden plot. So she focused on health issues for mothers and children. And in so doing, she saw life hanging by a thinner thread than we are used to. A baby dies because the father will not allow his wife to take it to the hospital; another little girl's name is Maybe,[25] as in maybe she'll live maybe she won't, because half her mother's seventeen children died as infants. A teacher tells me that instead of going to the gendarmes, he will kill the men who stole some of his cattle or, he says, "Maybe they will kill me." Death seems nearer. Right outside the concession, a rough circle of stones marks the grave of Masaba's husband, close at hand "so that we can think about him and greet him," and so that he can still be a presence in the family. A Senegalese man living in Paris wrote, "Down there, there existed between death and myself an intimacy, made up at the same time of my terror and my expectation. Whereas here death has become a stranger to me. Everything combats it, drives it back from men's bodies and minds."[26] And despite all the hardship, the people laugh, too.

As we bicycled out of Diala for the last time—the first stage of our return trip to Bamako—I reflected on the past days: I had been living in a thatched hut with mud walls lined with cow manure; we had had to bring in our drinking water by bicycle and store it in a pottery urn; I had bathed in four cups of water a day; I had eaten tò almost exclusively. And yet, for the duration of my stay, I never felt the lack of anything, nor a longing for the comforts I insist on at home. It was about as far from my

25 Park found the same thing. "Thus, my landlord at Kamalia was called Karfa, a word signifying to replace; because he was born shortly after the death of one of his brothers."

26 From L'Aventure ambigue by Cheikh Hamidou Kane, quoted by McLuhan, The Way of the Earth.

American home and lifestyle as it is possible to get, but the lasting lesson of Diala was how little is enough when you have community.[27]

I was sorry to miss the fête celebrating the sale of the cotton harvest. However, I was eager to visit the Bandiagara Escarpment, a 125-mile line of cliffs a good day's bus ride north of Bamako. Known as La Falaise, it is the home of the fabled Dogon people. But first we had to get to Bamako. Along with about a dozen other passengers from Keleya, Emily and I crammed ourselves into a baché, a covered pickup truck that is the functional equivalent of a bus. My hard, blue American Tourister suitcase jostled incongruously with the colorful variety of bags and boxes and paraphernalia piled high on the roof, including a goat. The sides of the baché were lined with live guinea fowl trussed upside down. At last we were ready; some men gave the vehicle a push, and soon we were hurtling down the highway. Whenever we passed through a village where the inhabitants had optimistically placed speed bumps in the road, the driver simply went around them, at full tilt, even if it meant driving down the embankment. Only the goat bleated its protest, and finally let go with its bladder just as we reached the capital, to the fastidious fury of the passengers.

In Bamako, donkeys pulling carts cantered through the streets, their drivers beating them mercilessly. (The brutality of Malians to their animals was something I never came to terms with.) More enjoyable was an open pickup truck full of young boys playing musical instruments, talking drums and the Malian fiddle, all made out of wire and tin cans. Many of the stores had gaily painted walls advertising their merchandise or services, some of them elevated to an art form: a butcher with his meats, an amazing variety of fish for the fishmonger or a fat cook over a fire preparing various regional specialties. I particularly liked a radiator

---

27 Park put it this way: "I cannot, however, take leave of Woolli, without observing that I was everywhere well received by the natives; and that the fatigues of the day were generally alleviated by a hearty welcome at night; and though the African mode of living was at first unpleasant to me, yet I found at length that custom surmounted trifling inconveniences, and made everything palatable and easy."

shop where various mechanical parts were portrayed in a rather futurist style.

We were in Bamako for the rest of the day, and we made the most of our time visiting the markets for food, utensils and handicrafts. Carrots had come into season, and everywhere there were women with baskets on their heads sprouting dozens of bright orange fingers and giving new meaning to the term "carrot-top." Amid the bustle, a stately Tuareg man strode down the street, his sword in its leather scabbard clutched matter-of-factly in his hands. At a stall where craftsmen were carving wooden statues, numerous representations of *tubabs*, or white people, included Tin-Tin and a French *para*; one particularly, mounted on a horse, aroused my curiosity because it recalled so quaintly and irresistibly Noël Coward's "Mad Dogs and Englishmen": "When the white man rides, / the natives hide in glee, / because the simple creatures hope he / will impale his solar topee / on a tree."

There was more interest in wildlife here than in the countryside. In the fetish market, every conceivable pelt or animal part was laid out on mats: monkey heads and paws, blue and green birds, snake skins and the skins of wild cats that I would have sworn were endangered and pro-tected. Where the artisans' stalls were set up, crocodiles, hippos and all sorts of birds were everywhere: as stone and wood carvings, as motifs drawn in lines and dots on mud-cloth and calabashes and as wild-colored patterns printed on textiles. Under an awning, one old man sought to impress us with the realism of a painted statue of a cobra catching a bird at its nest by demonstrating with his hands how the snake slithered up the tree and pounced. In a magic shop among the skin boxes and amulets, I spotted a wooden bird, simple but shapely. "What do you do with it?" said I. "You look at it. It looks at you. You talk to it." A Malian conversation piece, I thought, and wondered if it talked back.

From Bamako, we planned to take the bus to Mopti on the banks of the Niger, and from thence a bush taxi to Bandiagara and La Falaise, anoth-er couple of hours. As we traveled north into the Sahel, the countryside became progressively parched. Here and there, the flat scrubland was accented with a striking outcrop of red ferrous rock. Otherwise the dom-inant features on the landscape were the huge baobab trees. For the first part of the ride, the road took us through typical bush country. But beyond Segou, it was being cultivated much as Mungo Park found it when he passed quite nearby 200 years before. The entry in his journal reads: "Cultivation is carried on here on a very extensive scale; and as the natives themselves express it, 'Hunger is never known.' In cultivating the soil, men and women work together. They use a large sharp hoe, much superior to that used in Gambia." Not much seemed to have changed.

But I did little reading; as always there was too much else to look at on the bus. A chicken made a brief escape down the aisle; recaptured, it had to content itself with squawking protests for the rest of the journey. Next to me was a charming young woman with a round face and *retroussé* nose and a tiny baby on her lap. Whenever she turned to get something from her sack or bent over her baby, glowing curves of light brown skin appeared from under her *panya*; the baby played happily with a mobile phone the whole way. Across the aisle, equally absorbed in technology, a man Emily dubbed "Dapper Dan" because of his little goatee and indefinable air of self-importance spent the ten-hour trip fiddling with his pocket radio, tuning in to a station when one was within range and just twiddling the dial from static to static when one was not. In the seat in front of us, "Ants in his Pants," a rather slight man in a purple boubou, would jump up and down officiously checking out anything, no matter how insignificant, taking place anywhere on the bus. And in the middle of the backseat, an old man in a turban, impervious to the jolting ride, sat trancelike with his chin resting on the muzzle of his old rifle. The most exciting thing that happened was when, with only an hour to go, the bus stopped for evening prayers, and there was a halfhearted revolt at the delay by passengers who were more anxious to get home than to observe their devotions. But Allah won out, and we didn't get to Mopti until well after dark. We spent the night just outside the city.

The next morning we left humdrum human burlesque behind us and exchanged it, it seemed to me at least, for a more metaphysical experience. No longer on the *goudrone*, we headed into Dogon country over a dusty road, potholed but serviceable enough for our rattletrap taxi. I was aware that we were gradually climbing, and on top of the plateau, the air was fresh and cool. After the flat savanna around Diala and so much of the journey north, the countryside was getting more interesting, too. The landscape, though far from lush, was becoming decidedly greener, the vegetation making quite a contrast against the stark red bluffs. Craggy massifs rose up around us, and the ground was increasingly scattered with huge boulders. Outcrops sculpted by wind and rain took on weird and wonderful shapes that added to the growing sense of magic in the land. Here and there iridescent rollers and bee-eaters flashed from tree to tree.

As we crested one low ridge after another, a rhythm of anticipation set in: the next hill drawing us across its valley and up its slope revealing a further vista toward which the road would dip away before climbing into the distance once more. Down one of these hills, two men came walking, stopping to talk from time to time. They wore long blue robes and conical straw hats. Perhaps they were herders, or old men going out to their fields. But to me, they appeared as sages, philosophers discoursing together in a pastoral landscape. And suddenly an antique phrase slipped into my brain, *Et in Arcadia Ego*. It connoted some mysterious, wonderful past. But rather than its original meaning—the portent of mortality even in Utopia—my intuition was closer to the nostalgic memory reflected by Poussin's philosopher-shepherds as they contemplate the tomb of one who once upon a time lived in a happy paradise. The notion that Emily and I were visitors to Arcady, travelers now in time as well as space, was further encouraged by the rocky landscape—not so very different from the one in Poussin's painting. As it took hold, this idea entirely colored my perceptions of the land of the Dogon.

My vision of Arcady conjured up a notion of industry among those who dwelt there that enhanced rather than spoiled. Next to the road, the slopes were ribbed with lines of well-cut stones to hold back the soil and protect it from the erosion that was dissecting the plain elsewhere. Troupes of goats and sheep were grazing, watched by their herders reclining under the spreading trees. A stream flowed, its banks like an emerald ribbon across the dry terrain, and here and there especially brilliant splashes of green marked the presence of ponds that sank deep into the plateau. Around these and the temporary pools left from the rainy season the villagers were tending their crops—onions, eggplant and tobacco—in gardens neatly laid out like checkerboards, most of the soil having been brought in by hand.

While this perception was taking shape in my head, we approached the last ridge before the edge of the Falaise and the far horizon. Sangha, where we would spend the night, glowed in the late afternoon sun like a village in the thousand and one nights, its mud houses transformed into domes and minarets. The nearer we came, the more extensive were the signs of cultivation. Everywhere, fields and rocklines were neatly laid out. Low walls of broken stone awaited a basket or two of soil so that a crop could be planted. Small depressions had been augmented to hold the rains. On the outskirts of the village, women were tending their gardens. Beside the road, one particular rock, its surface dimpled with holes in which the pebbles had been played a million times, had been worn smooth by generations of old men congregating here for a game of mankala. Along the main street enormous baobabs loomed, their branches like roots as if the tree—as legend has it—had been planted upside down. Their trunks had a waisted look: as high as a man could reach, the bark, used for making rope, had been flayed in tiers two or three feet broad, leaving ridges so that the tree could still be climbed.

We had hired a guide, Mamadou, in Bandiagara, the gateway to the Dogon country. As always in Mali, the process was a performance in itself involving a cast of thousands. Besides enlisting Mamadou, we were introduced to a baby cayman (sacred to the Dogon) called Aba, and I refused an offer of twenty-five camels (one for every year of her life) for Emily's hand in marriage to a young man who styled himself "la lumière de La Falaise" (the light of the Falaise). Mamadou himself was, by contrast, shy and retiring, and at first, watching his lanky body draped over a chair in a corner, I feared he might be a bit glum. I needn't have worried. From his canvas porkpie hat to his flip-flops, all of which had seen better days, he cut quite a dash as he ambled ahead down the trail. And his serious demeanor readily broke into a wide smile. I guessed he was in his thirties, and he had lived around the Falaise all his life.

Now, as he led us into this fairy tale, Mamadou pointed out the ritual places and explained the taboos. Many of the Dogon are animists (hence the fetish market), and scattered about the fields stood upright stones washed white with millet milk where goats and chickens had been sacrificed to keep the water sweet, make the gardens grow or consecrate a particular fête. He led us through narrow lanes between the houses, surprisingly deserted, as if we were in a dream. Along one street, the walls of the house of the fetishist were honeycombed with rectangular recesses where various medicines and magic powders were stored. When I tried to take a photograph of it, two little boys suddenly appeared shouting at us. As we penetrated deeper into the maze of narrow lanes, a merchant barred our path to tempt us with ancient relics, leading us into his house and producing antique statues from under the bed to admire and buy.

If these were the initiation rites of a fairy tale quest, it was a welcome respite to escape from the alleyways. We followed our guide out of the village through the well-tended gardens by the river where little boys were catching fish with their hands in a mud-hole and a herdsman and his cattle seemed to be leading us into the setting sun. After we had gained a certain distance, Mamadou turned us around: there, spread out before us, lay the village, now burnished by the afterglow, with a full moon rising behind it. As we watched the light change from gold to aquamarine, Mamadou told us the story of the first Dogon. He was one of two brothers who, being trapped on the banks of a river by their enemies, would have been killed had not a crocodile carried them on its back to safety across the water. Here Mamadou interrupted his story to assure us that in a nearby village sacred crocodiles still play with the village babies in a pool. I could not help thinking of Aba's small but needle-pointed teeth.

Getting back to the legend, Mamadou went on to tell how the brothers reached Mopti, again at death's door, this time from hunger. The elder brother cut off his leg to feed his younger sibling. Then they parted, the younger to La Falaise where he started the Dogon tribe, the cultivators of millet. The other, with only one leg, remained in Mopti and begat the Bozo, the fishermen of the river. So the Dogon and Bozo are cousins, and if the Dogon's millet crop fails, they go to Mopti where the Bozo are obliged to give them fish. And if the Bozo need millet, the Dogon must share it with them.

As we turned back towards the village, a gaggle of young boys that seemed to grow as we walked surrounded us. The smallest child hammered out a tattoo on an empty Nescafé tin with a bone as if beating our retreat. The older ones sidled up to us offering trinkets of various kinds for sale. The younger children showed us drawings of Dogon dancers they had made with colored ballpoint pens. Having failed to get my attention with these, one boy tried the sympathy ploy on Emily: "I'm a student, and I don't have a pen." My whole vision of Arcady crumbled at his hands, outstretched now for presents instead of welcome: *"Bonbon? Cadeau? Bic?"* Candy? Present? Pen?

Suddenly I was overwhelmed with disgust, at myself rather than them, for unleashing the cynical side effects of tourism. I needed a catharsis, and I found it after dinner when I went into the artisan's *magasin* next to the hotel. I walked into the dragon's mouth with the specific intention of getting the best deal I could. I was ruthless. The artisan merchant was delighted to show me some beautiful statues by Dogon craftsmen and (allegedly) their predecessors, the Tellem. I settled on a wooden shutter carved with a sacred serpent and two crocodiles, and a Dogon wedding gift, a miniature montage of all the utensils of their domestic life, from the specialized knife for hollowing out a calabash to the ladder "so you can sleep together under the stars." He quoted his price; I told him that I respected his work, but it was more than I could afford. He came back at me with gentle encouragement. "Go on, state your price. Bargain with a smile." Reluctantly, I offered something less than a third of the asking price. "OK, now I will make another offer. You see, we do not get angry." And so it went, back and forth, offer, counteroffer. I was determined to stick well below half his original ask. Finally, he took my *cary cary*, or "absolutely last price," plus "a beer to drink your health." I was delighted by this nicety that saved face all round, and I accepted. The experience of bargaining had exorcised the memory of the children and helped reconcile my ambiguous feelings. After all, bazaars have a place in stories like Scheherazade's. As do portents: outside the *magasin*, a little boy was playing with the severed head of a black sheep. It was a call to mindfulness that behind the fairy tale lay some harsh realities. I shuddered as I remembered Mamadou saying matter-of-factly that the old practice of human sacrifice might still go on in some villages, voluntarily, in secret and only in great emergency.

The sun had risen but its rays had not yet reached the top of the plateau next morning when, leaving our taxi behind, we started our hike down the cliff. I was back in my fairytale world of omens and wise men; as we walked out beyond the village, a lamb skipped ahead of us, and a large centipede shuffled across our path, but no one killed it. Towards the edge of the cliff, the fields gave way to bare rock as if it were the edge of the world. Before us, an arid plain, already bathed in sunlight, stretched away from the cliffs to the hazy horizon like the sea. Beyond a barren ridge running parallel to the cliffs, the only features to break the monotony were blobs of green—the shrubs that dotted the dusty land-scape. But directly below us at the foot of the cliff lay a fertile strip where baobabs and tamarinds grew in profusion between the fields of millet and grass. From where we stood, it looked like a Garden of Eden, with the ridge a protective battlement for this Utopia against the wilderness.

The great Malian sage Amadou Hampate Ba wrote that "the deepest secrets of life are hidden in the bowels and tunnels of the earth. Myth tells us that life began in a grotto, grew in a well, and burst forth from a crevice."[28] Although I had not read it at the time, it makes a fitting fore-word for what still seems to me like a mystical descent. Like an African Virgil, Mamadou led us through a cleft in the rock down into the bowels of the cliff. Our path started along a dry streambed that must have been a torrent in the rainy season; along the cliff face, low caves had been excavated horizontally into the rock, refuges of the ancient Tellem peo-ple during clan disputes. In some places we had to scramble over great boulders, while above our heads, an occasional tree grew out of the ver-tical rock face, a triumph over gravity and drought.

For a while, we joined the course of a stream that fell in little cascades and brought this particular crack of rock to fresh, green life. Halfway down, where water bubbled out of the rock wall into a pool, the trees

28 Quoted in McLuhan, *The Way of the Earth.*

had grown into a deliciously shady grove. A party of women in bright cotton *panyas* were collecting wild grapes and filling their urns with water. The baskets, round at the bottom and square at the top in the traditional Dogon style,[29] were full of the little green fruit, and they offered us handfuls. They were not real grapes, but the flesh was pulpy and refreshingly tart. Between the spring and the village ahead, the feet of centuries had smoothed the ledge, sometimes perilously narrow, to a high, slippery gloss. Yet the women managed to pass each other effortlessly, even with heavy burdens on their heads, even in the skinniest places.

When the path opened up, we emerged into another magic world. Below us, the side of the rock face bristled with the thatched roofs of a village that seemed to float above a pasture, a natural corral surrounded on three sides by cliffs. Stone-and-mud huts arranged along a symbolic plan made up each family compound. A circular building at one end, where the women spend the days of their period, represented the head, with long rectangular buildings on the sides being the arms, and the courtyard in the center where rituals are performed, the heart. This "body" formed the axis of the house, the entrance to the concession representing the sex.

As we threaded our way between houses and granaries, a pair of elders welcomed us. They were reclining in the shade of the *togouna*, the village meeting hall, a distinctive open structure with a low ceiling designed to accommodate men only if they are sitting, which enforces decorum at town meetings. By contrast, the thickness of the thatched roof was much higher. Doubtless partly to provide some insulation from the rays of the sun, it is also insurance in case the roof wears thin before its time. *Togounas* can be rethatched only in special ritual years, and great misfortune would come to the village if the roof did not last to the next appointed year. The posts that supported its weight were carved with masks: owls, rabbits, snakes, and, most importantly, the form of Kanaga, the Dogon symbol of the creation of the world, with two "arms"

---

29 The Dogon basket is a representation of order in the Cosmos, uniting the sun (circle) and heavens (square).

pointing up to heaven and two rooted in the earth. Some of the houses had other animals in relief on their walls: a wild cat, an elephant and the turtle dove, carrier of messages, always represented on stilts to simulate flight. These were painted with the two colors most significant to the Dogon: white, the light of the sun, and red, the color of the moon.

Many of the wooden doors and shutters of the buildings were intricately carved with ritual scenes: rows of people, with arms lowered to indicate that they were watching a sacrifice, surrounded the central form of the Kanaga, often with the revered crocodile, which has the same shape, and the sacred serpent.

We completed our descent and entered the Utopia we had spied from the top of the cliff. The tall feathery grass we walked through and the multicolored birds flitting about the trees and bushes suggested that we were indeed in the garden of the gods. The contorted trunks of the great baobab trees added a further dimension of fantasy. An elderly man wearing the traditional Dogon conical hat, riding on the haunches of a steer, greeted us as he and his family made their gentle progress from one village to another. But there was a somber side, too. The fields of millet we passed, planted a good five weeks earlier, had still barely sprouted, there had been so little rain.[30] And the tranquillity of the place seemed all the more bittersweet because of the threat of the advancing tide of sand: the

30 The reader will notice that with my sojourn in Dogon country, the year has jumped ahead six months to a new season and indeed, the moon waxes and wanes with astonishing rapidity. In fact this account is made up of experiences encountered on three separate trips to Mali over several years, and I have taken some strictly chronological liberties. In defense, I would point to an interesting passage from the autobiography of Amadou Hampate Ba, who writes: "La chronologie n'étant pas le premier souci des narrateurs africains. . . . Dans les récits africains où le passé est revécu comme une expérience présente, hors du temps en quelque sorte, il y a parfois un certain chaos qui gêne les esprits occidentaux, mais où nous nous retrouvons parfaitement. Nous y évoluons à l'aise, comme des poissons dans une mer où les molécules d'eau se mêlent pour former un tout vivant." (Chronology not being the first concern of African narrators. . . . In telling African stories where the past is relived as if it were an experience in the present, in some sense outside of time, there is sometimes a certain chaos that troubles Western minds but which we find perfectly natural. We move there at our ease like fish in a sea where molecules of water mix together to form a living whole.) I had taken the book to read on the trip, since I was going to Bandiagara, where he was born, and I noted the passage with great delight, since my journals are a day-to-day hodgepodge of past and present made necessary by the frequent desire to describe things which were actually happening while I tried to catch up with events of the previous days.

ridge we had seen from above was in fact an enormous sand dune, whose advance the villagers were vainly trying to stem by planting trees.

We spent the night in a village at the foot of the cliff. It was a beautiful evening, and I lay down on my mat on the flat roof of a Dogon house and watched the stars come out. The Big Dipper was setting behind the edge of the plateau, in what seemed to be a race with the deepening dusk. For a moment it hung there in all its shining glory, and then it was gone as if it had sidled into a crevice in the rock, leaving the black sky to the Milky Way and a myriad of other constellations. There was no other light, until just before dawn when the finest crescent moon rose behind the mud-walled mosque. Its reflection floated briefly in the stillness of a water hole before being extinguished by the first rays, tinted red by the cliffs and the sand of the plain, of the sun. Simultaneously, the sound of pounding began, soon followed by the call of the Imam from the mosque.

The old men had already gathered under the shade of a mighty *fromagier* tree when, after an early breakfast, we went for a walk in the village. The path took us past the spot for making traditional medicines, a fissure in the rock sheltering a collection of small pots, broken and whole. Further on, large round pottery vessels representing, but not containing, deceased relatives had been set up by one family or another in shallow caves. The corpses themselves are buried in ancient Tellem houses, and Mamadou pointed high above us to where the rock face was literally plastered with their dwellings, like the work of a colony of enormous house martins. The Tellem, he said, were the first people to settle on the cliff, perhaps as long as a thousand years ago. In those days, it had faced a well-watered, wooded land and provided the people with a refuge from the wild beasts of the forest. The Tellem were pygmies, a gentle tribe that disappeared into the forest having been chased away by the more warlike Dogon, who were fleeing the advance of Islam.

It was they who had built the old houses we now were climbing over, one side carved into the rock, the other built out from it. This was sometimes a fairly nerve-wracking business as Mamadou would climb over crumbling walls, shin along wobbly beams and jump up and down on the old floors to demonstrate their solidity, all perilously close to a significant drop down the side of the cliff. Some of the buildings, though, were almost intact: round women's granaries that would once have sported a thatched conical roof, and square male storehouses with three windows. The remains of covered streets ran between walls that, although long abandoned, were protected from the weather by a natural overhang and in surprisingly good shape. Also, said our guide, the mud that came from the plain long ago when it was still forested was better and longer lasting than what they can dig today.

As we made our way back down to the contemporary village, evidence of female industry was everywhere. A flagstone slab, polished by generations of women's feet, marked the presence of a well. The circular hole in its center had been creased and indented by the lines of untold bucket-loads of water pulled taut over its lip until it looked indecently like a sphincter muscle. Just before we reached the houses, Emily noticed that the women were pounding millet on a flat rock, instead of in the wooden mortars she was accustomed to among the Bambara in Diala. According to Dogon custom, millet should not be pounded in the village because the husks are prickly and are likely to hurt the children's bare feet. In the shade of a wall where the houses of the village started, two young girls sewed their wedding garments. At another concession, a family was preparing vats of indigo, a truly royal blue, for dyeing. Again unlike Diala, where a whiff of smoke hung permanently in the air, there were few if any fires in the village. With the desert advancing and deforestation an even more serious problem than in the south, fires were extinguished as soon as the cooking was done.

As we hiked along the base of the cliff, we visited several villages over the course of the next couple of days. We would set off in the relative cool of the morning, but by midday it was very hot, and no matter what they say about "mad dogs and Englishmen," I was glad to spend the early afternoon hours relaxing in the shade of a concession. Each village had its own character, and not surprisingly we liked some better than others.

What was surprising, however, was my increasing susceptibility to the presence of omens, good and bad, as we approached them. It was nothing so obvious as a couple of children running away from us as we appeared. Rather it might be the impassivity of a lizard basking on top of a rock that seemed loaded with foreboding. Whether a roller remained on its perch and turned its head away or instead flew ahead of us to lead us in suddenly became of consequence. Again, I found some comfort in the words of Hampate Ba on the subject of symbols:[31] symbolism in African culture "is not abstract or mental, but concrete in the sense that an earthly symbol is like an echo or a concrete expression of an aspect of the primordial force. Things below are reflections of higher principles — living reflections which contain a presence."

One morning, just as it was getting very hot, we came to a natural amphitheater in the rock. Water should have been tumbling into it in a *grande cascade*, but the lack of rain had reduced its flow considerably. Nonetheless, the pool at the base of the cliff was still good-sized before it gradually seeped below the sands of the plain. When we got there, a herd of cattle had just arrived to drink, but at the foot of the falls where it was deeper and rockier, the coolness of the water was like a siren song. With a quick assurance from Mamadou that there was no guinea worm or schistosomiasis in the water, Emily and I clambered around over the rocks and slid in. As I swam, I looked across the pool to where, in the shadow of the cliff, a grove of trees stood out lush against the hot red sand and rock. Birds in a kaleidoscope of colors — green parrots, glossy starlings, bright blue rollers and appropriately enough a paradise fly-catcher — flashed about the branches, filling the air with their calls. The herd of cows had moved on, and to complete this tableau of the peaceable kingdom, an old Peul man with one astonishingly milk-white cow came down to the water's edge to wash.

My cap, which I had soaked in the *grande cascade*, was dry within minutes of setting off again to the next village, and as we walked, the bright orange sand seemed to further amplify the infernal heat. So we were content enough to laze away the afternoon under the *dougoutigi's gwa* while a procession of little boys and old women came by to hawk their wares. I had not seen a calabash made into a box before, but the women had baskets of them, dyed purple with embroidered designs on the lid. Most interesting was a little boy who produced a bracelet made out of twisted copper, which, he assured me, came from a Tellem tomb.

31 Quoted in McLuhan, *The Way of the Earth*.

We explored the village in the relative cool of the evening. A plat-form supporting what looked like four large breasts, Mamadou explained, was an altar for sacrificing goats. They lay the beast's head between the mounds, and the blood runs off it into special large canneries. Nearby, we came upon a scooped-out rock where humans were sacrificed. Strangers to the village would be caught if they came too close; two men cut the victim's throat while the village *Hogon,* or medicine man, held him in place. However, Mamadou assured us that the practice had been out-lawed at Independence in 1960.

Not long after we had gone to bed, Dogon-style on the roof again, a strong wind blew up and gusted all night. Dark clouds blew across the sky, and for a while I was afraid we were in for rain, which would have been very welcome to the village, but less so on our open rooftop. It was still very hot, and the effect was like being in a clothes dryer, made worse by the stench from the latrine, or *nyegin,* upwind. In the courtyard of the next concession just beneath us, a tethered horse nickered from time to time. It was not a restful night.

By morning, the sky was entirely overcast, and the cliff had disap-peared in the mist. But at least it was cooler. It turned out that it was the day the whole village went into the fields to collect the old millet stalks, which they would bring back to burn. From our roof the night before, we had seen a big blaze in the distance as another community did the same thing. As we left the village, a gaggle of children came running past us headed back the way we had come with shrieks of ter-ror. Ahead of us, a group of young men with spears were dancing around, generally whooping it up and trying to stab each other's toes. Some of them were beating talking drums under their elbows, and one was blowing on an antelope horn. The next moment, from out of the bush ran an apparition entirely covered with branches, dancing and twirling. There was more chasing as he joined the group, one of whom I now noticed was clad in a Superman T-shirt, which made an interest-ing juxtaposition with Birnam Wood. Then another man covered in leaves came running out from behind a rock, and the whole ensemble danced off back to the village. It was a rain dance, participated in indis-criminately by all the religious groups from the village, Christian, Muslim and Animist, and the shriveled fields of millet all around were witness to the need.

The wind continued to blow, fortunately at our backs, as we continued on our way, but the blowing sand seemed to suck all the color from the landscape. And then, out of this desolate scene a charming village appeared. Above it, a column of rock loomed like the Sword of Damocles. Rising alone out of the desert, it was the height of a ten-story building, and a pronounced overhang gave the impression it might topple over at any minute. Every year, a brave man scales it and conducts a sacrifice on the top to keep it steady. Should it fall, according to Dogon myth, it would signal the end of the world. The power of sacrifice was also evident in the village itself, which was laid out in five *quartiers*, only one of them situated at the very base of the cliff. The predominantly Muslim residents of the others avoided this particular *quartier* for fear that it would be struck by a rockfall, but its inhabitants were comfortable making sacrifices to ensure that any falling rocks would pass by on either side of their houses.

Our entrance was greeted by a miniature air force of children with propellers on sticks that whirled around as they ran toward us, and we knew that this would be our favorite village. As soon as we had disposed of our packs, Mamadou prepared tea. In Mali making tea — in little shot-sized glasses — is a domestic ritual that usually seems to fall to the junior male member of any group. Into a miniature kettle — usually of blue enamel, at least early on in its career — he puts a very generous scoop of green tea followed by three shot glasses of water. Setting the kettle directly on the coals of a little brazier, he brings it to a boil. Now comes the artful part: he pours and repours the brew, at first from kettle to glass. As it gets stronger — and after adding an even larger scoop of sugar and bringing it to the boil again — the adept makes the amber stream flow from glass to glass through an ever increasing distance to build up a "head." As always in Mali, the whole preparation is carried out with tremendous panache, right down to the rinsing of the tray before the first glass is proffered. Three *parties* are brewed one after the other from the same tealeaves, and everyone has their favorite. Mamadou described the character of each: the first and strongest, bitter like death; the second, gentle like love; and the third, sweet like life.

Our host was preoccupied, as was the entire village, with the drought. When I expressed the hope for rain, an old man with whom I had been bargaining for a wooden carving of a monkey took my hand and raised it three times to the sky as he muttered a heartfelt *"Abarika"* (an emphatic "thank you"; I had previously only encountered *Abarika* as thanks for the food at the end of a meal, at which time the response is "May it cool in your stomach") with each upbeat. A parade of children led by an old lady beating a drum ran through the village and out onto the path where they jumped up and down, chanting prayers. A group of women followed up the children's procession with a rain dance of their own. When I climbed onto the roof to watch, an old harridan disengaged herself from the crowd and approached, waving her spear in my direction. Apparently she thought I was taking photographs of the ceremony, and although my camera was nowhere around, she continued to glare at me suspiciously even after she had rejoined her friends. Meanwhile, with nothing to do in the fields, the young men hung about the concession in their designer dark glasses.

Wherever we went in the village, a little boy of about eleven went with us. Instead of asking for *bonbons* or *bics*, he said nothing but trotted ten or so paces either in front or behind, playing a tune on a Dogon flute. It was an enchanting accompaniment to our walk up to the old houses on the cliff. High up, at the end of a path, stood a pink and white painted building. It had been the house of the last *Hogon* of the village. A large sculpted head guarded the front of the courtyard where the animals were sacrificed, this time on an enormous breast, also pink. On either side of the door of the house itself was a carved black snake, the *Hogon's* symbol; above the lintel, sheep's jaws and monkey skulls had been plastered into the wall. Inside, the house was decorated with paintings of masks. In one corner, a baobab cord hung out of a hole in the wall of an old Tellem house marking where the old man was buried. He had died some years before, but no one had yet succeeded him because no one alive in the village had yet met the requirement: to have seen two festivals of *Sigui*, a celebration honoring the ancestors. Since this happens only every sixty years and the last one was in 1968, the village would have to wait another thirty years or so for a new *Hogon*.

Still climbing, we eventually came out to where the overhanging rock funneled into a low cave extending back into the cliff. Sitting in the entrance, as if in a reverie, was an old man. He had on a robe of indigo, and the only time he moved was to periodically strike a hand gong with the ring of his finger. Although he was not one himself, the old man said he liked to stay close to the dead *Hogon* and visited this cave every day. About the entrance were a variety of totems: a pottery dog, wooden statues of Dogon men and women, a mask; there were also a number of small pots and urns. It was a strange and wonderful sight to see the old man communing with whatever spirit it was he was finding there. At Emily's suggestion, I presented him with one of the kola nuts I had brought for just such an occasion, and he sent the little boy scurrying into the recesses of the cave to store the nut in a calabash of water collected from the rock.

We spent the night fearlessly in the *quartier* below the cliff. We had come to the end of our sojourn in Dogon country, and, we thought, if our number came up, what a way to go! As always, the evening produced its share of fascinating tidbits; one was a French shotgun, "much adapted" and proudly displayed by our village host, that his father had brought back after serving in the French army during World War II. We had in fact met hoary Malian veterans on a number of occasions, all fiercely proud of their contribution.

The next day, it was time to return to civilization. Our way first led us through drying riverbeds. A small herd of cattle was gathered around the last remaining water, while its owners—a group of Peul men, the traditional herders—rested in the shade of the mango trees. Until we started our climb back up the cliff, I had thought of it as having a fairly monolithic face, but here the rock wall was broken and indented, which made our hike considerably gentler. We reached the top, and from our perch on the red rock rim towering over the plain, the face of the escarpment stretched away into the distance. On the other side, over the slightest rise, the plateau crumbled away to reveal before us a little oasis in the rock. In the middle was a pond with waterlilies. Around its edges, rice was growing, and every nook and cranny in the surrounding rocks were planted with millet. The harmony of contrasts—the water in the dry rock, the touching husbandry in the wilderness, the green against the red—offered a glimpse of perfection as arises only in dreams.

As we climbed up the opposite side of the valley, I paused at the top of a cleft and looked back at the harsh features of the plateau, split wherever it could support so much as a trickle of water by the cool green stripes of trees laden with wild grapes. I was hot and out of breath. A sudden shaft of cool air funneled up the chimney from below was like a benediction on all I had just found and where I had just been. I felt as if I had been to the same spiritual place where Amadou Hampate Ba began his epic tale, *Kaidara*.

> *It was in the mysterious, distant country of Kaidara*
> *which no one can locate exactly*
> *nor tell us when or where the story took place.*
> *It was only a few years after the mountains had hardened,*
> *when the world forces were just finishing carving out the river beds.*[32]

To get from the rim of the Falaise to Bandiagara and a bush taxi, Mamadou had laid on two motorbikes, one driven by himself and the other by a friend who had six fingers on one hand. Emily and I each got on the back of one, and we shot off, out past the pools with their brilliant green terraces and the sacrificial stones bleached by millet milk. A kettle of Egyptian vultures soared above us as we headed for the rocky bush, where one of the motorbikes shortly got a puncture. While the tire was taken to a nearby village to be mended, I sat under a tree and watched the baking countryside. A field away, cattle wandered along the exposed bedrock of a dry riverbed. I had frequently been impressed in Africa with how quickly figures materialized out of the emptiest landscape, and not long after I sat down, the bush yielded up its denizens in the form of a very serious little boy of perhaps nine or ten and an even younger girl. The little boy was incredibly polite and stood there looking thoughtful. At length, he spoke. These were his millet fields, he said solemnly. His face was delicately featured and reminded me of the shepherd boys of

32 Amadou Hampate Ba, *Kaidara*.

North Africa painted by Sargent. Meanwhile his little sister hung from a branch of the tree, slowly turning her beautiful face from side to side so that her enormous eyes swept around like the beam of a lighthouse. Responsibility and Beauty were soon joined by Indifference, another little boy, who lounged against a rock, turning his back on us. After a while, Responsibility sent him off to bring their hoes and calabashes from a nearby field, and back they went to work, breaking the soil and mounding it ready to receive the millet. It was market day in Bandiagara and as people passed on their way, they chided me. "Why don't you do some work and help them?" However, our motorcycle escort soon reappeared, Mamadou clutching in his hand a bottle of Castel, the local beer, still cold for me. It was a welcome sight. The froth ran over my beard as I gulped it down and said goodbye to the Dogon.

We headed back to Mopti, the "Venice of West Africa," from where I was to go on, this time alone, to the ancient city of Djenne, famous for its great mosque, by baché again. It was after dark when we arrived, and I got my first sight of the city from the roof where I awoke the next morning at eye level with a black kite patrolling the street for offal. Right below me, the market, a plaster compound the size of a city block, was beginning to come to life. Beyond the rooftops, the great Niger flowed, and it was there that I headed. I knew I had plenty of time before my baché would leave; regardless of what the schedule says, departure time is a function of the number of people aboard. Mungo Park experienced the same thing waiting for a caravan to start, complaining that "though the day of our departure was frequently fixed, it was always found expedient to change it. Some of the people had not prepared their dry provisions; others had gone to visit their relations, or collect some trifling debts; and, last of all, it was necessary to consult whether the day would be a lucky one." While waiting for a quorum to arrive I explored the city.

I set off down an alley, attracted by the bright stripes and squares of Dogon wedding blankets draped on its walls and spreading out over a stall. Made of long narrow strips sewn together (a Dogon loom extends across most of a courtyard), some were in traditional white and black while others incorporated the red, yellow and green of the flag of modern Mali.

Rouge vif	Living red
Jaune d'or	Golden yellow
Pré vert	Field of green
Promesses d'or	Promises of gold
Récoltes de sable	The harvest of sand
Poudre d'or	Gold dust
De nos yeux	Of our eyes
Sangles de verdures	Belts of green
Sans blé de Dire	Without wheat of Dire
Sans granges du Seno	Without the granaries of Seno
Sans riz de montagne	Without rice from the mountain
Le soleil la lune	The sun the moon
Nous rougeoyant vifs	Turning us a living red
À longueur du Niger.	The length of the Niger.[33]

Along the broad hard of the riverbank, pirogue after pirogue was pulled up. Each one had its own fanciful pattern painted on the prow: elaborately constructed geometric designs made up of squares or roundels in yellow, red or green with the occasional highlight in black. Big rusty ferryboats lolled on the river bottom, waiting for the rainy season to refloat them and for there to be enough water once again to make the trip to Timbuktoo. As it was, the river was still receding, leaving behind it a moraine of plastic trash along the waterline. On the opposite shore, I could make out the domed huts, either thatched or covered with skins, of a Bozo village, and a regular traffic of pirogues shuttled from one side of the river to the other loaded with fish. In the main square, a Tuareg in a

33 Malian poet Léon Niangaly's poem "Motifs de couleurs."

black turban was giving children a ride on his camel, four or five at a time.

I had been accosted several times by someone whose brother or father or uncle had a shop full of antiques that might interest me, so now I followed a young man into his *magasin* to look at his collection of Dogon carvings, knives, guns and other artifacts. He indicated a Bambara pistol that looked like nothing more than the crudest wooden model of a six-shooter with a metal barrel drilled into the stock. I wondered if it was the local version of an ethnic joke, but back in Diala, when I described it to one of our friends, he insisted it could fire. The pièce de résistance, which he produced from his pocket with great ceremony, was carefully wrapped in a grimy bit of cloth. It contained a little bronze figurine of a warrior on a horse. He said it was Sundiata Keita, the Malian equivalent of King Arthur, a thirteenth-century hero who defeated the tyrant Sumanguru at the battle of Kirina and united Mali into a kingdom that flourished for the next century, astounding contemporary travelers with its richness.

There was plenty to look at in the baché station, as well. An old man was making the rounds with a balophone, playing a rather monotonous three- or four-note phrase over and over again. But as he approached, his strokes got faster and faster and more intricate and syncopated until I was mesmerized as his gnarled hands made the hammers fly over the instrument before me. Little boys threaded their way through the crowd, begging for alms. Some were leading victims of river blindness by the hand; others were *garibous*, boys under the care of the Imam for whom begging was part of their religious training. In either case, begging appeared not so much a failure of the social services as a part of the culture. Mali is a Muslim country, and alms for the beggars invite a blessing on those who give them.

Finally, the baché was full; it was an incredibly decrepit vehicle and by any reasonable standards wildly overloaded. As a precaution, I gave some alms to an old blind man who gave me his benediction for the journey. There was an angry chatter from the starter and an indescribable grinding of gears, and we were off. Throughout the whole 100-plus miles to Djenne, I doubt we ever went faster than 20 mph (I couldn't tell because the speedometer had long since gone).

✌❦✌

Our first stop was at the police checkpoint just outside Mopti. I was trying to catch the attention of a boy selling roasted peanuts when I became
aware that a noticeably unfriendly gendarme in crisp green uniform was
demanding to see my passport. His inspection revealed that I had not
registered with the police in Mopti, and I was peremptorily ordered from
the baché and led away to the post. "Search the vehicle," he ordered his
subordinate over his shoulder. I wondered about whom I should be more
apprehensive, the policeman or my fellow passengers, who were clearly
in for a monumental delay. In the office, his superior was both more
genial and less smartly dressed. Nevertheless, I had committed a serious
offense and would have to return to Mopti at once, report to the chief of
police and have my visa stamped. Having already waited nearly three
hours for the baché, this seemed like the end of the world, certainly the
end of my trip to Djenne. Trying to keep my cool, I explained that I had
come all this way to see the great mosque, the largest mud structure in
the world, and if I had to return to Mopti now, I would miss it. This was
met by shrugs, but somehow I felt the mood was changing, and eventually I was allowed to proceed, much to the disgust of the arresting officer.
To someone who has witnessed officials in British and American airports
browbeating uncomprehending visitors from developing countries, it was
interesting (to say the least) to experience the shoe on the other foot.

To my relief nobody in the baché seemed perturbed in the least at the
delay. *Insh'Allah* — it is all as Allah wills it and pointless to complain. I
wondered how living in the moment, the Buddhist's mindfulness, was
related to the passive reliance on the will of Allah that made my fellow
passengers so patient. As we trundled through the countryside, scrubby
and desolate, I mused on the difference between this attitude and our
own. In committing myself to the unpredictability of transportation in
Mali, I had made a conscious decision to shake off the habit of considering only points A and B and never the time and space and experiences
possible in traveling between them. Djenne might be my destination,
but getting there by baché was sure to be no less interesting.

I was not disappointed. The ride lasted seven and a half hours and was, by American standards, quite uncomfortable. Among other things, we had a flat tire, and I slammed the door on my thumb, turning it an impressive shade of blue-black. But at one point we passed a Tuareg on a camel loping through the Sahel. At another stop, a patrol of Malian soldiers, their faces almost completely swathed in khaki turbans against the dust, caused a momentary frisson as they swept through the village in a pickup truck in the bed of which a large machine gun had been mounted.

Nearing the market town of Sofara, a steady stream of brightly painted donkey carts brightened the highway. Our entry got briefly but inextricably tangled up with a herd of sheep and various passersby as they pursued and tackled the animals fleeing before us. The market itself was a riot of exotic sights, sounds and smells, little different from the ones Mungo Park passed through in 1805. As we left, two huge tractor-trailers containing whole villages and their goods were already on their way to the next market, the people clinging to the sides, a tangled mass of humanity in the dust.

Wherever we stopped, there was always somebody playing a makeshift instrument or singing. A blind boy came up to the window playing a beautiful but repetitive melody on an instrument consisting of a wire string stretched between a coffee can and a short length of cane. Another little boy was beating the planks of a donkey cart with two sticks, using it as a balophone. Perhaps the most unforgettable was a little *garibou*, one of the beggar boys under the care of the Imam, with long eyelashes, who sang another repetitive but haunting song in his rough unbroken voice. A verse from Coleridge's *Kubla Khan* sprang into my head:

> *A damsel with a dulcimer*
> *In a vision once I saw:*
> *It was an Abyssinian maid,*
> *And on her dulcimer she played,*
> *Singing of Mount Abora.*

Now I knew the tune that she had sung, and like Coleridge still wish I could "revive within me Her symphony and song."

The sun was turning into a fiery copper disc as it settled into the bank of dust that was obliterating the horizon when an elderly man leading his cart stopped to chat beside the baché. The sides of the cart were decorated with the hearts, clubs, spades and diamonds of a deck of cards. On the seat, his wife sat demurely, covered in a beautiful indigo *panya*, a gold ring in her nose. It was a mesmerizing picture, and it was at that moment that I caught my thumb in the car door. This made our driver very unhappy; despite my assurances that it was entirely my fault, he still felt responsible.

As always, we stopped for evening prayer at dusk. The glow of the moon struggled with the dust as all around me turbaned men in white and black robes knelt toward the east, which in Bambara is *Koran*. Well after dark we finally drove into the main square in Djenne. Before me was the largest mud castle in the world, the great mosque, with another full moon rising behind it. It was an unforgettable sight, and the discomforts of the day melted away as I bought supper of beans and fish from a street vendor and devoured them on the spot.

Djenne, located in the Inner Niger Delta, was founded in the ninth century, probably after an epidemic had swept through an earlier city, Djenne-Djeno, less than a mile away. It was believed that if water from the river were to flood a house, it would bring the evil spirit into it, and so in order to protect their new city from the river, the chief called for a special sacrifice: a young woman who must be beautiful, an only child and a virgin. No one in the city could be found who possessed all these characteristics, until an elder from a Bozo village some distance away heard about the need, and knew that his daughter Tapama was destined to be the one. The wall where she was interred alive can still be seen. Djenne soon became a commercial hub in the trade routes of the western Sudan.

In the twelfth century, the chief converted to Islam, and his palace became the great mosque of Djenne. It was desecrated 400 years later when the mosque was occupied by the carousing troops of Pasha Judar, a Spanish mercenary who conquered the city with a Moroccan army in 1591. The Peul king, Sekou Amadou, finally drove the Moroccans out in 1810, but the mosque had been defiled. Nonetheless, it would have been sacrilege to destroy the great building himself, so the King had all the rain gutters blocked up, and demolition was left to nature. It took twenty years, but the old mosque finally collapsed in 1830. Not until 1905 did a great mosque grace the marketplace again, and its building represented a rare harmony of African and colonial interests. The French had taken Djenne in 1893, and the local administrator at the time was an enlight-ened man who respected local customs and particularly the marabouts, the Muslim holy men. When he sought to become governor of the whole of French Sudan, he asked these men to bless his efforts. This they did in exchange for his promise that he would rebuild the great mosque. The very next day, the appointment came through, and the mosque was built in one year. Every year since then, the mud walls of the building have been replastered voluntarily by the citizens of Djenne.

Standing in its huge open square, the mosque may be the most impres-sive building in Djenne, but its streets of mud houses have a beauty all their own. The oldest walls—some of them from as long ago as the thir-teenth and fourteenth centuries—were built using balls of mud mixed with shea butter, the same that we had seen being made in Diala. A num-ber of houses had painted wooden windows, their shutters adorned with silver stars reflecting the Moroccan influence. In the courtyard of one such building, we peered down into a sacred well, built for a half-Moroccan, half-Malian princess who wanted to drink from the water of the river in the privacy of her home. When the well was dug, some hundred feet deep, it was said she could look into its reflection and see what was going on in the Kingdom of Morocco as well as Timbuktoo. This is unfortunately no longer the case, but the waters still serve for medicinal purposes.

In the late afternoon when the sun was not so fierce, we walked out to Djenne-Djeno, the ancient city, crunching over shards from a city that thrived from 250 B.C. to the ninth century and only finally gave up the ghost in the 1300s. In some places, the foundations of houses were clearly visible, the *boules* of mud still resisting the test of time. Great urns, many of them intact, seemed to sprout from the earth, being con-tinually uncovered by the wind and the river that floods the site in the rainy season. At any moment I expected to spot the head of Ozymandias.

As we walked, Hamadou, my guide in Djenne, said, "I want to travel, so that I can return." It seemed reasonable that a guide should be infected with the same wanderlust as the clients he serves, and tourism was the only way he could earn enough money to gratify it. We talked about the pros and cons of tourism as it advances on Mali. Tourists bring jobs, new ideas, a higher standard of living. At the same time, Hamadou was acutely aware how tourism breaks down the very traditions that make the people so agreeable. Children asking for gifts — *bonbon? bic?* — were a prime example. Emily was shocked at the forwardness of kids in the tourist areas of the north; in her unspoiled, unknown Bambara village, it would be disrespectful for a child to address an elder or a stranger before being spoken to, and he would very likely get slapped for his pains. I remembered old Masaba wielding a stick at a cluster of kids who were getting too loud, saying, "These kids have no shame."

Hamadou told me that Malian people assume that tourists arrive with a preconceived agenda to exploit them. Mungo Park made several references to similar conversations: "The notion of traveling for curiosity was quite new to him. He thought it impossible, he said, that any man in his senses would undertake so dangerous a journey, merely to look at the country and its inhabitants. . . . it was evident that his suspicion had arisen from a belief that every white man must of necessity be a trader." And in connection with the ivory trade, "They cannot, they say, easily persuade themselves, that ships would be built, and voyages undertaken, to procure an article which had no other value than that of furnishing handles to knives, etc., when pieces of wood would answer the purpose equally well."

Perhaps such suspicion is partly the legacy of colonialism, but it is also curiously logical in a very poor country. Why would *tubabs* spend what to most Malians is an unimaginable amount of money to come and look at their mud huts? Some ulterior motive could be the only possible explanation to such a perplexing question. It set up a curiously ambiguous relationship between Hamadou and me; if I asked his help in bargaining in the market, for instance, whose side was he supposed to be on? Or alternately, on which side was his bread buttered? In the less touristy south, Emily's Malian friends would tune out when we went to the market together — and only later tell us that we had paid far too much.

At what point does development aid become tinkering with what we do not understand? Here was a way of life as unspoiled as any I had ever seen, and it worked in so many ways. Every little thing we did to change it—even saving a baby's life—ran the risk of putting it a little out of balance. My time in Mali made me all the more convinced that we need humility in the panaceas we offer. We must be very sure that our ways and intentions are both the best and for the best. On the other hand, everyone I spoke to loved America, and many wanted to go there. On the side streets of Bamako, families and friends clustered around a television to watch *Dynasty*. The price in the U.S. of various items—my camera, the tailor's sewing machine—was a constant source of interest, but I could never decide whether my answer should go high or low; the implications of either seemed unfathomable.

An immense gulf separates tourists from the people of Djenne—or Mali, or any developing country. The visitors have the means and the leisure to cross oceans and continents to get there. Perhaps even more importantly, we take it for granted as if it were a right. At a tourist site in a developed country, such as in my home state of Maine, this division is less marked, but I wonder if we nurse the same underlying suspicion of our tourists. And do we, despite it all, treat tourists with the same kind of appreciation as honored guests that they do in Mali? For all the hang-ups in intercultural relations, the phrase I heard most often, in villages, in the markets, even as I was being frisked by the security official at the airport, was *Adiarra an ye kosebe k'i nana anfe Malila*—It pleases us greatly that you have come to visit us in Mali.

The solo trip back to Mopti was not nearly so exciting as the one outward bound, except when at my favorite guard post, one of the African passengers got into a fight with one of the gendarmes and would have been carted off but for the physical intervention of several other travelers. Taking no chances this time, I checked in with the chief of police and then headed for the bus to Bamako. I got some oranges and bananas from a *tigi*, and sat down to await events. An army man, who had been on the bus on the trip up, was there again with his rifle, swaggering self-importantly. We had dubbed him Ranger Rick. Now he was showing off his bayonet. He was sporting a white bush hat a little too large, which somewhat undermined his bravado. Meanwhile, three men who had loaded our luggage onto the roof of the bus stared down at the crowd from their perch like the gargoyles of Notre Dame. At last, the driver began to call the names of the passengers. When he got to mine, "Bagayogo, Draman," a tall African dressed in an immaculate grand boubou in front of me turned around and said with a smile, *"Eh bien, vous étiez les esclaves de ma famille."* ("Well, well, you were my family's slaves." He meant the Bagayogos.)

Soon we were on our way. I needn't have worried about my visa; under the benign eye of Ranger Rick, we sailed through the checkpoint. An hour later we stopped for evening prayers. The bus emptied, leaving me alone with two women and a baby. As usual, *tigis* selling food and drinks surrounded the vehicle. They were very persistent, never taking no for an answer, with good reason it turned out: time after time I watched my fellow passengers display not the slightest interest in their wares, only to buy something just as the bus started up again.

Ten hours later, back in Bamako, I was still trying to make sense of it all. Considering our orderly (and blessedly comfortable) lives, it is hardly surprising that experiences so different should shake one up so profoundly. At the same time, I wondered if there wasn't more to it than just the shock of the new. I thought of the evenings around the communal bowl of millet and the atavistic tug I felt time and again as I watched or engaged in the basic routines of the day in Diala. For all the differences from my habitual lifestyle, there remained in them something subliminally recognizable as the same. The most unexpected moments would resonate with a mind-bending sense of déjà-vu. The young herder in the sunset and the girls with their wedding garments in the Dogon village brought the tune of Edith Piaf's western song, "Eden Blues," to mind: *"En descendant la fleuve argent qui roule jusqu'au Nevada . . . Les filles s'appellent Soledad, les garçons gardent les troupeau-eau-eau-eau-eaux."* The Little Sparrow's wail at the end of the verse goes straight for the heartstrings. Two brothers—one wiry and angular, the pillar of a rustic community, whose fortune is in his herd of cattle; the other plump and jovial, the successful merchant in Bamako among the sacks of millet in his warehouse—might have been a country squire and a merchant out of Henry Fielding's eighteenth-century

England. More distant, but just as arresting, was Amadou Hampate Ba's account of his mother, dressed as a man like an African Fidelio, infiltrating a French prison (in Bougouni, the next market town beyond Keleya) where her husband was being held in *durance vile*.

A day or so later, on my way back to the United States, I found a clue in just as unexpected a place. The plane stopped in Brussels for a couple of hours, and I scooted into town to go to the museum. There, in a sixteenth-century Dutchman's vision of a Middle Eastern town,[34] the activities happening all over the canvas were the same ones I had seen in Emily's village only days before; it could have been Diala today. In my mind, distance on the map had been replaced by distance in time, but Africa no longer seemed so far away, and its very exoticness rang a strangely familiar bell. I remembered my daughter asking me if she would ever again find such pure happiness as in her village. It was a challenge to the foundations of all we are taught: happiness is moving forward. Suddenly, her question made all the sense in the world. Is there really no way to grow in a village like Diala? As I listened to the pounding mortars and watched the repetitive rhythms of life, I had been forced to admit that growth would have to be measured differently here. And when a group of boys exploded from a neighboring concession, each one with a bicycle tire as a hoop, it had been hard not to envy such unalloyed fun. Looking for a word to describe what affected me so much, I settled on "real."

The visceral excitement aroused by my visits to Mali has always haunted my dreams long after my return. The first morning—back in my own bed and luxuriating in its clean sheets and the comfort of home once more, neither asleep nor awake but hovering between past and present—I clutched at the host of sensations as if they had been a dream: the uneven soil underfoot, the taste of bush bread in sweet coffee, my nose continually stuffed up from the dust and above all the repetitive patterns that are the essence of Mali. I struggled to block out the familiar sounds of home for one minute more in order to let the memories and the rhythms stream in, undiluted, one last time. The endless pounding of

34 Breughel's *The Census in Bethlehem*.

the women grinding millet, the benedictions at parting, the greetings and their responses called out wherever you go. . . .

"You and the morning."

"Did you pass the night in peace?"

"Peace only."

"Greet the people of your village for me."

"They will hear it."

Lay of a Lizard in Love

L'écho de ce pays est sur,
J'observe, je suis bon prophète;
Je vois tout de mon petit mur,
Même tituber la chouette.[35]
—René Char, "Complainte du lézard amoureux"

WINE GOES BACK to Provence, promised Ford Madox Ford, "the will be astonishingly visible." Indeed it was. Most spectacular were the mountains to the north, stretching beyond the jagged humps of the Dentelles de Montmirail to the perpetual snow of the Alps and Mont Blanc. But for 360 degrees, overwhelming natural drama unfolded below me. Westward beyond the turbid Rhône, the Camargue disappeared into the unbroken distance. Tectonic forces took over once again to the south in the wild Vaucluse and the Luberon: olive-green waves with crests of white limestone that rolled towards the Mediterranean and collision with ever expanding Marseilles and the smog-enshrouded refineries of Fos-sur-mer. Sweeping eastward, the view finally melted into the horizon along the rocky coastline of the Riviera above which the Italian Alps emerged pale as ghosts.

Just days after arriving for a three-month sabbatical in Provence, I was standing at the top of Mont Ventoux,[36] where I had made a determined pilgrimage in order to mark the anniversary of Francesco Petrarch's ascent of the Windy Mountain on April 26, 1336. As far as we know, the

---

35 The echoes of this countryside have a safe sound. / I am keeping watch and I am a good prophet; / I can see everything from my little wall, / even the owl as she staggers forth.

36 *Mont Ventoux* comes from the Latin, *Mons Ventosus*, or Windy Mountain.

fourteenth-century poet was the first person to climb it, at least for fun. He tells us he met a shepherd on the way up who, as a foolish youth many years before, had gone to the summit in the line of duty and thought the Italian mad to try it. When he got to the peak himself, Petrarch could see all the way to the Pyrenees in one direction and into the boot of Italy in the other, this latter evoking a literary sigh of homesickness. To view the features of a whole country from a height of 6,250 feet must have been astonishing for a fourteenth-century mortal, almost as inspiring a perspective for the times as was, in our own, the first view of the Earth from space.

How much Mont Ventoux has changed over 650 years or so is hard to tell. From a distance, its naked, scree-filled slopes are the mountain's most striking feature, and they give it a desolate aspect. During the heat of summer, they have a parched look of almost intolerable ferocity, while in winter, the snow suggests the Olympian indifference of an iceberg. However, in the description of his ascent, Petrarch mentions great beech forests and seductive dells, and one can imagine them in the folds of the foothills whose contours stand out in the late afternoon rays of the sun. On his climb, they more than once lured the poet from the proper path, prompting many a parable about the wretched human condition and especially his own unworthiness on account of his hopeless passion for the otherwise married Laura. So overcome was he by these illuminations, he tells us, that he descended the mountain in complete silence and retired to his room in the inn to write his 6,000-word account of the expedition that very night. It should be required reading for every hiker. In it he reflected on such important topics as how to choose a hiking companion—neither too chatty nor too taciturn, neither too simple nor too sagacious; Petrarch lists another half dozen qualities in which he looks for the middle ground—the spiritual lessons offered by the climb, and the feeling inspired by doing it "because it's there."

Rather than follow Petrarch's path of pious introspection, I had chosen Mont Ventoux to start my own exploration of the inextricable skeins of nature, history and landscape that were coming to life in the Provençal spring. The Space Age structures that inelegantly straddled the mountain's peak in front of me seemed to point to a science fiction future that was far from reassuring. One, which looked rather like Darth Vader's helmet, declared itself to be a military installation and off-limits to civilians. But the perimeter fence was in a sad state of repair and looked as if no one was watching it. Another geodesic dome–like construction turned out to be an enormous soccer ball on a pedestal celebrating the World Cup, which was, the year being 1998, capturing the hearts of 60 million French men and women.

As I gazed at the Provençal landscape spread out below me, the sense of continuum was altogether more heartening. On all sides, wherever a plot could be worked, the lands were being cultivated as they have been for centuries. With their villages and castles, their orchards, vineyards and fields of lavender and hay, the maze of lanes and byways, they are beyond question part of a human landscape. And yet the imprint of the human demands made upon them — for shelter and protection atop the hills, for sustenance and commerce on the slopes and in the plain — seems above all to advertise that sense of proportion that the Holy Roman Emperor Frederic II prized so highly. They suggest an amicable entente with the earth, one that so far has been tempered by the implicit knowledge that if she is to produce, nature must also be nurtured. Ford Madox Ford, whose 1935 book *Provence* was serving as my vade mecum, has this to say: "If I write of Provence a little as if it were an earthly Paradise . . . [my] purpose is none other than to induce my readers . . . either to settle in the land, . . . or at least to model their lives along the lines of the good Provençal and his Eden-garlic-garden." From my perch in the clouds, I could see the traditions of centuries of farmers continuing to maintain the happy effect of *"la nature en bonnes mains."*[37]

It was a yearning for the simplicity of the "Eden-garlic-garden" over the stultifying politics and vicious intrigue of the papal court that induced Petrarch to leave his career as a clerk in the Pope's treasury at Avignon.[38] He also needed to escape his impossible love for Laura, but

---

37 "Nature in good hands" is the sobriquet for the French Nature Park in the Pas de Calais, but it is equally applicable in the Midi.

38 Pope Clement V, finding conditions in Rome too chaotic and dangerous, had removed the Holy See to Avignon in 1309.

his decision to become the pioneer rusticator was as unprecedented a step as his ascent of Mont Ventoux a decade before. In 1345, the poet decamped to the Closed Valley—Vallis Clausa, the Vaucluse—where he found a haven on the banks of the River Sorgue in the town of Fontaine-de-Vaucluse. It was a day's ride away from Avignon and at the time the back of beyond.

As I hiked into the wild rocks nearby, through a pasture smelling of rosemary and wild lavender, I wondered how far afield Petrarch rambled. He tells us he followed the shepherds' paths up into the mountains, wandering alone by day or night, another most unusual pastime for a successful scholar and writer in the fourteenth century. "In the high mountains and harsh woods I find some peace"; he wrote in one of his poems, "and every habitable place is for my eyes a mortal enemy." His sonnets are filled with fantasies and daydreams of Laura gathered in the wilds.

> Clear, cool, sweet, running waters
> Where she, for me the only
> Woman, would rest her lovely body,
> Kind branch on which it pleased her
> (I sigh to think of it)
> to make a column for her lovely side. . . .
>
> Where the pine or mountain casts its shade
> I sometimes stop, and on the first stone seen
> With all my mind I etch her lovely face.[39]

The gorge ahead meandered through the plateau. Water had ground its undulating designs onto the rugged terrain all around. High up along the cliff's face, tiers of inaccessible balconies carpeted with broom and thyme seemed to wait for some mythological figure to grace them with her appearance. Did Petrarch imagine himself with Laura in one of these canyon bowers? Was it on one of the boulders strewn below that his

---

39 Petrarch, *Selections from the Canzoniere and Other Works.*

imagination etched Laura's lovely face six and a half centuries ago? Where water continues to scoop and polish the rocks into pools and natural basins, did he clamber over their slippery sides to refresh himself with a swim; and did he let himself be pulled by the current of cold blue water down a stream groined in the rock? Penetrating these open tunnels, the poet surely sensed in their curves and hollows the reassuring presence of the *Magna Parens* herself.

A short-toed eagle, called more picturesquely *Jean-le-Blanc* by the French, soared over the barren crags, putting an end to these speculations. The morning sun made the bird translucent as it scanned the ground for prey in the garrigue. *Jean-le-Blanc* is an eagle, but it hovered and rode the wind as if it were Gerard Manley Hopkins's kestrel.

> *I caught this morning morning's minion, king-*
> *dom of daylight's dauphin, dapple-dawn-drawn*
> *Falcon, in his riding*

Somewhere across the rugged fields the eagle disappeared in a dive; seconds later it flew up again with a snake—a *couleuvre*, its favorite food—clutched in its talons. As Hopkins exclaimed, "the achieve of, the mastery of the thing!"

After the intensity of the bright dry path, the canopy of a magnificent live oak engulfed the trail with cooling darkness. A spring trickled from a natural limestone bench, little more than a patch of dampness, but the mossy surface was very green after the sun-bleached rocks. This oasis was as intimate as the gorge was awe-inspiring, and encountering the shade of the poet and his immortal love seemed quite possible, perhaps in the song of the blackcap—a voice Petrarch thought more melodious than the nightingale's—that came from deep within a hawthorn bush.

In the Palais des Papes in Avignon, not far from the cold stone walls and meager fireplaces of the office where Petrarch kept his books, one enters a room covered in murals that give an impression of the natural world Petrarch encountered. Painted at the time of the Avignon popes, they depict various hunting scenes against a dense background of shrubs and trees and leaves. A man with a falcon on his wrist is about to go hunting, while elsewhere others lure game with birdcalls and set ferrets after a rabbit. Young boys are engaged in taking eggs from bird's nests, and in a pond peasants demonstrate four different methods of fishing. A strip of blue sky is all that relieves the predominant dark green tones, which give the illusion of having entered a forest.[40]

Much as Thoreau paid social visits to Concord from his retreat on Walden Pond, Petrarch used to make his way of an evening up a precipitous path to pay a call on his friend the Bishop of Cavaillon.[41] From a pinnacle just above the poet's dwelling, the ruins of the Bishop's castle still stand watch over the stream. On either side, the limestone rock formations rise ever more steeply. Along the cliff-tops, kestrels and jackdaws fly about the gaping mouths of caves where prehistoric humans once found shelter. Below, the Vallis Clusa narrows into its breathtaking cul-de-sac. Here, fed by subterranean springs, an open pool glows bluish green in the perennial shade of its sheltering cliffs: the Fontaine de Vaucluse. Just half a mile upstream from his hermitage, here Petrarch could find inspiration aplenty.

The Fontaine is a symbol of purity, as penetrating and impenetrable as the stare of the nude in Ingres's painting of La Source. A natural font— twenty or so yards in diameter—has been sculpted by the water of ages right into the base of the towering limestone precipice. From the brightly lit cliffs above to the refracted depths of the water in the cave below, just such a place must surely have been in Loren Eiseley's imagination when he wrote "The Lost Plateau."

That lost plateau is a land of running water
drawn from invisible torrents in the sky,
crags, sinkholes, jumbled strata
     and always the water pouring

---

40 Not far from this room, in the Pope's bedchamber, the walls are decorated with hundreds of birds perched among the leaves of an endless pattern of ivy against a blue sky; trompe l'oeil birdcages hang in the window casements. Pope Clement VI had a particular fondness for nature, and this provided a setting for the live nightingales he had brought into his rooms so that he could hear them sing.

41 Petrarch conducted his "Walden" experiment exactly 500 years before Thoreau!

from cavern to cavern, basin to basin cascading
deeper and ever deeper till no rope, no ladder,
not even the hardiest of the climbers there
could reach rock bottom for there is no bottom,
only the sheer plunge of the water falling
into abysms that upset the ear
till voices cry out where there are no voices,
till tumult shouts and has a voice to speak,
but in that chaos like the primal chaos
in a still pool where cold stalactites drip
their solvent crystals into shapes uncertain
swims slowly, slowly a prophetic fish. . . .[42]

Nothing can detract from the awe inspired by the aquamarine water bubbling up from the bowels of the earth. Not the graffiti left by nine-teenth-century visitors who hired tar brushes from street vendors to inscribe their name and the date of their visit on its walls. Not the groups of students from the local high school slipping and sliding on the steep bank as they flick pebbles into the pool speckling the surface of the water with dust.

Nor has anyone resolved the secrets of the Fontaine. Not even Captain Cousteau — "not even the hardiest of the climbers there / could reach rock bottom for there is no bottom" — who was able to dive only to a depth of 150 feet. In 1985 an underwater robot did finally find, at about 900 feet — almost the height of the Empire State Building — where the water-filled pipe leveled off and tunneled under the mountain. On the way down, the robot found a school of fish.

A fig tree that grows out of the rock above the pool gives an idea of the maximum height of the waters. At full flood, some 30,000 gallons of water pour out of the Fontaine de Vaucluse every second, spilling over the basin's lip in a torrent, a description of which deserves the French flair of a local guidebook: "*Surgissant d'une nuit profonde, la rivière se*

---

42 Loren Eiseley, "The Lost Plateau," *Notes of an Alchemist.*

déverse dans une chevauchée fracassante parmi d'énormes blocs de roches qui semblent avoir été mis exprès en travers du chemin d'eau."[43] Climbing down among these enormous rocks, careful not to slip on the patches of dark moss that spot their sides, one enters a world of falling water. It was spring, the river was high and from all around the sound of the water filled the air. Bleached and rounded, the rocks reminded me of a boulder-strewn page from one of Babar the Elephant's early adventures: the animals that Polomoche turned into stone. Where the stream tumbled into little pools, a dipper bobbed about before flying straight as an arrow down the stream. As the summer progressed, the level in the basin would fall, the river making its appearance at a point beneath the broken rocks lower and lower down the slope towards the town. That year, by July, it would drop by as much as a meter a day—twenty meters or more since April—and the old men would say that they had never seen it so low.

In the Romanesque church in Fontaine-de-Vaucluse, in a heavy gilt frame, a picture of a bishop subduing a dragon caught my eye. He is St. Véran, the monk who brought Christianity to Provence in the middle of the sixth century and the first Bishop of Cavaillon. The dragon is the Couloubre, a dreadful creature that lived in the wild mountains around. The story goes that St. Véran used to get away from his Episcopal duties and retire to Fontaine-de-Vaucluse to meditate in an anchorite's cave beside the river. Upon returning one day to his retreat after an afternoon's fishing in the Sorgue, he encountered the Couloubre. As it leapt at him, the saint made the sign of the Cross and dealt it a blow with a sharp stake. Then, picking up a chain he used to secure his boat against the current of the river, he threw it around the monster's neck and pulled for all he was worth. As the Couloubre writhed in agony, the flailing of its tail carved out the fantastic formations—"*qui se découpent, le soir, dans le soleil,*" according to a *Chronique du Val-de-Sorgue* — that adorn the Vallis Clausa. Finally, the saint dragged the monster out of the valley and over the mountains from whence it flew off to die in the snows

---

43 Surging out of a profound night, the river pours itself in a shattering ride amid enormous blocks of stone that seem to have been put across the flow on purpose.

where the Durance rises. St. Véran raised a chapel wherever on its flight a drop of the dragon's blood fell to earth.

Outside the church, as I looked up at the rugged cliffs with the sound of the rushing water still ringing in my ears, it seemed obvious that St. Véran's struggle against his dragon was a metaphor for the struggle of the new religion against the old. The forces of nature were at the heart of the pagan cults; where better to look for the source of the strength of their champion than this magic spot? As I went on to encounter the Couloubre and the saint touching down from place to place across the region, their dual presence would be a leitmotif that rippled through my quest. And I couldn't help but speculate on the dragon's connection with the — by comparison — little *couleuvre*.

I might have wanted to think about the symbolic harnessing of nature for spiritual salvation, but when I looked for St. Véran's cave, I found it had been turned into a storeroom for a merchant's wares, Provençal handicrafts as found in any resort town of the region. Ever since Petrarch's day, Fontaine-de-Vaucluse has been a mecca for tourists eager to behold one of nature's wonders, but one must concentrate hard to remove from one's mental retina what Ford Madox Ford complained of, as long ago as 1935, as a "Coney Island display of publicity."[44] The way to the Fontaine is a gauntlet of souvenir shops and fast-food places. Cheek by jowl with the ice cream shops, like a bird of ill omen, sits the Musée de Justice et Châtiment, more honestly known by the local children as the "torture museum." Here for ten francs they can goggle at the depths of depravity of which humans are capable. A mile above it all, another eagle hung on the wind before gliding off over the rim, as if the ghost of Petrarch were shaking its head at so much commotion below.[45]

44 In a provocative literary somersault, he puts part of the blame on Petrarch, arguing that a "great man cannot get off the responsibility for the quality and behaviour of his admirers, because his poetry or doctrines will have had a large share in moulding their characters and demonstrations."

45 Walden Pond has suffered a similar ironic fate, at least in terms of visitors; on a summer's day, its beach is filled body-to-body with sunbathers, with Thoreau's ideas about nature the last thing on their minds.

Navigating my way through the crowds—dodging a continuous onslaught of tourists, more school groups and dogs—mounting claustrophobia drove me off the path in search of a little respite from the hubbub. I found it along a stretch of greensward beside the river, calm for the first time since the stream spilled out of the basin and tumbled over a quarter mile of boulders. Here the waters of the Sorgue take on their famously sensual character. Along a promenade free of souvenir stands, fishermen cast their lines in the shade of a row of plane trees; young lovers strolled, and old men walked their dogs, enjoying the soothing sights and sounds of the stream. Petrarch drew an engaging sketch of a heron with a fish in its beak on the banks of a stream, and this is surely the place one will come closest to finding such tranquillity in Fontaine-de-Vaucluse today.

Bubbling down through Fontaine-de-Vaucluse *ville*, the stream flows under a bridge and turns the mossy paddles of a decorative waterwheel, a memento of some point in time between Petrarch's day and ours when the waters of the Fontaine were put to more lucrative effort than the inspiration of a poet. Where herons once fished, mills for making paper were built, the last one only closing in 1968. Its retirement was short-lived. It has been reborn as a demonstration of the old industry and supplies *folklorique* paper made from cloth on which to print the words of the *Marseillaise* and saccharine poems suitable for souvenirs for the million sightseers who visit the Fontaine each year. Looking back at the green flood surging towards one, however, captures the imagination with a longer-lasting song. It banishes the tawdry displays that stretch along its edges to the periphery of consciousness. In a visual joust between purity and vulgarity worthy of Petrarch, nature in all her resplendent vigor shines through and puts to shame the dross that has accreted on the shore.

In my imagination, it is hard to stop the Sorgue long enough to do justice to its allure. Of all the rivers I know, it is the most magical. Athena-like, it springs full-blown from the forehead of a mountain. Wherever it flows, sun and water dance in a *perpetuum mobile* of color and liveliness. The water glistens from emerald green to jade in an interplay of light and shadow; damselflies with metallic blue wings and bright red bodies flit from beam to beam, wherever the sun has managed to penetrate the leaves of the trees overhead. Below the surface, fernlike plants undulate in the cold, clear current, rippling the smooth surface as its waters flow onwards, deceptively inexorable. If there is a river running through paradise, it must be very like the Sorgue.

A few weeks later, a friend and I took a canoe to find out what happens to the river before it reaches L'Isle-sur-la-Sorgue, our market town. As it flows out of Fontaine-de-Vaucluse, the stream cuts through a diminishing order of limestone folds. Paddling between them was like witnessing the final spasms of Cretaceous energy that lifted up the Vaucluse. Tough little green oaks sprang from the striations wherever their roots could pry open a crack in the rock. As the valley spread out, we entered an avenue of plane trees on either side of its banks, their roots runneling down over the bare earth into the river. Napoleon decreed that the roads of the Empire be lined with trees so that his troops could march through the hot southern sun in the shade. As much as anything I know, the sight of a line of trees on either side of the road, their evenly spaced trunks mottled green and brown by peeling layers of bark, sometimes circled with a stripe of whitewash, tells me I'm in France.

Of a sudden, the shade was gone. Only a line of tree stumps remained, and instead of luxuriating in a green tunnel, I could see all the way across the Provence Country Club golf course to the cliffs of the Vaucluse. One last great skeleton at the end of the rank kept ghostly watch over its fallen comrades. The culprit, I learned, is an organism, the *chancre rouge*, whose spores infest the trees, starting at the roots. Once infected, it is all over, and to stop the spread of the disease, the trees must be cut down as quickly as possible, along with their unaffected neighbors downstream, since water is one of the organism's most effective vectors. My paddling companion told me that the *chancre rouge* is alleged ("in good Gallic fashion," he said) to have come into the country with American ammunition boxes at the time of the Mediterranean landings in 1944 and to have spread—somewhat more slowly than Coca-Cola—up through Provence.

Further downstream, other trees, oaks and willows, took over, and the river regained its intimacy. Around a bend, an altercation had developed. A group of middle-aged Parisians that we had seen shouting and splashing each other's canoes in fun were now being hectored in earnest by a fisherman from the banks. You are scaring away the fish and stirring up the bottom, he yelled. *"Il faut pas chier partout!"* he added in a heavy Provençal accent. This is private property, and I've been paying taxes on it for forty years. You have the right to pass, *mais quand même* . . . . The current plunged onward and took us out of earshot.

The beauty of these waters has been sung by other writers since Petrarch. Writing in the 1950s, Marie Mauron recalled the Sorgue of her childhood in her classic memoir of Provence, *Lorsque la vie était la vie.*[46] Although much of what she described of the beautiful green river is still apparent, before her chapter is over Mauron has painted a bitter picture of the impact of pollution— *"les poissons morts, le ventre en l'air, les moribonds taches de pourriture"* [47] — in what she calls "this century of death." As I let the current take me and I thought of how seductive the Sorgue still is, I asked myself what must it have been like seventy-five, a hundred years ago? The question raised another infinitely more alarming one: How do we keep track from generation to generation of the steady degradation of our world? How many times have I been told, first by grandparents, then by people of my parents' generation, "Oh, you should have known it when . . ."? And now I tell my children the same thing, and they understand its import as little as I did.

Mauron capped her jeremiad with the ultimate curse, *"Les poètes se taisent."*[48] But in this, at least, she is not quite right. René Char was an outspoken defender of the Sorgue long before environmentalism as a movement existed in any organized sense. Only three years after the end of the Second World War, during which he had been an active member of the Resistance, Char wrote a poetic drama for radio about the Sorgue. Its subject was the struggle against factories that were polluting the river

---

46 *Quouro la vido ero la vido* in Provençal; she wrote it in both languages; *When Life Was Life*, in English.

47 Dead fish, belly-up, moribund stains of putrefaction.

48 The poets are silent.

and killing the fish (*"les poissons morts, le ventre en l'air"*), thus destroying the livelihoods of the local fishermen. Pierre Boulez wrote the music for the radio piece and later turned it into a cantata, *Le Soleil des eaux*. The cantata brought him to prominence as a leading modern composer. The very title, "the sun of the waters," evokes the Sorgue, and the score produces a blend of sound whose vitreous volume masterfully captures the play of the one on the other. "La Sorgue," the second of Char's two poems Boulez set to music, begins:

> *Rivière trop tôt partie, d'une traite, sans compagnon*
> *Donne aux enfants de mon pays le visage de ta passion.*
>
> *Rivière où l'éclair finit et où commence ma maison,*
> *Qui roules aux marches d'oubli la rocaille de ma raison.*
>
> *Rivière, en toi terre est frisson soleil anxiété,*
> *Que chaque pauvre dans sa nuit fasse son pain de ta moisson.*
>
> *Rivière souvent punie, rivière à l'abandon.*[49]

The powerful verses are at once evocative of the river and deeply personal, almost to the point of obscurity, in their imagery.

We reached L'Isle-sur-la-Sorgue, five miles downstream, and landed at a municipal park of benches and plane trees that boasted the pathetic title *"Réserve pour la Protection de la Nature."* It reminded me that Ford Madox Ford uses the matter of parks to declare his sympathies with the Provençal temperament. He disparages English parks and pooh-poohs "the liberty they give to Nature to demonstrate its vitality." His sympathies are entirely with the foreigner who sighs, "Ah, but give me the Luxembourg Gardens, with the clipped and orderly trees, the aligned

---

49 René Char, "La Sorgue" (translation by J. H. Brumfitt): River setting forth too soon, at one bound, without a companion, / give the children of my country the face of your passion. / River where the lightning ends and where my home begins, / which rolls the rubble of my reason down the steps of forgetfulness. / River, in you the earth is a tremor and the sun anxiety, / may each poor man, in his night, make his bread of your harvest. / River often punished, river forsaken.

statues of the Queens of France. . . ." The English preference for wildness in their landscape architecture he regards as a deviation from such a healthy point of view, lamenting as a loss when "the Englishman became de-Latinised, a lover of 'Nature,' a compendium of the names and habits of the few birds or of the extremely limited fauna of his country. . . . For," he sniffs in conclusion, "it is one thing to love birds and another mentally to pin them down on the entomologists' cork board or so anthropomorphise them with anecdote. . . . And that is really what differentiates Latin from Septentrional Earth worship." I yield to no one in my love of "clipped and orderly trees" and "aligned statues," but give me an untended island sanctuary along the Sorgue (with birds I am happy to name) over that carefully ordered, bleak municipal *"Réserve"* every time!

At L'Isle, the Sorgue turns north on its way to the Rhône. But to the south, a fertile plain wraps around the Vaucluse and, extending eastwards, forms a valley with the Luberon range before gradually dissipating in the wild hills beyond Apt. Like the portico of an enormous natural amphitheater, the western approaches of the region are framed by L'Isle on the Sorgue and St. Véran's Cavaillon on the Durance. It was into this valley that the Bishop dragged the Couloubre from Fontaine-de-Vaucluse and from here that the mortally wounded beast finally escaped.

The plain is watered by the little Calavon River. Rising in the mountains to the east, it starts off sensibly flowing south towards the sea. But the limestone massif of the Luberon blocks its course and turns the river westward to join the Durance at Cavaillon, the waters of the two rivers no doubt allowing the city its chief claim to fame, its delicious melons. On the way, the Calavon passes under an elegant Roman bridge built at the turn of the Christian era, the Pont Julien. When I got off my bicycle to inspect it one day, the bridge's three graceful arches seemed disproportionate to the algae-clogged flow. It was summer by this time, and the river was little more than a green trickle, not the vibrant color of the Sorgue, but the dense green of eutrophication. Its waters had been sucked almost dry to irrigate the fields along its banks. Some years ago, a factory making the local specialty, candied fruit, discharged so much waste into the river that farmers found they were spraying maggots on their crops. Since then, local citizens have made a concerted effort to improve the Calavon's water quality, but it is reckoned too small a stream to catch the politicians' attention.

And yet, it is not inconceivable that Hannibal and his men trudged along the Calavon's banks on their way from Spain to outflank Rome. The Via Domitia, the oldest of the Roman roads across the Alps, ran beside it. And just down the road from my perch on the Pont Julien, a Roman staging post is still memorialized in the name of the hamlet that grew up on its site: La Bégude, which I was told indicated a drinking establishment and derived from the Latin verb, *bibere*, "to drink."

The Calavon valley is the country's *primeur*, supplying market stalls all over France each spring with the first fresh fruits and vegetables of the year. René Char painted an intimate portrait of the heavily cultivated countryside in the playful "Complainte du lézard amoureux" (the other poem set to music by Boulez in *Le Soleil des eaux*, and the source of the verse at the beginning of the chapter). It is an animal's view of the fields of sunflowers and their cypress hedges that begins:

> N'égraine pas le tournesol,
> Tes cyprès auraient de la peine,
> Chardonneret, reprends ton vol
> Et reviens a ton nid de laine.

The poem radiates the summer warmth one sees rising from the land. As in an Impressionist painting, Char brings them to life through the mere mention of goldfinch, sunflower and cypress, and our associations do the rest. It ends:

> Qui, mieux qu'un lézard amoureux,
> Peut dire les secrets terrestres?
> O léger gentil roi des cieux,
> Que n'as-tu ton nid dans ma pierre![50]

50 Do not pick at that sunflower, / your cypress trees would be most disturbed, / goldfinch, fly off again / and return to your woolly nest. . . . Who better than a lizard in love / can tell the secrets of the earth? / Oh sweet and airy king of the heavens, / would that your nest were in my rock!

Bicycling through the fields and orchards, I became aware that I was crossing a living tapestry dominated by squares and circles that told of human activity on the land at its most beautiful. If you lived in Provence, Ford Madox Ford believed, "you could afford to look at life and make patterns out of it—as did Cézanne at Aix-en-Provence."[51] In the plain, strips of vineyard had the order and discipline of a military cemetery. Rows of lavender made purple stripes against the bare red earth. Freest of all, the wind slithered like an amoeba across the wheat. Where the relentless blast of the mistral—the awesome wind of Provence that blows for three, six or nine days but always in multiples of three, according to local lore—would otherwise roar unchecked, live fences of cypress and poplar trees had been planted to interrupt the flow of the wind, underlining the haphazard arrangement of the fields as they narrowed toward the vanishing point. As I climbed into the foothills, the contour of the land introduced refreshing curves to man-made lines. Natural folds set the straightest row adrift, wrapping it around earth's body. And from the vantage of a terraced square in Gordes, one of the hilltop towns of the Vaucluse, the orchards appeared in the distance like patches of stippling.

When my family and I took up residence in a hamlet halfway down the mountain from Gordes earlier in the spring, the air had a raw damp smell to it, cut by a whiff of coal smoke from someone's hearth. Farmers were ploughing their soggy fields, and in the hedgerows just beginning to green in the hills, great tits flitted about the leaves of the live oaks, building their nests. Mournful in the dank woods, a little Romanesque chapel of St. Véran—witness to a drop of the blood that spilled from the dreadful Couloubre on its final flight—stood simply among the bare trees, its only covering a shroud of ivy.

51 Ford Madox Ford, *Provence*.

Though cherry and almond blossoms had already turned their orchard worlds to white, the vineyards were still black and grotesque and without a trace of green. With last year's growth mercilessly amputated, they reminded me of an ominous image from another of René Char's poems, one of his most obscure: *"Dans la nuit tragique de la préhistoire les quatre doigts tabous de la main-fantôme."*[52] He was referring to the walls of a prehistoric cave where the print of a hand, mutilated save for the thumb, bears silent witness to a ritual sacrifice that encouraged who knows what outcome, millennia ago. Just so, row on row of fingerless arthritic hands now covered the hillsides, like the phantom hands of our prehistoric ancestors praying for the warmth of renewal. Above them, ready for another year of discipline, iron trellises on which the tendrils would be spread-eagled as they grew formed ranks of X's that marched across the vineyards, turning them into a procession of medieval flagellants weighed down by their crosses.

There is something of the medieval torture chamber about French horticultural technique. Explaining his success with roses, a gardener once told my mother succinctly, *"Il faut être impitoyable,"*[53] with Gallic emphasis on the last word. Where else would they make a pitchfork from the trunk of a single *micocoulier* tree, its branches trained to become the tines? In the villages, the courtyard of many a house sports a mulberry tree, its branches cruelly pruned; by midsummer it offers an umbrella of dense shade, but when we arrived the one on our patio spread its naked arms from a trunk as lifeless and artificial as the Pope's staff. In the public squares, the plane trees beneath which the men had begun to get out their *boules* and play in the chilly evening air were similarly pollarded and bare.

For the first few weeks, the days were overcast, and even when the sun broke through at noon, the light was drab. But a few days of the mistral, and one day the sun popped over the horizon into a golden sky absolutely devoid of cloud or dust.

---

52 "In the tragic night of the prehistoric age, the taboo four fingers of the phantom hand."
53 You must be pitiless.

It was still cold and gusty but sunny and bright; color was returning to the world. The vineyards no longer seemed dead but asleep in the pink-brown soil. An exquisite light engulfed the valley, bringing the Luberon mountains close and showing up every bulge and dimple on their flanks. Midway across the valley a glorious hump of green like a velvet dragon's back glowed as if in a landscape only Claude Lorrain could have imagined. The setting sun gave the crooked branches of our mulberry tree the substance of flesh. Soon the irises that van Gogh[54] loved would begin to bloom, bringing a passing splash of color to the dry stone walls that lined the roadsides and ran seemingly forever across the land. The earth had come back to life.

As it did, we reveled in the trails that meander through the hills of the Vaucluse and Luberon now blooming with hedges of blue rosemary. Despite the rugged terrain, we were as likely to come across groups of middle-aged ladies—some time after we heard them, to be sure—pushing each other up over the rocks or dangling their feet in a cold stream, and dressed as if they had come straight from the market. Scattered all along the paths, spent shotgun cartridges gave ample evidence of the Provençal farmer's passion for hunting, and at a trailhead, a passionate message—*Chasseurs déstructeurs!*—scratched across a signpost attested to the ongoing struggle to control their excesses.

It is an emotional fight between David and Goliath that has raged from the halls of the European Parliament down to the town hall, with the Chamber of Deputies generally fighting a rearguard action to forestall any more enlightened legislation that might come out of Brussels. Fifteen years ago, I represented the International Council for Bird Preservation at a protest in the Bordeaux region against the spring shooting of turtledoves. The French riot police kept the badly outnumbered *écolos* in one village, while thousands of *chasseurs* demonstrated in another. (*"Touche pas aux tourterelles!"* was their ironic cry, as well as *"Pas de discussion avec les écolos."*) At one point, our speeches were interrupted

---

54 Van Gogh spent most of the last two and a half years of his life in Provence, first in Arles and then in St. Rémy.

while the police detonated a homemade bomb found in the square. When the Conseil d'état the next day ruled that the hunt was illegal, the hunters vowed to thumb their noses at the law.

In Provence, the local hunters' committees manage the shooting rights on all properties of twenty hectares or less. Property boundaries everywhere proclaim *"chasse garde"* or *"chasse réserve."* Larger landowners can organize the hunting on their land for themselves, and it is simply assumed that they will. Woe betide him who does not. A late-night phone call will generally take care of it; otherwise the loss of a valuable horse will do the trick. On the land, the hunter is king.

That the local attitude to nature is first and foremost utilitarian was nowhere more clearly demonstrated than on an interpretive sign at the edge of an area where roe deer had been successfully reintroduced. On either side of a description of the project, pictures of wild animals were arranged in two unmistakably anthropocentric classes—the good (boars, partridges, rabbits and hares) and the bad (weasels, raptors, snakes and foxes). Not surprisingly, the "good" species could all be cooked, and the "bad" species were those that share our taste for game but eat it raw. The official rationale for this utilitarian ethic is *valorisation de biodiversité.* Or as our cleaning lady said after my son discovered, to his great joy, a snake: *"On peut aimer les animaux, mais quand même!"*[55] A species is worth what we can get out of it, and so it can be classified quite simply as good or bad.

And if it is bad, then one must do unto it as St. Véran did to the Couloubre. Continuing my search for saint and dragon as allegory for the relationship of man and nature, I stumbled one day—I was about to prop my bike against it—onto one of Provence's delightful and virtually unknown curiosities, the *Morvelloux.* Carved at the base of a gigantic rock by an anonymous sculptor hundreds of years ago, the saint stands over his dragon. Some imagination is needed for the detail, because wind and rain and time have left little more than an outline of either. In the mysterious *Morvelloux,* I could see a reflection of my ambivalent

---

55 The snake was a *couleuvre,* totally harmless, but the close etymological relationship with the *Couloubre* was unmistakable.

appreciation of both victor and vanquished. I share Ford's admiration of the human joys of the meridional way of life, but I am uneasy with the attitude towards nature that accompanies it. It is not the conviction that man is the center of the universe that troubles me, but that he can do what he likes since there is always time for confession. This, combined with the assumption that our species' ingenuity will solve whatever problems we create, leads to hubris and leaves little relevance for restraint.

☦§☧

As the Sorgue is a poem vibrant with light and water, and the valley a pastel of arcs and lines, so the uplands belong to the unrelenting world of stone. No matter which path I took, my consciousness barked its metaphorical shins on stone, either massive cliffs, outcrops and natural megaliths, or the fractured rocks of all sizes that were on their way back to the dust. Where river and plain were ingratiating, the limestone hills of the Vaucluse and Luberon were at first sight pitiless.

Perched atop wild pinnacles, the ruined ramparts of many a castle hung ominously over the land. To this day a symbol of oppressive cruelty, the fortress of Baron Meynier of Oppede, chief instigator of the murderous suppression of the Vaudois[56] in 1545, stared balefully from the flanks of the Luberon at the towns in the valley its lord put to fire and the sword. Rising straight out of the rock from which their blocks were cut, the walls could not but inspire respect as a magnificent feat of medieval engineering. Arched gateways opened directly onto sheer drops of hundreds of feet. Incised in the stone wall at the entrance to the inner keep, an extraordinary face leered out at me: a green man or a devil?

But the world of stone has also been tempered by a kinder hand. The rocks are easily broken and trimmed by the mason's hammer. Lovely necklaces of dry stone walls adorn the countryside, enclosing farmers' fields, marking the boundaries of their properties and turning the sweat

---

56 Adherents of the twelfth-century religious reformer Waldo. A contemporary of St. Francis, Waldo espoused a brand of asceticism that, unlike the Franciscan order's, did not find favor with the Pope of the time.

of human effort into grace. Over the ages, the wall-builders, eschewing mortar, have laid their lozenge-shaped stones flat upon each other, mile by mile, tier by tier, year by year. The final row is stacked vertically like teeth or dragon scales, the stones squeezed together tightly to give stability to the ensemble. The walls have been made and remade since they were first built, their upkeep and repair an ongoing proposition. The local telephone book has seven and a half pages of masons listed (compared with only two for lawyers).

Besides the walls that run out in every direction, dry stone construction is integral to a building style in exquisite harmony with the land. On any walk through the countryside in this part of Provence, sooner or later the rambler will come upon the beehive roof of a *borie*, half hidden behind a tangle of scrub oak or hawthorn. The woods and fields are full of them, lonely cabins used chiefly as temporary shelters for shepherds, as sheds to store tools or as granaries. Extraordinary workmanship and effort went into their construction, which required not a single wooden brace or rafter or beam. Sometimes the ages have taken their toll; what once was an ingeniously constructed dome has seemingly melted into a puddle of loose stone. But what a welcome sight it must once have been to a weary traveler, the floor strewn with leaves, dry and clean smelling, to make a comforting carpet or even a mattress. When they were built is anyone's guess since the construction techniques, handed down from generation to generation since Neolithic times, have changed little over the millennia. A few masons kept the art of building a *borie* alive as late as the beginning of the twentieth century.

Gordes has a Village des Bories, a *folklorique* attraction for tourists who come by the charter busload. But on an excursion into the Luberon, I came upon a ghostly unknown village made up of these mysterious structures, lost in the middle of a wood. On its outskirts, old walls around old fields still kept the forest at bay. Some enclosures still provided pasture; others had been invaded by cypress and broom. A high wall encircled the village itself. Houses varied in size and shape; some were rectangular while others had an interior curve like a snail shell. All had the classic corbelled vault. Cisterns carved out of the limestone and covered to prevent evaporation and keep the water cool and clear showed the same skillful stonework as the houses. Between the walls of the houses and their courtyards ran narrow streets that converged at the entrance, in the middle of the village, of a magnificent hall, now roofless. Here at some time in the past—perhaps around the eighteenth century when agriculture flourished in Provence—a community depended on a balanced relationship with the land and celebrated the fruits of its labors: the olives and grapes they cultivated, the sheep and pigs they kept in the corrals along the inside of the village wall.

Across from the lost village, the little town of Goult perches on its hill. Protected from the ravages of the mistral, its steep southern slopes bask in the sun, bearing witness to another pastoral endeavor raised in stone. From top to bottom, stone retaining walls have turned the hillside into a wedding cake of semicircular terraces where orchards and crops were once cultivated. Today among the overgrown olives, jays bounce from tree to tree or fly from level to level over the deserted gardens, but in olden times, when the lowlands were fever-ridden marshes, the town's inhabitants grew their food here, in the shadow of the castle walls. The ensemble is a monument to ingenuity and common sense. As well as maintaining the hillside, the terrace walls trap the heat of the sun, taking the edge off the chill of early spring nights and adding to the length of the growing season. As well as leading from terrace to terrace down the hillside, the paths provide a system of gutters to trap and distribute runoff from the rain. Nicely situated in a cozy nook, a little stone cabin provides what must have been a place of leisure for the old farmer. Here he could sit, in shelter or shade depending on the season, and contemplate his peaceful domain through the unusually large window.

A few miles to the east, a hill of sunset red, Mont Rouge, interrupts the familiar cultivated fields. Here human industry and the land have incidentally produced another monument, this one a fantasy of breathtaking beauty. The cliffs of Roussillon have been mined since Roman times for the vibrant hues of their ochres, and wind and rain over the years have done the rest. The resulting shapes and their fantastic colors would seem possible only in an hallucination. The red is, they say, from the blood of the Couloubre, and I can believe that the dragon still haunts the quarries. Where the old galleries run back into the cliff, the caves produce the eyes and mouth of a gigantic reptile; lower down, the outcrop has been forged into flat pyramids like the angular scales on a dinosaur's back; cirques hollowed out of the hillside have left enormous columns with onion domes. All these are painted with a fiery palette of orange, crimson, eggplant and yellow. At the bottom, a pine wood is slowly working its way up the gullies, bringing with it the high summer sound of the *cigale*; no musical accompaniment could be more fitting. And nothing could set off the brilliant reds of the sand to better effect than the green feathers of the evergreens: jewels of blood and gold laid out on a green baize cloth.

In the pine woods that surround Mont Rouge, occasional ochre arches or turrets emerge unexpectedly as if by a fairy's spell before the forest opens out to rolling hills covered with vineyards. They belong to the local winemaker. He sells his wines by the bottle, but also by the gallon direct from a pump for about the same price as a gallon of gas in the United States. (Prices, reflecting our different national priorities, are neatly reversed; French gas is of course much more expensive, about what one pays for wine in America.) He came to France in the sixties with nothing in his pocket, a *pied-noir* refugee from Algerian independence, and built up this vineyard that now covers several hundred hectares. He is a man of few words, but this he knows as he gazes over the green rows that ride over the rolling hills in the early evening light: "*C'est un paradis.*"

From my lookout on the ramparts of Gordes, I followed the farmers' tracks as they zigzagged across the irregular checkerboard of fields, pale lines that merged and divided as they diminished into the distance. Little villages—more accurately, clusters of houses—were sprinkled liberally about the valley, the red of their tile roofs appearing haphazardly through the branches of the shade trees that surrounded them. Perhaps starting with a single farmer and his family, the original farm—in one of the oldest, loopholes in its solid walls attested to a time when brigands roamed the valley and a farm had to double as a fort—has been added to over the centuries. As the family increased and prospered generation by generation, the campus grew organically around its courtyard as the need arose, much like an African village and with the same sense of community. Some of the hamlets around our house in Gordes were still inhabited by the families from which they took their names—Les Gros, Les Martins, Les Imberts—although most had been to some extent gentrified by newcomers. In one, the date of construction carved over the lintel of an addition hinted at its own story: An 8, the eighth year of the Revolution or 1799.[57]

Out on our bicycles, my wife and I came upon a little *hameau* seemingly lost in time in a marshy tuck in the plain. A faded sign painted on the plaster of a run-down house indicated where its *boulangerie* is no more. Wild boar trotters were nailed to a barn door like trophies. In the courtyard, bunches of pink, blue and yellow flowers were drying on the same lines as the laundry, and an older couple working their garden spoke to each other in Provençal. I was told that the hamlet is the last in the Vaucluse that remains unchanged.

Like the villages, the boundaries of field and orchard have evolved organically, a function of generational distribution. Most of the landholdings are relatively small. Not to be found here are the vast green deserts that pass for cornfields further north, or the yellow expanses of mustard that make the countryside around Dijon so lonely. Apart from a few farms surrounded by their own fields, most of the plots are pocket handkerchiefs of land, the original properties having been split up and recombined as children married and their parents died. As they have passed into different families, either as dowry or inheritance, ownerships

---

57 The revolutionary calendar was, in its own distorted way, an interesting variant on the man-and-nature theme. "This was also an attempt to reconstruct time through a republican cosmology . . . an opportunity to detach republicans from the superstitions they thought embodied in the Gregorian calendar. Their [the calendar's creators'] efforts were directed especially at the rural world, to which the vast majority of Frenchmen still belonged. In keeping with the cult of nature, the twelve months were to be named not just after the changing weather (as experienced in northern and central France) but in poetic evocations of the agricultural year." Simon Schama, *Citizens*.

have broken into pieces that are rarely contiguous. Today, a farmer may find he owns bits of land all over the place.

So long as the whole of an ownership is big enough to produce and its parts close enough together to manage, it can survive despite its fragmentation, and the traditional patterns of agriculture endure. But land cannot be infinitely subdivided. In the inevitable logic of generational division, the cultivated plot is destined one day to become too small to provide for a family. Then it must make way for a new house without a concomitant investment in the land.

On her wedding day, a local farmer gives his daughter what is now an olive orchard for her new home. Who could regret such a thing on this fine June Sunday as bride and groom proceed down the steps of the medieval castle in Gordes—which is also the *mairie* or town hall—under an arch of daggers formed by the groom's air force buddies? Another acre or so of agricultural land may have gone, but in return, a family—and who knows, perhaps a community—has stayed intact. The new house will use the traditional stone, and the town's architectural consultant will ensure that the design is traditional. The beaming father, flushed with pride from bushy moustache to military crew cut, stands at the heart of the happy crowd of wedding guests, the life and soul of the party. He might also be chuckling at the irony of the new house's dry stone façade, mandatory to maintain the integrity of the landscape. In his grandparents' day, undressed stone was the least expensive means of construction, and as soon as he had a little money in his pocket the farmer would plaster it over, adding status to his house. Now when his descendants renovate these same buildings to sell as vacation homes, they remove the plaster to reveal the "chic" dry stone, as if the buyers arriving from the city were hankering for a humbler past.

The cumulative aspirations of resident and visitor alike are nibbling away the lovely landscape of squares and circles that has basked in the warmth of its harmonious proportion to nature for so long. The TGV has brought Provence practically within commuting distance of Paris, and books like A Year in Provence have made it all the rage. Cars with local license plates are being outnumbered by those with Parisian or German or Belgian ones. Houses and tennis courts spring up amid olive orchards and vineyards, bestriding the landscape without even a passing glance at nature. On a hike into the Vaucluse, where the year before there was nothing but rosemary and thyme and wildflowers, our trail is interrupted by the pink gash of a driveway cut straight uphill through the garrigue, trumpeting the logic of convenience rather than nature's design. In the midst of the dry aromatic vegetation, the house at its end constitutes a considerable fire hazard. It made me think of a chemistry class at school when that one last titrated drop of potassium permanganate suddenly turned a colorless solution red. I wondered when, somewhere on this fertile plain, that one house too many would in the same way irrevocably change the landscape. A few days later, bicycling to the top of the Luberon, I got a vision of the future that is not so very far away in either time or space.

It was a hot day, and the long ride up had been a grueling one. Towards the end, when every downstroke of my thigh muscles against the pedal seemed as if it would surely be the last, an Egyptian vulture flew by, not twenty yards away along the side of the mountain, a hopeful look in its eye. I once saw that look on the face of an elderly subscriber at the Boston Symphony Orchestra who all his life wanted a particular seat in Symphony Hall that was held by a lady even older than himself. One season, on his way out after the first concert, he observed to me with satisfaction, "She's weakening." So, the vulture and me.

But neither of us could have been feeling much in the way of satisfaction at the "weakening" of the farmland spread out below us. In the gap from the end of the Luberon range to where the Alpilles rose in the west, the future that worried me a few days before had become the present. High-rises on the outskirts of Cavaillon were the most obvious, but signs that the landscape is passing the point of no return were everywhere. The lines of trees that bounded each plot bespoke suburban ornament rather than agricultural need. It was no longer the Durance that provided geographical continuity but the Auto-route de Soleil on its way from Marseilles to Paris. Power lines marched across the landscape regardless of its natural features. No matter how green it looked from above, this was no longer a rural landscape.

I was only too happy to turn my face to the wild unfettered view looking north. A flock of jackdaws flew off over the wild Combe de Vidauque, whose ridges tumbled away to the plain. On their flanks, back-lit larches overlaid a herringbone pattern on the rounded shapes of the red pines glowing in the midmorning sun. Somewhere below, a chapel to St. Gent, Provence's answer to St. Francis, nestled against the feet of the wild mountains. I discovered it while cycling along a back road beyond the Morvelloux. It is just a simple plastered façade in the middle of a lit-tle lawn with a couple of cypresses and a well-tended orchard of almond trees, but the building seemed to bless the little garden with its warmth. The sunlit atmosphere of perfect calm was an invitation to enter its precinct, and I had felt compelled to stop and enjoy what St. Gent had to offer.

It can hardly be coincidence that Provence's most beloved "saint" came by his sainthood not through the church but through popular acclaim. Frédéric Mistral, Provence's original poet laureate, gives a delightful account of a visit to St. Gent to cure him of the fever when he was a boy:

The old people gave the young a lively account of what they had been told. "Gent," they said, "was the son of peasants like ourselves, a good lad from Monteux, who at the age of fifteen withdrew to the wilderness to dedicate him-self to God. He tilled the soil with two cows. One day when a wolf killed one of them, Gent caught the wolf, harnessed it to his plow, and made it work, yoked to the other cow. But in Monteux, after Gent left, it did not rain for sev-eral years. The people of Monteux said to Gent's mother, "Imberto, you must bring back your son, for not a drop of rain has fallen since he left." And Gent's mother, after much searching and calling, finally found her son. . . . And since his mother was thirsty, Gent stuck two of his fingers in the rock of the cliff to give her a drink, and two fountains gushed forth, one of wine and one of water. The fountain of wine has dried up, but the fountain of water still flows, and it's a sovereign remedy for bad fevers.[58]

58 *The Memoirs of Frédéric Mistral.*

One could hardly ask for a more graceful parable of the happy balance between man and nature.

Restored myself, I bicycled on along the top of the Luberon amid countless wildflowers—poppies and groundsel—until the mountains dropped off in a jagged rump of ridges and combs, made, it is said, by the frightful thrashings of the Couloubre in its death throes. It is also here that the little Aiguebrun stream cuts the Luberon in two. It rises not far from a sleepy little hamlet located at the very end of the road, a village most of whose buildings are *maisons troglodytes*, homes carved into the rock. Just beyond the houses, a series of terraced pastures fans out from the village. A path, still paved in places with stone cobbles rounded and smoothed by centuries of use, skirts around them before dropping several hundred feet to the riverbed. In places, the stream has cut right into the base of the steep calcareous cliffs, leaving an overhang big enough to block the sky. In others, it bends away, creating little pastures between the rock face and the oak and willow bushes that follow its course.

I found it a gentler, moister world than the gorges of the Vaucluse. Where the sun could penetrate, rills and pools sparkled between mossy rocks that shone a dazzling green in its rays. In the shade, water-magnified stones lay round and smooth and blue on the river bottom. From the dense cover along the banks came a constant symphony of birdsong— nightingale, blackcap, chaffinch, blackbird—for which the ripple of the water provided a continuo. And to this was presently added the irregular rhythm and sonorities of bells, giving it the gloss of an African rhythm band: a shepherd was bringing his flock of sheep down to graze on the little streamside fields in the late afternoon.

Sitting on our terrace that evening, I realized I had never experienced the impact of man on the landscape in so moving and omnipresent a way as in this basin. The terraced fields, the cobbled paths, the little pastures: the work and care that have gone into the land over centuries were a living presence. Our mulberry tree was now bearing luscious black fruit; the Pope's staff had greened again as it did when Elisabeth's prayer secured for Tannhäuser his redemption. A magpie and a hoopoe chased each other around the garden. As the sun went down, thunderheads over the Luberon turned an extraordinary pink, and after they disappeared in the dark, summer lightning glimmered in the distance. Later that night, it turned into a stupendous thunderstorm, the mountains jumping out of the dark beneath jagged bolts of lightning and thunder echoing off the rocks.

The next night—our last in Provence—we went to dine with friends who were staying in a chateau a steep drive up to the top of another hill town nearby. It was not as high as Mont Ventoux, but for 360 degrees we had a view of the whole valley. As we lingered over our food in the high-walled garden, our children played soccer. An extra-strong kick, and the ball soared over the wall and down onto an invisible village street. As it rolled and ricocheted down the hairpin course like a ball in a pinball machine, we could trace its zigzag progress down the hill by the cries of the boys in vain pursuit, their voices—now nearer, now farther—amplified by the paving stones of the town. The scene evoked for me a feeling of haunting melancholy not unlike the end of Albert Lamorisse's magical film about childhood, *Le Balon Rouge*. It was hard to tell whether my melancholy was about a personal ending—the close of a delightful sojourn in Provence—or something more ineffable that had to do with the future of the countryside itself.

Arlésienne Suite

Who would list to the good lay
Gladness of the captive grey?
'Tis how two young lovers met,
Aucassin and Nicolete,
Of the pains the lover bore
And the sorrows he outwore,
For the goodness and the grace
Of his love, so fair of face.

Sweet the song, the story sweet,
There is no man hearkens it,
No man living 'neath the sun,
So outwearied, so foredone,
Sick and woeful, worn and sad,
But is healed, but is glad
'Tis so sweet.
—*Aucassin and Nicolete,*
translated by Andrew Lang

A QUARTER OF A CENTURY later, the opening lines of the
Provençal *cante-fable* came effortlessly to mind at the sight of
the castle of Beaucaire, its white tower gleaming just across
the Rhône from Tarascon. Only the tower recalls the town's past glories,
but in early summer, the park inside the ruined battlements was heavy
with the scent of lilac and broom, and from the depths of the bushes,
nightingales sang, just as they did for Aucassin:

At Beaucaire below the tower
Sat Aucassin, on an hour,
Heard the bird, and watched the flower,
With his barons him beside,
Then came on him in that tide
The sweet influence of love
And the memory thereof.

Aucassin, son of the Count of Beaucaire, loved Nicolete, a baptized Saracen. His father would have none of it and had her imprisoned high up in a tower. However, Nicolete escaped, and the lovers ran away through forests and deserts. At sea, they were separated by storms and pirates until eventually they found each other once again and became Lord and Lady of Beaucaire. I was exposed to this lovely piece of twelfth-century literature as a child. My sister found an outlet for her artistic temperament and talents in an extraordinary acting school run by two elderly Boston ladies, friends and colleagues of our great-aunt. Their productions, immaculately designed and directed in the basement of a rather drab hotel, were regularly reviewed on the theater pages of the *New York Times*. They were a formidable pair of women. When the owner of the hotel was found floating facedown in the East River under suspicious circumstances, they never even considered canceling the opening, which was the next day. Far from it; at the reception, one was heard to confide, "Too awful, but such good publicity for the theater."

So my brother and I never really had a chance when the same iron-willed lady called my mother some days later to tell her that the next play under consideration was *Aucassin and Nicolete* and that my sister might play Nicolete, if only. . . . "We need more boys," she sighed. "You do have two sons, don't you?" A pause, then, "Katie would be so marvelous, made for the part. . . ." I can imagine her voice trailing off. At all events, my mother got the point. Protest was useless; my brother and I were sacrificed to our sister's theatrical ambitions and with a dozen or so other little boys were dragooned into becoming soldiers, shepherds or courtiers, all the vassals of the Count of Beaucaire. The family photograph album contains a picture of the cast of *Aucassin and Nicolete* on the set, which was painted in the colors of an illuminated parchment from a medieval Book of Hours. Most of us are covered from head to toe in chain mail with only an opening for the eyes and mouth. Nevertheless, my brother's and my unbending personalities, easily recognizable, stand out from the crowd. My father labeled the photograph "Reluctant Thespians."

That year, my parents took me to Provence for the first time. The sights and sounds, smells and touch must have made a deep impression because they have tumbled inside my head ever since, ready for any chance association, as if I had always known them and what Ford Madox Ford calls "the frame of mind that is Provence." The warmth of the Mediterranean night, the round embrace of the parasol pines overhead, and the soft feel of their needles in the dust underfoot. The intoxicating fumes of low-octane gas and hot tarmac giving off its heat in the dark, mixed with the comforting smell of the afternoon's leftovers of wine and cheese and bread in the back of the car. The dim light diffused through the curtains of beads or strips of plastic tape that hang in the doorways so exotically, and a street decked with strings of naked lightbulbs leading to a stage where a beautiful young woman with dark skin and black hair sings. For years, right through my adolescence, I could recall the tune of that song until it was blotted out, like stars are by city lights, by other melodies quintessentially French: the syncopated raciness of Darius Milhaud's *Le Boeuf sur le toit*, the naïve coquetry of the soun track of Jacques Tati's *Mon Oncle* and the smoky heartbreak of Edith Piaf's "Milord."

One of the places we went that summer was, of course, the Camargue, the delta of the Rhône that is one of Europe's premier birding spots. It is equally famous for its white horses, which were the subject of another fable—this time a film—that had already beguiled me, *Crin Blanc*.[59] Although conceived for the screen rather than a castle hall, the tale is as ageless and captivating as *Aucassin and Nicolete*. It is another story about love, this time between a boy and a horse. As with the medieval play, the essential dramatic ingredients are all there: constancy, perfidy and

59 *White Mane*, also by Albert Lamorisse.

courage. To save the horse, little Folco must first win its confidence and then overcome the greed and hatred of the local *manadier*, or horse breeder. He does, but unlike Aucassin and Nicolete who enjoyed "Many years in shade and sun, / In great gladness and delight," Folco pays the ultimate price: boy and horse swim out to sea "to a beautiful isle where children and horses are always friends." In addition to the boy and the animal, the film has a third protagonist: the Camargue itself.

The land has the classic triangular shape of the delta, its northern apex at Arles, its base the Mediterranean coast running from Aigues-Mortes eastward to Fos-sur-mer. It is a savage place, parched in summer and flat. Only the occasional line of tamarisk bushes running beside an irrigation ditch, or the tall reeds at the edge of a lagoon, or here and there, like a white overturned boat, a *cabane* — one of the huts traditionally used by the *gardians*, the cowboys of the Camargue, to escape the harsh environment—breaks the horizon. Above all, the Camargue is windswept. There is nothing here to stop the mistral, the ferocious wind that blasts down the Rhône valley and is the bane of Provence. In his famous *Letters from My Mill*, Alphonse Daudet wrote, "Like the sea, uniform in spite of its waves, the plain conveys a sense of solitude, of immensity, increased by the *mistral*, which blows without relaxing and without obstacle and by its powerful breath seems to flatten and so widen the landscape. Everything bends before it. The smallest shrubs keep the imprint of its passage, and continue twisted and bent toward the south in an attitude of flight." The mistral drives even animals crazy, and for humans, it is considered an extenuating circumstance in murder cases.

In the Camargue, one enters an etymological world that is as mysterious and evocative as the land itself. In the words for its natural features, the language seems to achieve an almost perfect synthesis, a visual equivalent of onomatopeia to summon up the landscape. The local word for lake, *étang*, fierce and murky like the choppy waters of the Étang de Vaccares;[60] a shallow sheet of water, *gaze*, as hard and bright as the light

---

60 The Étang de Vaccares is the largest body of water in the Camargue, a shallow brackish lake that covers some thirty square miles and is now a nature reserve.

reflected off it when the mistral has cleared the air. *Sansouire*, how better to sound out the greenish haze of these flood-prone lands covered as far as the eye can reach with *saladelle* (sea lavender) and *salicornia* (glasswort or marsh samphire)? And *salins*, the man-made lagoons, as basic as the salt they have produced since the Middle Ages using water from the Mediterranean and the fierce summer sun of the Midi. The sandbars that appear in some of the shallower lakes are called *radeaux* (literally, rafts), while the narrow irrigation canals are *roubines;* after the sibilant alliteration of *sansouire, saladelle, salicornia* and *salin*, they seem to provide a reassuring resolution, like a simple chord in a chromatic sea. Above the waterline stands the Phoenician juniper, or *mourven*, its skeleton, bleached and twisted, often the only break in the flat, gray-green land.

The origin of the word *Camargue* itself is a thought-provoking exercise in the possibilities of parallel evolution. In his book *Camargue,* Michel Droit[61] offers a number of theories: *Camars*, an early god; *Caii Marii ager*, the field of Caius Marius, the Roman general who defeated the barbarians outside of Aix in 102 B.C.; *Ca-mar*, in the Celto-Ligurian dialect meaning "field covered with water"; or, from the *langue d'oc, cara-marca*, "dear frontier," or even more likely given the seemingly endless space, *n'a cap marca*, "having no frontier." As it disappears into the mists of time, each one lays claim to an inherent and indisputable logic. Out of their meanings layered on top of one another, the face of this enigmatic land begins to emerge.

Like so many mysterious places, the Camargue seems to invite definitions in threes. It is made of silt, salt and water. Its qualities are expanse, light and silence. More cosmically, it is the land of sky, earth and water. More prosaically, what visitor has not inscribed on a postcard, "the land of white horses, black bulls and pink flamingos"?

The influences that have shaped the Camargue are also three: the river, the wind and man. Long before it reaches the sea, the Rhône has let go its burden of debris scoured from the Alps. Before it was banked

61 Michel Droit, *Camargue.*

and channeled, the river spilled out over the delta and deposited fine alluvial silt that now lies to a depth of over fifty feet and contains never a stone. The annual floods also flushed away the salt constantly swept in by the sea, but continual meddling since the eighteenth century with the Rhône's natural flow has left the soil of the lower Camargue increasingly salty. Today, only plants that are at home in a harsh environment survive, and they provide pasture for the bulls and horses that are at the heart of the Camarguais way of life.

According to Dr. Luc Hoffmann, who has studied the area all his life, two vectors form a crosshair of dynamics that defines the Camargue's ecology.[62] As the sea gets closer, the salinity of the soil increases. As the main flow of the river gets closer, sand gives way to river silt. The critical factor is wind: the mistral being far stronger than the winds from the sea, it keeps the sands of the Mediterranean at bay over most of the delta. However, in the west where the shoreline runs longitudinally, crosswinds have covered the alluvial mud with sand, giving the Petite Camargue its distinctive aspect. Here thrive the grapes that make the delicious *vin de sable*,[63] the rosé wine of the region. Around the courtyards of the farms, parasol pines take the place of plane trees, and their pine needle domes glow in the sunshine, lightening the landscape. Where the Étang de Vaccares is bleak and foreboding, the Petite Camargue captivates with a gentle façade.

The Rhône, the mistral . . . and man. However wild it may appear, the Camargue has been managed by humans since ancient times. The land is laced with canals dug for irrigation and drainage. Under the Romans, it was the wheat basket of Provence. Michel Droit eloquently described the human factor: ". . . all his art and all his talents have, in fact, been devoted to preserving this spontaneous harmony, dating from time immemorial, between sky, earth, water, wind and animals. His presence has never succeeded in reducing the space, in tarnishing the light

---

62 L. Hoffmann, *An Ecological Sketch of the Camargue.* Hoffmann, heir to Hoffmann-LaRoche and a Ph.D. in biology, runs a biological field station that I first visited in 1977.

63 Wine of the sand.

or in breaking the mystery." While much of what he wrote is still true fifty years later, cultivation is increasingly squeezing the man-made wilderness from all sides, ineluctably reducing the "space" of the Camargue. Much of the land toward the apex of the triangle is under rice. Not only is there little "mystery" in a field of rice, there is growing conflict between the advancing cultivation and the breeding colonies of thousands of flamingos. As the two get closer, the rice fields are providing a new source of food for the birds, not the rice itself but tiny crustaceans that thrive in the flooded paddies. So far, so good. But as a flamingo stalks its meal, its shovel-like bill and large webbed feet wreak havoc with the plants, and as flamingo numbers multiply, so does the wrath of the farmers. Will the "light," in this case the gorgeous pink of the *flamant rose*, be tarnished, too?

It was this bird that drew me first to the Camargue. Brought up with the magnificent diorama of flamingos flying into an everlasting sunset at the Museum of Natural History in New York, I had high hopes of the Camargue when my parents took me there at the age of eleven. But the closest I got to a flamingo was what I would think of now as a delightfully dilapidated hotel called the Flamant Rose, just off a long straight road lined with plane trees. I had no clear idea of how to find the real thing, having thought that the Camargue would simply produce flamingos wherever we looked. My parents were in something of a rush to get back to their castles and cathedrals, and we never got as far as the salt pans where the flamingos congregate and which are hardly attractive for anything other than bird-watching.

It was many years later that I finally added the greater flamingo to my life-list. The day was cold and windy and colorless. In the distance across the water of the salt pans, far from the tropical glamour I had expected, a whitish mass that I first took to be an island turned out in fact to be a colony of more than 12,000 pairs of nesting flamingos. Closer by, along the sea wall that holds back the Mediterranean, a band of a dozen or so of the great birds looked decidedly chilly. Some stood up to their breasts in the cloudy water, their necks wrapped around their bodies, looking more like dirty pink feather dusters blowing in the wind than Alice's croquet mallet. Others strutted sedately, each claw planted purposefully one in front of the other, their legs and bills a most synthetic-looking pink. As they moved, the improbable kinks in their necks and the odd angles of their legs combined to give the impression of an invisible hand writing slightly awkward hieroglyphics. Suddenly, an ungainly trio rose and attempted to fly into the teeth of the mistral. There they were, hardly thirty yards from me, stretched out and beating their wings for all they were worth, all to no avail. At last revealing their gorgeous color, they hung in the air as if they were in a wind tunnel. All I had to do was stand and watch, marveling at the contrast of the crimson coverts and black tips of their wings, brilliant even on so grim a day.

Since the 1960s, when for several years no colonies bred at all, ecologists from the biological field station at Tour de Valat, deep in the Camargue, have significantly strengthened the Camargue's flamingo population, among other things by mass-producing the muddy stumps that serve as their nests. But disaster can strike from unexpected quarters. One year a Mylar balloon escaped from a child's clutches and blew into the colony. Its shiny surface glinting in the sun spooked the birds, and they flew up from their nests in a pink cloud, abandoning their eggs and young.

I have been to the Camargue many times since, and one of the things that keeps pulling me back year after year is the instructive way it parsimoniously doles out its treasures one or two species at a time. Early on, I found the complete array of European herons and egrets; it was particularly satisfying to spot for the first time the mousy form of a Squacco heron, its plumage like a perfectly toasted marshmallow. It took several visits before I had seen all three of that glamorous page-full—the hoopoe, bee-eater and roller—which sets all the other plates in a British bird book to shame. A year or two later, on an outing with Roger Tory Peterson, I finally saw the pratincole, its sinister, almost batlike flight making it quite a different bird from the one whose picture in the field guide had intrigued me for years. Like Scheherazade, the Camargue always leaves something to tempt me back. And each time I return, the birds that I have previously found welcome me like an old friend.

As I follow the dusty track beside a canal on one of the famous white horses, rainbow-colored bee-eaters fly in and out of their nests in the high banks, while swallows dip and glide over the water. Wild birds and animals are in general unconcerned by the presence of people on horse-back, allowing one to get quite close. In the shallow brackish waters of a *gaze*, hundreds of delicate birds are making their living by probing the mud with their beaks: avocets with retroussé bills, black-winged stilts teetering into the deeper water and a myriad of smaller waders that we call peeps and the French, *limicoles*. Snowy egrets and gray and purple herons are on the lookout for fish, and the rattling song of the great reed warbler explodes from the reeds at the edge of the marsh. A small band of white horses grazes on the salty vegetation, and cattle egrets wander among them, riding on their backs as if they were in the African savanna. Further off, a slow black caterpillar spreads out over the green horizon where a herd of bulls is crossing a *gaze*. *Gardians*, the cowboys of the Camargue, keep the animals together with judicious prods of their tridents, whose crescent shape bisected by a central prong is the symbol of their way of life: man on the landscape.

As we ride on, the land gets progressively more barren and the plants increasingly hardy. The mud has dried into a crazy paving of black cracks; squinting against the brightness of the summer sun, the irregular reticulations form black patterns on my retina. When I open them again, the dazzling contrast of the white salt drying in the *salins* is like a block of ice dropped into boiling water, enough to make the eyeballs burst. Soon the barren beach appears with an inevitability that is emotional as well as geological. Here Aucassin and Nicolete must have wandered before taking the ship that led them so far astray. Into the leaden Med-iterranean that rolls towards us, little Folco and White Mane headed out towards their beautiful never-never-land. And now we are flying over the damp sand at full gallop, grateful for the high back and pommel of the very utilitarian Camarguais saddle.

On the way back to the stable, the young woman who has been my guide holds my attention. Her every move exhibits independence and reaffirms her relationship with her animals and her land, and I wonder, not for the first time, where on earth one could be brought into a better life. Her family have been *manadiers* for generations, some raising bulls, the others horses. A part of the family business includes a stable, on the edge of Les-Saintes-Maries-de-la-Mer, advertising *promenades à cheval* for those wanting to experience the Camargue on horseback. When I first saw it, it seemed appropriate, here in the south of France, that the name of the enterprise, Le Sherif, should have both Arab and Wild West associations. (As it happens, the Camargue was an early locale for making cowboy films in the days when movies were still silent.)

Sensibly, new construction in the area has been concentrated in Les Saintes-Maries-de-la-Mer, so that elsewhere in the Camargue, it can be rigorously controlled. Based on its renown as the gypsy Mecca, the town is also a major tourist center. But what you see first, as you approach Les Saintes-Maries-de-la-Mer, is a massive shape that materializes out of the featureless wilderness. Refracted by the heat streaming off the baking land, it appears to hover on the shiny horizon like a mirage. As you get closer, the outlines of a twelfth-century fortress church come into focus, and the dark brooding form takes on the color of honey. But the church still retains its sense of mystery even in the midst of tawdry tourist trappings. It marks the spot where, according to legend, Sts. Mary Jacobe and Mary Salome first came ashore after their miraculous voyage from Palestine.

In the wave of persecution that swept through Jerusalem some years after the Crucifixion, the two Marys, sisters of the Virgin and mothers of several of Jesus' disciples, were set adrift in a small boat without oar or sail to find a martyr's death at sea. According to the Christian story, they were accompanied by Sara, a young black servant. When she saw their bark floating away from Jerusalem, Sara ran down to the shore calling after them, begging to be allowed to join in their martyrdom. The saints could not turn their rudderless ship around, so one of the Marys threw her veil over the waves, and the girl stepped across it to the boat and thus accompanied the saints to Provence.

But according to another more poignant version of the story, which rings truer to the spirit of the Camargue, Sara was a princess of the land, a priestess of Mithras and the cult of the bull. Having the gift of foretelling the future, she knew that the old gods were destined to give way to the new religion radiating out of Jerusalem, and she was waiting to greet the holy boat people when they arrived. According to this version, it was her own veil that she threw over the waves, walking upon it to the boat to bid them a reverent welcome.

Surely it is this Sara who is the patron saint of the gypsies and reigns in the crypt beneath the fortress church. Every May, the Romany come to Les-Saintes-Maries from all over Europe for the feast of the Holy Marys. The night before, they keep a vigil before her shrine. In this land of the bull, could the crypt not once have been the subterranean temple of Mithras, a place of pagan worship long before the Christian era? The legend of the holy boat would have served the purpose of bringing the old worship into the body of the new faith. And just as the Christian legend of the Saintes-Maries co-opted the pagan one, Sara's gracious bowing to the inevitable served to keep the old ways alive, not far beneath the surface.

Another saint who came from Jerusalem with the two Marys—St. Martha, Mary Magdalene's sister—went on up the Rhône to Tarascon, where a dragon was terrorizing the city. The Tarasque had come out of the river and lived in a murky forest nearby. (Tarascon was then a village called Bois-Noir, Black Wood, referring to the place where the dragon lurked.) St. Martha confronted the beast and subdued it with the sign of the Cross. Some say the creature sounded to the depths of the Rhône and was never seen again; others that the saint led it back to Tarascon by a silken halter, whereupon the townspeople stoned it to death. As with St. Véran and the Couloubre, the story sounds like a parable of the conquest by the new religion of the old nature worship. The Tarasque, identified with the great river Rhône, would symbolize the evil of the old ways, which the Church was bound to destroy. In the fifteenth century, King René d'Anjou, known as "the good" for his liberal instincts and interest in the local history of his lands, instituted the popular festival celebrating the town's deliverance from the Tarasque, which continues to be observed to this day. And St. Martha is buried in the little church just opposite King René's magnificently restored castle, which stares proudly across the Rhône at the ruins of Beaucaire.

Stories like those of the St. Marys, St. Martha and *Aucassin et Nicolete* blow over the Provençal countryside like the scent of its wildflowers. The play of pagan and Christian, nature and man is finally distilled into pure delight, a whimsical descant that decorates the physical testimony of the timeless dance of man and the earth. Often, they are manifested in local festivals that can be traced back to pagan times, the old gods and their powers recognizable in all but name. Existing in the heart of the people, they express the soul of the land, what the French pack into the single word *terroir*. In the Provençal landscape, the breath of the past still whispers in the branches of the olive trees and the nightingale's song, and in the festivals that the Good King René set such store by. As the returning nightingale sings in the old Provençal tune that Frédéric Mistral used for his poem "Magali":

> *Sir, you have a good memory*
> *To have remembered me so long.*
> *It will always be my wish*
> *To spend summers here with you.*
> *To your love I will respond,*
> > *Warbling sweetly;*
> *Day and night I shall sing*
> > *Here around you.*

Another Provençal myth tells how Hercules, on his way back from Spain, where he had completed one of his labors, was challenged by an army whose chiefs were none other than the sons of the cosmic union of Earth and Neptune. Having used up his own arms, Hercules called upon his father for help, and mighty Jove obligingly let fly with a barrage of stones that defeated his enemies. The barrage also formed La Crau, a plain that, away from the aquatic influences of sea or river, is the closest thing to a desert in Europe. Rather than a moody paradise like the Camargue to its west, La Crau is like a moonscape. It is the ancient bed of the Durance from a time when the river flowed south directly into the Mediterranean. While the Rhône has deposited its load of alpine stones long before reaching the delta, the Durance comes straight out of the mountains, scattering stones and pebbles all over the plain. It is still doing so as the river rushes past Cavaillon towards its rendezvous with the Rhône itself.

The utter otherworldliness of the Crau is by turns alluring and frightening. Apart from the occasional remains of a shed, the only visible features on its monotonous surface are piles of stones a couple of feet high built at regular intervals in all directions. They give the plain a pimpled look. During the Second World War, fearing that its flatness would make an attractive landing ground, German soldiers erected these cairns to prevent Allied gliders from using the Crau in their jump from North Africa into occupied southern France. It must have been grueling work in either the blazing sun or the roaring wind. La Crau is not a land of half measures. Unfortunately, this extraordinary habitat of pebbles and aromatic herbs has been nibbled away year by year since the sixteenth century as irrigation schemes have brought water from its mother, the Durance, to her long-abandoned land. Once watered, it has proved to be surprisingly fertile, possibly because of the sheep that have grazed on its meager vegetation for a thousand springtimes.

I went hiking here one day in early June twenty years ago with a birdwatching friend from the biological field station. As we walked, the scent of crushed thyme rose from the stony ground under our feet. All other vegetation had already been desiccated by the summer sun. In every direction, the land dissolved in a mirage of sparkling water. Of human beings, there were none, except in the distant green horizon where a tractor flickered through the heat as it plowed up one more strip of desert. Overhead, a different kind of mirage streaked past, returning to its nearby base. Where the Crau stretched away into the haze in the southeast, a vast monolithic structure shimmered in the distance, a supersecret French air force installation. Bird-watchers covered in all kinds of fancy optics (as I was that day) are advised to give it a wide berth.

We had not been walking long before a covey of lesser bustards took alarm and flew off, keeping close to the ground before alighting and disappearing in the scanty undergrowth some distance away. It boded well, and a flock of bee-eaters hawking over the occasional skeleton of an asphodel added a further sense of anticipation. But after that, nothing stirred in the heat. Just as the Camargue made me work for her bird species, so did the Crau. I had to wait for another year to find my first sand grouse, the place's totem, and still another to spot a lesser kestrel flying about the broken roof-tiles of a ruined farmhouse. La Crau is the only breeding site in France for either bird.

As well as explaining a remarkable landform, the legend of Hercules and La Crau is yet another explanation of human victory over nature, but with a difference: it hints at a more productive resolution than do the stories of St. Véran or St. Martha. The saints contented themselves with killing their dragons or driving them away. On the other hand, once he had defeated them, Hercules taught the Ligurians, the ancient tribe of Provence, to cultivate the land and weave cotton and wool. Hercules taught the people how to live with nature. At least for a while. As more and more of the Crau was cultivated, a British visitor to Provence[64] was able to write optimistically a hundred years ago, "In another century probably the sterility of the Crau will have been completely conquered." Until recently, it seemed that his prophecy would be fulfilled. For most of the twentieth century, the insult of Marseille's solid waste—at a current rate of a thousand tons a day—has been added to the injury of the plough. In the 1980s, environmentalists adopted a policy of triage and focused their efforts on saving the more diverse Camargue. Today, less than a third of the original Crau is left, but local efforts are reviving the hope that what remains may yet be saved and, with it, its unique wildlife.

Each spring since at least Roman times, the Crau has seen herds of sheep gather on its stony soil. From February to June, they feed on the vegetation not yet burned by the sun. Then their shepherds lead them to greener pastures in the Alps. The *transhumance* is an annual migration that once took ten days or more on foot. Then in the 1950s, as ever more vehicles filled the roads, the sheep became the source of serious traffic congestion. In the department of Bouches-du-Rhône, they were banned, and the animals had to be transported to their summer pastures by truck. However, according to a local newspaper, *transhumance à pied* may be making a comeback. The sheep, it seems, find it less traumatizing than a rapid, jolting journey and arrive at their summer pastures in finer fettle

64 S. Baring-Gould, *In Troubador-Land.*

the traditional way. Moreover, with a truckload costing 5,000 francs, it is much cheaper for the shepherd.

The traditional start of the journey is celebrated with the *Fête de la Transhumance* in the town of St. Rémy, just across the Alpilles, which border the northern edge of La Crau. Getting to St. Rémy early, I settled on a sidewalk café on the main street and watched the world go by. Occasionally a van drove past announcing, to the sound of recorded Provençal pipes, "The herds leave the Plateau de la Crau at 10:30, two kilometers from town." For the best seat in the house, the price was one cup of coffee. I have a mental list of "quality of life indicators," and I give high marks to any culture that lets me sit at a table in a café for hours, watching the world go by, and nursing one *café crème* if that is all I want. It is not the coffee but the time that is important. We could save all the wilderness left in the world, but if we are not allowed the time to drink a cup of coffee, what will it have gained us?

From the top of a tree just outside the town came the insistent voice of the chiffchaff, its endless song insinuating itself into the sunniest aspects of the countryside. And then at about eleven, the main street of St. Rémy was transformed into what my neighbor, sitting on a bole of a plane tree, had assured me would be a "reever of ships." (It took me a moment or two to translate this correctly into a "river of sheep.") Three thousand sheep surged forward, swarming around anything—a recalcitrant donkey, for instance—in their path. Their shepherds herded them on with good-natured yells. From time to time a group of handsome brown sheep with long upright horns ran past. They seemed in more of a hurry than the rest, when necessary climbing over the backs of the animals in front to get ahead. An old fellow with splendid moustaches brought up the rear in a fiacre with his family, all of them dressed to the *folkloriques* nines. Very soon it was over; 3,000 sheep had passed by, leaving a reever of sheets.

The Alpilles run east and west. Up their rugged slopes, scrubby oak groves give way to bushes of gorse and broom and then finally dense *maquis*, the home of the Dartford warbler. The peaks are improbably jagged, and on the naked cliffs a pair of the seriously threatened Bonelli's eagles looks down from their lofty perch on an uncertain future.

Along the slopes, bare rock breaks out of the cover of broom, and from crack to crevice the blue rock thrush flits about. From the north, the approach to the Alpilles is guarded by what is left of the Roman center of Glanum. Its walls grew out of the natural bastions of the foothills. Even before Roman times, a prehistoric settlement had thrived beside a sacred spring here, and a cave in the rocks above it had allowed those early inhabitants to watch the pass into the mountains from comparative safety. The pass is still used by a modern highway, the D27, which crosses the Alpilles at this point, but the process of cutting the road through the last of the mountain—perhaps to avoid the Roman remains—has sadly truncated the setting of the ancient sanctuary. However, next to a temple to Hercules the healer, the sacred spring still fills a Roman swimming pool with water. While trying to win the heart of the lady of nearby Les Baux, Peire Vidal, the greatest of the medieval troubadours, is said to have appealed to Venus and won her assistance by riding backwards on a hog around just such a spring at midnight. At Glanum, the long reach of history connects the Courts of Love with the Roman goddess and in its turn the sacred spring of the ancients.

Such a mélange of past and present is literally bottled on the slopes of the Alpilles, not five kilometers away. Where Druids once worshipped the mother goddess, from whence wine was shipped to Rome, in whose halls the troubadours vied in the Courts of Love: the ruins of the Château Romanin cling to the jagged foothills.

And here a new cathedral of sorts has been built, in the heart of the mountain itself, to store the wines of Château Romanin. It combines the oldest concepts of engineering design—even the royal cubit as the basic measure—with an almost futurist vision of ecological perfection. "The whole framework," say the builders, "resonates at the same frequency as that of the Earth (7.8 Hz), which of course enables the wine to stay 'alive.'"

Château Romanin cultivates its vines according to the rules of "biodynamics"—based on the philosophy of Rudolf Steiner—and aims "to stimulate the harmony existing between the cultivation of vines and their environment (the cosmos and the soil) so that the characteristics of the environment can better express themselves." Instead of synthetic chemicals, the fields are fertilized with cow manure and sprayed with infusions of nettles to improve the circulation of the sap, a solution of the cinders of the grape worm to ward off the depredations of its kind and a "decoction of horsetail" to protect the leaves from the fungus. Beyond organic treatments, la biodynamie takes into account the positions of the moon, the stars and the planets in determining the propitious day to carry out the various steps of wine-growing. Each part of the plant is associated with one of the elements: the roots—the earth, the leaf— water, the flower—air. Most importantly, the fruit is fire, and the vini- culturalists of Château Romanin carry out all important work on the vines when the position of the moon can best reflect down to earth the influences of the fire-related constellations. Finally, in the cellar that sings the same song as the Earth, the bottled wines are stored in "the ideal geomagnetic position, three degrees geographic north-east."

After I was introduced to a bottle, I noted more succinctly in my jour- nal, "Sounds flaky but tastes good." And it is, in fact, the wine served at the Oustau de Baumanière, one of the best restaurants in all of France, just the other side of the Alpilles. The winemakers of Château Romanin have captured the spirit of the earth, air and water of Provence. The taste has the brightness of the landscape in the summer sun, and through it a subtler flavor makes itself felt that could be, for all I know, the distil- lation of the joys and sorrows of the land.

The harmony of biodynamics is a far cry from the hardscrabble world of Marcel Pagnol's Jean de Florette or even Ford Madox Ford's mordant summation of what is considered good luck in Provence: "You only need not to have the maladie among your vines for one season when the vines of most of your neighbours have shrivelled under the mildiou, the oidium or the pourridié. And that is Nature and how men wish to live with Nature for Provence."

Mildiou, oidium (where the "decoction of horsetail" comes in handy) and pourridié aside, the relationship of man and nature in Provence reflects a marvelous historical symbiosis combining all the faults and glo- ries of the civilizations that have from time to time overrun the land. "For the Provençal . . . ," wrote Ford,

Nature is a matter of little squares in the orange, sun-baked earth. . . . You go out at dawn from your mas that has frescoed walls; between a forgotten shrine that contains a IXth century Christ and the field from which they are just disinterring the Venus of Arles who looks upon you with sightless eyes; with a tiny knife before the dawn is up you remove an infinitely tiny but superfluous leaf from a tiny plant; between clods the countenance of every one of which is as familiar to you as the face of your child and that tomorrow you shall reduce to fine earth, you lead with your hoe threads of water to the base of every plant that is as familiar to you as the clods, your children and the names of your saints, bull-fighters and poets. The sun rises and scorches your limbs whilst you prune your vines; your throat knows the stimulation of the juice of your own grapes that you have pressed, of the oil of the olives you have gathered and crushed, of the herbs you have grown in the mess of pottage of your own beans, of the cheese whose whey was pressed from the milk of your own goats.

Ford sums up his peroration to the Provençal farmer by invoking his obedience to "the laws of the arts, the requirements of beauty and the divine dictates of Nature and the beloved earth."

Ford's rustic idyll is more easily found in the undistinguished towns of the plain whose raison d'être remains as it has always been, to serve the daily needs of the people from the countryside around, rather than tourists and urban refugees. Beneath their pollarded plane trees, young men and women take part in the *boules* tournaments, side by side with the gnarled and wrinkled old men whose arthritic posture still seems to calculate the perfect trajectory for the *boule*. Places like Cavaillon, the city of melons, have languorous, tree-shaded squares, but of "sights," only one, rather dilapidated, Roman arch. Carpentras, surrounded by its market gardens, has a traffic system that is designed like a snail shell and so disorients visitors that they head for the hills, either the Dentelles de Mirail to the north or the Vaucluse to the south. Plan d'Orgon has a plain fortresslike church past whose impressive buttresses the D99 runs straight, leaving the town in a cloud of dust, fumes and noise.

But on a summer Sunday afternoon, on the other side of Plan d'Orgon's municipal park, highway traffic does not disturb the local audience enjoying the *course taureau*. Under the shade of the plane trees that surround the small sunken arena, the village band plays a familiar Provençal tune, a march that is certainly easy on the ear. The first time I consciously put a name to it was at an orchestral concert, but my reaction was one of recognition: "Oh, *that* old thing." Bizet's *L'Arlésienne*. It is one of those ingratiating tunes that is absorbed without even knowing it—surely a testimonial to its traditional roots—and runs through our heads until we ask, "Now, where the devil does that tune come from?" It is quite possible that I heard it originally in its proper setting in the arena at Arles.

The bull enters the ring, sometimes with a rush but as often at a purposeful trot. Under his wicked glare, nine young men in white, armed only with a comb in one hand, jump into the ring. This is not a *mise à mort*—a fight to the death—but a serious contest of skill and daring. On each lethal horn, the bull sports a little rosette, which one of the men will succeed in picking off with his comb. For a while the men sidle around the animal; then one runs at the bull, feints and passes in an effort to snatch the rosette. The bull charges, swinging its head. When its horns get too close for even a daredevil's comfort, he leaps from the sand onto the high railings that surround the ring, and hangs there while another man gets the beast's attention and distracts it. If the bull does not swerve to face its new enemy, he hurls himself out of harm's way over the barricade that protects the spectators. It must be a close call as to which has the potential for more physical damage, a swipe from the bull or a crash landing against the cement base of the arena.

The bulls themselves have their own particular tactics: one repeatedly pries off a beam from the barrier with its horns, launching it into the air in a satisfying shower of splinters and foam. Another jumps right out of the ring and runs around the inside alley until it is finally driven back with vigorous thwacks of the Camarguais trident. Throughout, the action is accompanied by a breathless play-by-play commentary, invariably exciting some of the younger members of the audience to join the mêlée.

The bull is the link with their land. On a Sunday afternoon in the arena, the animal seems to be the familiar thread that runs forever through life like the custom of going to church. The cowboys whose lives are most tied to it have their own prestigious brotherhood. Its traditions are a celebration of man and the land in the Camargue that goes back to the fifteenth century. The aim of the age-old Confrérie de Saint-Georges, now as then, is "*renforcer la rigueur du travail. Il y a de plus en plus de jeunes parmi les amateurs, et il est important qu'ils apprennent a travailler le plus sérieusement possible.*"[65] Under the banner of St. George—another dragon killer—the brotherhood continues to pursue its mission faithfully: maintaining the way of life of the Camargue.

On the first of May each year, the *gardians* gather to celebrate a ritual mass in Provençal outside the church of Notre Dame de la Major in Arles. Afterwards they lay a bouquet of sea lavender at the foot of the statue of their poet, Frédéric Mistral, before going on to demonstrate their skills in the local version of a rodeo in the old Roman arena. The arena crowns the top of the hill in the center of the town, and all streets lead up to it. A "double tier of sixty arches, as white and vacant as the empty eye-sockets of sixty giant skulls," is how the art historian James Pope-Hennessy described the 2,000-year-old structure when empty. But when it is filled with an expectant audience, the skulls come vibrantly alive as rows of residents and visitors alike line its ancient tiers. Daudet likened it to "a dead language come to life again, having lost its cold scholarly look."[66]

To the music of Provençal pipe and drum, upwards of fifty *gardians*—each astride one of the white horses of the Camargue—file into the ring, as did gladiators 2,000 years ago. Under black moleskin jackets, they wear the patterned shirts of Provence: little diamonds or even bull's heads on a background of solid color, red or yellow or blue. Most of them sport black flat-topped hats like the cowboys they are. Riding pillion behind each *gardian*, one of the famous Arlésienne beauties sits side-saddle to accommodate the long velvet or satin skirt of her traditional attire, her black hair pulled up in a comb and a lace shawl covering her

65 From the local newspaper: "To reinforce the work ethic. There are more and more young men who love this life and it is important that they learn to work as seriously as possible."

66 Daudet, *Numa Roumestan*.

linen bodice. Halting in front of a box where once some Roman legate might have lounged, the *gardians* attend to one more ritual: the swearing-in of the new captain of their *confrérie* and the solemn handing over of their flag by the outgoing leader.

As soon as the ceremony is over, the show begins. In a series of contests, horses race around the arena, their riders dodging and weaving. As much as the expertise of the men, it is a display of the amazing agility of their mounts, bred and trained, like American quarter horses, to turn on a dime, wheel, stop and cut out cattle. The movements are the same as in *White Mane* when the *gardians* tried to capture him, and some of the riders are boys no older than Folco. To start with, several *gardians* on horseback round up a young bull, springing off their horses to wrestle it to the ground. Even when young, the bulls are very aggressive, frequently charging the riders, sometimes getting their horns underneath the horses' bellies. When necessary the Camarguais trident comes in handy to throw an animal; whatever respect these men have for the bull, it does not soften their disposition to it. The priest of Mithras, after all, had no compunction about cutting the bull's throat.

After this demonstration of utilitarian prowess, the *gardians* compete in games that mix equestrian skill with romantic gallantry. A cowboy rides up to another to challenge him, and they go at it, the one trying to steal a bandana from the other's arm. Then in a competition reminiscent of a medieval joust, each *gardian* takes a short lance and runs full gallop toward a small ring suspended in midair, trying to carry it home on its tip. In another game, Arlésienne damsels ring the arena holding plates of oranges, and the horsemen try to snatch one as they gallop past and hurl it into the crowd; this is a surprisingly difficult feat, and today only a twelve-year-old boy manages to complete his circuit without a miss.

The final game contains all the pageantry of the troubadours. Holding a bouquet bestowed by his lady, each cowboy must avoid two of his comrades who race after him trying to steal it. The daring ones taunt their pursuers by dangling the flowers in their faces, and the darting and backing of the horses are amazing to watch. In the end, the gallant presents what is left of her bouquet to his lady, giving her three kisses, which are loudly reproduced on the PA system. If a rival thinks he has stolen a respectable handful of the bouquet in the preceding fracas, he will barge into the "winner's" presentation and disrupt it. And if there is an indisputable champion and his reputation warrants it, he may find himself hounded by an impromptu posse made up of all his comrades.

In between the games, men and women in traditional garb dance the *farandole* to Bizet's music, as if to return to its roots the tune the composer borrowed to color his music for *L'Arlésienne*. The dance is older than the arena itself; in some of the pictures adorning Greek vases, dancers join hands and step its figures just as they still do through the streets of Arles. As I watched I admired again the life of the *gardian* and the satisfaction he must have at the mastery of his craft.

I wondered, too, about the way his character has been shaped by the nature of his land and his heritage. His land has itself been shaped by the needs of the people who have made their lives here, and in this dry land, the greatest need is water. Twenty centuries of human waterworks adorn the landscape still: Roman aqueducts that brought water from the mountains and medieval canals that reached the sea, sixteenth-century irrigation schemes that fertilized the Crau and eighteenth-century flood control projects that made the Camargue as we know it now. Ironically, one made a wild desert into a cultivated plain, the other a breadbasket into a saline flatland.

And his heritage: an ancient Greek dance and the ceremonial games of the Romans; the cult of the bull and the garlands of the troubadours; pagan and Christian saints versus the dragons of devastation, human or natural. For 2,000 years, through good times and bad, the people and the earth have played and fought. Man's dominion is not in any doubt in Provence, but within the folds of the land, history and husbandry have produced a landscape to warm the heart.

The next morning, my last for a while, a full moon is paling well above the horizon as the sun comes up. Over the pastures, the sky is alive as the birds come in to feed: flamingos, ducks, *limicoles*. A coypu, the large muskrat-like immigrant from South America that has successfully carved a niche for itself in many a European fen, swims across the canal. White horses mill around, and as I watch, a young stallion cuts out a new mare and annexes her to his band. A pair of young rivals gallop past, letting each other know who is who, and reminding me of the movie I saw so long ago, even as they force me to move smartly out of their way. As I stroll into the morning, a glorious spring day unfolds, the trees greening, the larks singing. With snow-covered Mont Ventoux in the background, I make a pledge to return to the Camargue. At the same moment three wild boar, *sangliers*, two adults and a young *marcassin* still striped, appear out of a thicket. It seems like a benediction upon my vow.

Epilogue

For the Beauty of the Earth

For the Beauty of the Earth

I've been running through rains
And the winds that follow after
For one certain face
And an unforgotten laughter;
I've been following signs,
I've been searching through lands
For a certain pair of arms
And a certain pair of hands.

I've looked everywhere
That you can look without wings
And I've found a great variety
Of interesting things.

An occasional sunset reminded me,
Or a flower growing high on a tulip tree,
Or one red star hung low in the west,
Or a heartbreak call from the meadowlark's nest
Made me think for a moment: "Maybe it's true —
I've found him in the star, in the call, in the blue!"
But it never was you —
It never was anywhere you —
Anywhere, anywhere you!
—Maxwell Anderson, Knickerbocker Holiday

BREATHING IN, breathing out. Five hundred, maybe a thousand people were breathing in, breathing out. Two steps on the in-breath, two steps on the out. Slowly the procession spread and contracted in the light drizzle like an organism of its own, swaying forward behind the frail figure in his Buddhist monk's habit. Occasionally, the note of the mindfulness bell would call us back to our selves; the body would halt, pause, then sway on again.

It's harder to stick to one's breathing in a parking lot outside Boston than it was in the Malibu Hills. A month earlier, I had spent Easter week there with the Zen master Thich Nhat Hanh and 200 environmental activists. Some were practicing Buddhists; others, like me, were absolute novices. We were there to take time out from the environmental struggle, to recoup and to learn new ways to protect the planet. "Inter-being" and mindfulness are at the heart of Thich Nhat Hanh's teaching. Everything exists in everything else, and therefore our every action has limitless repercussions; inter-being is the spiritual side of chaos theory. Mindfulness through meditation brings body and mind into one "in the present moment," and its practice is based on the most basic human function of all, breathing. "Let the earth nourish and refresh you," he said. "You have only to breathe in and breathe out to have the sun, the moon, the sky, the mountains; to have eyes to see, ears to hear, feet to climb." When I learned that the master would finish his American tour with a day of mindfulness in Boston, I hurried to sign up. As if to make up for the parking lot, Hanh gave us a lovely new *gatha* for the occasion.

"Breathing in, I am a flower; breathing out, I feel fresh." I focused on a maple tree, not a flower. Seen in the gray light of the mist and the town, it was just another maple tree. Breathe in, breathe out: it was no longer so uninteresting. The leaves of its canopy, the bark of its wood, the branching of its trunk: every plane had its own geometry, every surface its kaleidoscope of patterns. Twigs hanging down wove hieroglyphs in the air; the droplets of rain at their tips were fresh, and there was an overwhelming sense of more. . . . *How many little miracles we miss if we only wait for the "meaningful" encounter. To rate the eyes of a weasel over the clock of a dandelion is arbitrary. . . .*

"Breathing in, I am a mountain; breathing out, I feel strong." The patterns now so clear were but the first layer of an onionskin. It would take a lifetime to peel back all the mysteries. I felt I could stay there forever. *. . . No miracle here: seek and ye shall find. Nothing earth-shattering, just a little private revelation. Searching for the spectacular is unnecessary; it is all around us. . . .*

"Breathing in, I am still water; breathing out, I am a reflecting pool." The rain keeps up a steady tempo of expanding circles that join and flow. The pools on the blacktop focus the texture of legs, the color of clothes, the leaves; they float upside down as in a camera obscura. . . . *The surface of the water strips away subjective distractions and penetrates the personal aura that surrounds us all like a smokescreen. . . .*

"Breathing in, I am space; breathing out, I feel free." Down a steep bank and across a wide field, we are finally off the tarmac. Eyes down, and grass is everywhere; eyes up, suburban trees reach for the gray sky. Searching for beauty, searching for meaning, for something unexpected: a twig from the maple tree lies on the grass, its leaves fluttering in the wind that ripped it from the parent tree. . . . *pattern in the leaves and breeze; their delicacy belies the strength they can command. . . .*

Many years before, I had taken a class in outdoor photography. My instructor used his camera as a pathway to finding the natural essence of anything, no matter how mundane. Then, my object was calibrated in terms of the angle, light, distance and relationship with surroundings that would find the artistic order in a chance encounter, turning thing into composition. Through the right combination of these the full expression of anything—an orchid or a dead leaf or even a crumpled cigarette box—would be revealed. Meditation turned out to be a better and deeper way. Instead of striving after an exercise in aesthetics, we were searching for nothing less than transfiguration.

> *Consider the lilies of the field, how they grow; they toil not,*
> *neither do they spin:*

And yet I say unto you, That even Solomon in all his glory was not arrayed like one of these.

As the objects revealed themselves, so nothing was really inanimate. Could a flower reveal itself to a flower? I wondered. Unlikely, but it could reveal itself to me, and leave me feeling that it had done all the work.

❧❦❧

I have searched all my life for a practice that would allow me to celebrate Earth and nature as they deserve, to penetrate their wonders in the least branch, pool or leaf. It is a personal quest for something ecstatic or revelatory, something that will make my cheeks tingle or bring tears of wonder to my eyes. Something like Schubert's "Die Allmacht," which we sang in the school Glee Club when I was in the third or fourth grade. As a hymn to nature that ranges from the terror of the storm to the beauty of the flowers of the field, it is incomparable.

> *Great is Jehovah the Lord. . . .*
> *At his command the trees put forth their opening leaves*
> *And valleys wave bright with golden corn:*
> *With lovely flowers the fields are decked,*
> *And stars in glory fill the vault of heaven.*

We performed it in English, and the heartfelt prayer at the end gives me goose bumps just as it did when I first sang it. I heard it then, and I hear it now as the consummate prayer to Earth.

My personal passion is fired as well by a conviction that a quest into the visceral appeal of nature—and for a way to express it as powerfully as "Die Allmacht"—is of the utmost urgency for the world. Regulations may make us take care of our air and waters and land. But cleansing our psyches is an altogether taller order. Like the search for the White Buffalo, it has no end. It is not a geographical journey; nature is still all around us. Nor is it a quest for the exotic; I remain convinced that nature is found in the best of our species and its works and is especially present in the familiar. Rather it is a treasure hunt like a walk on the beach, hardly aimless wandering and yet even less a methodical search. I am an inveterate beachcomber, the kind of whom Robert Louis Stevenson said, "It is perhaps a more fortunate destiny to have a taste for collecting shells than to be born a millionaire." Given time on a beach, one can abandon oneself, leaving tide and chance and footprints to do the rest. Thus has many a beach rewarded me with its most precious polished stone, "as small as a world and as large as alone."[1] In the same way I have been lucky enough to find a few nuggets that point the way to the numinousness of nature, pleasing and right—at any rate to me. They are like salts I have been adding to a beaker of solution a pinch at a time. One day it will become supersaturated and crystallize. One final molecule, or a speck of dust, and the whole thing will precipitate into a harmonious configuration that I will be able to comprehend.

I am not yet prepared to think of this inquiry as spiritual or sacred or mystical, still less religious, tempting as those adjectives sound. Coupling any one of them with the wonder inspired by Earth is much in vogue, which is a good sign but has led to undiscriminating use that has eroded their full meaning. *Spiritual* is too solemn for the dance of sand along a windy beach, and *sacred* too overused to do justice to the enormous gnarled yew tree beneath whose shade I once sat and which was worshipped by Druids 2,000 years ago. My dictionary defines *mystical* as "having a spiritual meaning or reality that is neither apparent to the senses nor obvious to the intelligence"; what about the physical exultation in the rise of the full moon? Only *religious* carries to me enough weight to embrace so overarching a theme as our relationship to Earth. But it resounds too strongly with our desire for order to be able to do justice to the magnificent chaos of a mountain pass, and appeals too much to a need for hierarchy to be able to appreciate things that ooze.

Perhaps my resistance to such terms is a legacy from that encounter in the Meditation Room in the United Nations building in New York. The space was, after all, set up as a place of meditation beholden to no

---

1 "maggie and millie and molly and may," e. e. cummings.

religion, where delegates could follow their beliefs regardless of creed. How right that the room's single monument should have so forcefully conveyed the power of Earth. Walking into the Meditation Room, one senses the indescribable that lurks behind the day-to-day view of our planet. As I try to penetrate it, the surface of that monumental block of iron ore in its beam of light shimmers in my mind. But Earth itself remains ineffable and remote, not willingly accepting my homage.

Instead I have had to fall back on the intercession of genius as found, for example, in Mahler's Eighth, *The Symphony of a Thousand*. It starts with a colossal rendition of the medieval prayer *Veni Creator Spiritus*, the inspiration for which, according to Mahler's wife, Alma, came to him full-blown in his woodland studio at their retreat in the Alps. "He composed and wrote down the whole opening chorus to the half-forgotten words. But music and words did not fit in—the music had overlapped the text. In a fever of excitement he telegraphed to Vienna and had the whole of the ancient Latin hymn telegraphed back. The complete text fitted the music exactly. Intuitively he had composed the music for the full strophes."

> *Veni, Creator Spiritus*
> *Mentes tuorum visita,*
> *Imple superna gratia,*
> *Quae tu creasti pectora.*[2]

The rest of the work is a setting of the final scene of Goethe's *Faust*. From the rustle, hum and crash of forest, mountain and cataract are distilled the words of the Mystical Choir. *Das Ewig-Weibliche zieht uns hinan.* The Eternal Feminine draws us onward. From the Creator Spirit to the Eternal Feminine, the symphony is an instinctive song of praise to the *Magna Parens*: as reflection of the Divine; as meeting place with the Divine; and as nurture from the Divine. Metaphor, matrix and mother.

A colloquial idiom that embraces something so vast faces a challenge at best, and what we have so far is far from "best." Environmentalists

---

2 Come, Creator Spirit, visit our souls, fill them with grace, Thou that didst create them.

have done a poor job of building a vocabulary commensurate to the importance of their issue. We have nothing that kindles inspiration as did the beautiful language of the King James Bible. Rather we express ourselves in jargon and tired cliché. Not only have we been ignoring an all-important tool in spreading the word, we have been heading in the wrong direction. No self-respecting forest or river wants to be called a *natural resource*. There is more mystery and excitement in a bog than can ever be encompassed by the term *wetland*. How can words so impoverished hope to inspire? Stalest of all is *environment* itself. A dull Latinate word, it leaves us no room for nuance or further shade of meaning, and the sense in which we use it is not even the primary definition of the word. Worse, it has no synonym.

The English language, normally so rich, presents the environmental essayist with an unexpected lacuna. Moreover, our attempts at enriching the lingo are generally impossibly self-conscious (*Gaia*, although I have some sympathy with the ideal), quasi-technical (neither *ecosystem* nor *biodiversity* is ever likely to appeal to a stylist) or hopelessly contrived (*biocentric*—even my computer underlines it in red). This dearth is no piffling matter. Language will avenge itself, said the Austrian polemicist Karl Kraus. How we use or abuse or overuse words counts. When we say, "they fail us," it is more truthfully our imagination that has done the failing.

German, as it happens, has a far better word for *environment* that appropriately sounds as if it came from some mythic past: *Umwelt*, literally "world around." But perhaps we should not be surprised that the notion of "world around" has been so irrelevant or foreign to our thought processes in the past. I was twenty-five before our world saw Earth whole for the first time. Our ancestors calculated that it was round, more or less, and mapped the continents and oceans, the rivers, lakes and mountain ranges. But the spheres on which they drew their findings were icons that spoke mostly of human decisions—national borders, cities, time zones. They were the tool of the discoverer or the empire-builder or the merchant. The view of Earth as our only home that came back from space in 1969 showed us ourselves for the first time: a living planet that we could call beautiful. If 500 years' familiarity with globes took away some of the surprise, the human wonder in the words of the astronauts who had

actually seen it made us start to look at Earth with fresh eyes. It had a different power than the cold monolithic catafalque that had awed me in
the Meditation Room. Our consciousness was altered, and it is no coincidence that the first Earth Day happened just nine months later and
attracted so many. The difference is in what scientists called—and we
had now been able to see—the biosphere, but it has a more venerable
name, nature, the Great Mother.

Nature is our intermediary with Earth, making it physically possible
for us to call the planet our home. CEO-turned-environmentalist Ray
C. Anderson describes Earth's evolution over millions of years with
almost anthropomorphic—if the word can apply to a planet—tender-
ness. "What begins as a very toxic and hostile environment gradually is
detoxified and sweetened as each species, through its metabolic processes, prepares the hostile environment for the next species, and the
next, gradually sweetening Earth's evolving biosphere and preparing the
way for those that preceded us, and for us."[3]

Nature intercedes on our behalf metaphysically as well, insofar as it is
through her manifestations that we approach Earth's unforgiving presence. Never forget that what we do with this now sweetened place makes
little difference to the planet itself. Sometimes I think it is rather like
death. Earth's grandeur is so potentially overpowering that our profound
connection with it needs to be hidden away in order for us to get on with
our lives, with only the occasional glimpse of nature's attraction to affirm
the intimation that it is there and all we have. For all but a few—monks
and artists perhaps—it is more comfortable psychologically to leave the
raw force of nature's presence overshadowed by layers of custom and the
bustle of workaday existence.

In his study of environmental perception,[4] Yi-Fu Tuan quotes Sir
Kenneth Clark of *Civilization* fame: "I fancy that one cannot enjoy a pure
aesthetic sensation for longer than one can enjoy the smell of an orange,

3 *Mid-Course Correction.* Ray Anderson is founder and CEO of Interface, Inc., one of the
world's largest interior furnishings companies. Yes, he uses the proscribed "biosphere," but
"sweetened" makes up for it.

4 *Topophilia: A Study of Environmental Perception, Attitudes and Values.*

which in my case is less than two minutes." Sir Kenneth was speaking of his appreciation of art, but it is no different with experiencing nature. Trying to open up to its light is not unlike the fate of ever-frustrated King Tantalus. Near my home the other morning, the surface of Casco Bay reflected and mixed the pinks and greens of dawn. In the shadow of an island, an occasional ripple picked up the yellow of the sun, and the wake of a pair of ducks, almost invisible themselves, left a momentary arc etched in the glassy water. The beauty of the moment took my breath away, but the sensation was impossible to articulate. Nor, after that initial feeling of wonder, was I able to give such an overwhelming scene its due by enjoying it at length. Hardly had I brought it into focus before the ethereal glimpse of birds and reflections was snatched away, as self-reflecting stimuli muscled their way into my thoughts. Light and color were still there, and just as objectively beautiful, but the pristine moment of revelation, unobstructed by preconception when the sight shone right into my soul, had gone.

Neurologists believe our brains are wired so that repeated exposure to an experience or image leads to habituation or reduced response. At the same time, our minds leap to intellectual activity rather than contemplation, and I find it impossible to decide whether it is the cause of this emotional theft or an attempt to mitigate it. As I contemplated the scene that morning, the ducks I saw did more than provide a graceful detail; my awareness of habits, even the act of identifying them (they were black ducks), quickly took over. It was a way to hold on to that fleeting moment. And as I admired it and marveled at its complexity, the image ripened into a glorious memory to be stored in the mind's eye. In about Sir Kenneth's two minutes, I had come full circle.

What I experience in workaday mode as the gradual blocking out of nature by the overlays of an increasingly busy world, Jungian psychology explains as the inevitable separation from nature in the development of human consciousness. A man born 200,000 years ago scarcely distinguished himself from the world around him (the Umwelt). To the extent that he did, it was instinctual based on biological signals, a growling belly or a rush of adrenaline as he lived the life alternately of predator and prey. Otherwise he was one with the elements, sensing changes in his environment, be it a coming storm or the approach of a pack of animals, intuitively as if they were all but features of a single organism. "He fed with the gazelles on grass; with the wild animals he drank at waterholes; with hurrying animals his heart grew light in the waters." So is Enkidu, the "man-as-he-was-in-the-beginning," described—around the third millennium B.Ç., remarkably early in the Rise of the Ego stage when the bond with nature had been finally broken—in the Epic of Gilgamesh.[5]

It was only a hundred thousand years before Gilgamesh was written that the separation from nature had got well under way. The Neanderthals needed ritual, probably honoring the dead with burial and perhaps even decorating the pits with pebbles and flowers. Another 50,000 years or so and the Cro-Magnons had an objective enough idea of their surroundings to become our species' first artists. The animals with which they decorated the walls of caves like Lascaux, Altamira and Chauvet give a clue to the web of magic these early people felt they needed in order to control the unpredictable caprices of nature. My friend Walter Christie, a Jungian psychiatrist, characterizes this stage as "exhilarated by the new magic and conscious enough to recognize a specific relationship with the Great Surround and make rituals in worship of it, but terrified that a small slip will result in eternal pain, for the moment lasts forever."

Some time during the next 40,000 years, *Homo sapiens* gave up its nomadic ways in favor of agriculture and settlement. A complex system of myths and taboos must have been necessary to protect the clan's villages and fields. Recognizable wants and fears—a good hunt or a period of drought—were reflected in a world of portents in nature or the heavens that came to be personified in the Great Goddess. During this time, from about 15,000 to 1500 B.C., in Walter's words, "Nature becomes the repository of all the warring impulses within the human psyche." And of the same period, historian Riane Eisler writes, "Religion was life, and life was religion."[6]

The recent discovery at the bottom of the Black Sea of a settlement that was inundated 7,000 years ago suggests the event that has come

5 *Gilgamesh*, translated by John Gardner and John Maier.
6 *The Chalice and the Blade*.

down to us as the biblical Flood. Scientists say the Mediterranean broke its banks and turned a freshwater lake into a saltwater sea almost overnight. The water may have advanced fast enough to widen the surface of the lake by as much as a mile a day. I cannot help wondering if it might have been a natural catastrophe such as this that gave the final push to a people hovering on the edge to complete its separation from the Great Goddess. All of their myths and taboos had been for naught.

The Gospel According to St. John tells us, "In the beginning was the word," and in the word, man demonstrated that the divorce from nature was complete. Whoever wrote the Epic of Gilgamesh 5,000 years ago, with its theme of the fear of inevitable death and the quest for immortality, had an Ego that was no longer absorbed in the Great Surround. Not only is the story a literary milestone in the progress of thought towards the written—and therefore potentially immortal—idea. In it we find a hazarded explanation of whence we came and how we were civilized. Enkidu is brought out of his wild state by sexual seduction. At the end of six days and seven nights with the priestess,

> . . .Enkidu was glutted on her richness
> he set his face toward his animals.
> Seeing him, Enkidu, the gazelles scattered wheeling:
> The beasts of the wilderness fled from his body.
> Enkidu tried to rise up, but his body pulled back.
> His knees froze. His animals had turned from him.
> Enkidu grew weak; he could not gallop as before.
> Yet he had knowledge, wider mind.

"Wider mind" is where we are now. "Knowledge" has been gathering like an insulating blanket of snow since our hunter-gatherer ancestors first started to put down roots and lay the foundations for our great civilizations. We have done away with mystery. We think, therefore we are. Nature, which used to abound with gods, is now scientifically measurable, and we have realized at least part of that ancient biblical bequest, "dominion" over it. But we are playing with fire.

The truth is that pollution and the irreversible changes we wreak on *our* environment are *our* problem, not the planet's. Earth watched impassively eons ago as the toxic chemicals that we are now digging up[7] were buried out of harm's way in the lithosphere; it stood by as the biosphere that we are now disrupting was organized; it shed never a tear for the mass extinctions of creatures that for a while its bounty supported. Writes Victor Rozek, "Ours is a planet without conscience or regret. It simply doesn't care whether it is populated by dinosaurs, cockroaches, humans, or three-headed trylobites." With or without us, Earth will continue on its axis unmoved, like the oak tree that silently engulfs the strand of barbed wire wound too tightly around it. And as the wire once encased inside the living wood rusts slowly away, so will the monuments to our folly last awhile in the geological strata until they are finally broken up or crushed by tectonic forces. *Sic transit gloria mundi.* To me, this is despair.

Some speak with Malthusian equanimity of the threat of disease or other catastrophic natural counterattack that might bring our species back into line with Earth's ability to sustain us. Others, with lofty detachment, take the "long view": Earth will survive whatever we do, say some extraordinary rationalists, so in the end it doesn't matter if we pave nature over. Fundamentalists take using up Earth's bounty as an obligation, although presumably it ceases to exist after Judgement Day. I can only describe these points of view as dangerous heresy. They lead to a couple of equally awful scenarios. Either our species struggles on in a concrete landscape from which all but the hardiest opportunists have been driven; we are left alone in a world of urban animals, where a squirrel may be the closest we get to a wild thing. Or our species succumbs—one can imagine any number of self-inflicted deaths—leaving nature to start again amid our collapsing roads and constructions. I recall the special melancholy of a pair of Danish tombs in a forest clearing in the Virgin Islands. That a member of the species that built them could bear witness to their losing struggle for immortality against the promiscuous forest redeemed them. How terrible those monuments would have been in a world bereft of human fellow-feeling.

---

7 One of the Hopi prophecies chanted in the film *Koyaanisqatsi* says, "If we dig precious things from the land, we will invite disaster."

In either scenario, the coup de grâce will have been the heartbreak of a species deprived of the comfort of the forests and savannas that spawned it and the wonder of the oceans and high places to which it always aspired. Keeping nature to be inspired by is every bit as critical to our species' survival as are clean air and water. The evidence that we must do so is all about us, and the consequences of failure are clear to anyone who has a mind to see: the fulfillment of the macabre nursery rhyme that ends T. S. Eliot's poem "The Hollow Men." "This is the way the world ends, / not with a bang but a whimper."

I am too selfish to go along with such despairing nihilism. Into my head comes the music of Brünnhilde's acceptance of all-knowledge as she prepares to redeem the world.

> *Weiss ich nun, was dir frommt?*
> *Alles! Alles!*
> *Alles weiss ich:*
> *alles ward mir nun frei!*[8]

It is the finale of *Götterdämmerung*. Her new wisdom combined with love allows her to reconcile man and nature, which she does by immolating herself, the old gods and the earth, and purifying the Ring, the symbol of adulterated nature whose curse has brought them all to moral ruin. This she bequeaths to the Rhine-maidens, who are pure nature. There have been many interpretations of Wagner's *Ring*, but for me the Jungian one of development from animal innocence to human consciousness and finally to renewal and reconciliation with nature holds most consistently true. Brünnhilde's act in the final moments of *The Ring* is a powerful symbol of the resolution we now need, although it must be less catastrophic to do us any good.

Wagner portrayed the reconciliation of nature and wisdom as redemption more forgivingly in his Grail myth, *Parsifal.*[9] The poem makes it abundantly clear that Parsifal, the Holy Fool, represents "unciv-

---

8 Have I learned all that avails thee? / All things, / all now I know: / all is clear to me!

9 Coming from a Christian background, I find it easy to slip into thinking about the

ilized" nature. Like the earliest humans, he feels nothing for anything but his immediate needs. He is on an aimless quest to better himself, having once seen a troop of knights in the forest, but his wanderings have only made him more like a wild animal without sense of good and bad. The Knights of the Grail, on the other hand, have lost their purpose having lost the sacred Spear. To get it back for them, Parsifal must first develop consciousness. This he learns from the seductress Kundry, whose kiss makes him feel the pain of his mother's grief for the first time.[10] At that moment he is overwhelmed with fear and sorrow, but his "nature" sees him through, and when the wizard Klingsor throws the Spear at him, he catches it and makes the sign of the Cross:[11]

Mit diesen Zeichen bann' ich deinen Zauber:
Wie die Wunde er schliesse,
die mit ihm du schlugest,
in Trauer und Trümmer
sturz' er die trügende Pracht![12]

The symbolism is, of course, Christian, but the image of the closing wound can be seen as an environmental metaphor, too. At the end of Act II, Parsifal has his personal enlightenment. The Third Act sees it become universal. Interestingly, it is Gurnemanz, a representative of the "civilized" order, who understands the significance of the reconciliation in the most beautiful passage in the whole four-hour-plus opera, the

---

development of planetary consciousness in terms of redemption. It is a template that I am culturally disposed to understand.

10 As with Enkidu, seduction is the key, although Parsifal's answer is abstention.

11 I saw Wieland Wagner's production of *Parsifal* at Bayreuth in the mid-'60s. In the program he sketched out "Ein psychologisches Schema" in the form of a cross of which Kundry's kiss formed the center. The main stem traces Parsifal's development from unity with his mother symbolized by the swan to his—and the Grail Knights'—salvation symbolized by the dove. It starts with The Mother (Der ewig weibliche Urgrund) and "Die leidende Natur weint über Parsifals Fortlaufen" representing "Das Gute," and ends with The Savior and "Der leidende Gott weint ob der Menschheit Schmach," "Das Göttliche."

12 With this sign I rout your enchantment. / As the Spear closes the wound / which you dealt him with it, / into mourning and ruin / may it crush your lying splendor!

Good Friday Spell. If the text is heavy with Christian dogma, the music that accompanies it is all nature.

> *Das merkt nun Halm und Blume auf dem Auen,*
> *dass heut das Menschen Fuss sie nicht zertritt . . .* [13]

In order to revel in this beautiful place, we had to grow, like Parsifal, apart from it. As in any experiment, the results were unpredictable, and as in any evolution, trade-offs were made and wrong turns taken. We wandered and made our own mistakes. But our divorce from the natural world allowed us to acquire wisdom. Now our task is to resuscitate our ancient identification with nature and allow it to inform us. Only then will we be able to close the rift between man and Earth and heal the wounds we have inflicted on nature. It won't happen by itself. The second renaissance will not arrive by simply wallowing in the warm bath of New Age muddle and feel-good confections that pass themselves off as a spiritual approach to nature. It will take discipline. The job ahead will be akin to that of the New England farmer grafting a young scion onto an old apple stock. It will take the puritan's intellect as well as the husbandman's craft to make the graft and have it take hold. If the graft were successful, the fruit would be nothing less, in Judeo-Christian terms, than a return to the Garden of Eden.

I have as unabashed a belief in humanity's central position in the web of life as any fundamentalist. When all is said and done, every manifestation of nature is a gemstone in the rough waiting to be polished by an appreciation of its beauty, and only we have that gift. However relatively short a period *Homo sapiens* still has to be let loose on the earth—on the scale of the biblical six days of Creation, we have had hardly a second so far—this is the "quality time," or should be. I want me and my genes to be a part of it.

Where we differ fundamentally—the fundamentalist and I—is in our conclusions and especially our perceived responsibilities. Joseph Conrad

---

13 Now grasses and flowers in the meadow know / that today the foot of man will not tread them down. . . .

wrote of our responsibility to what he called "the sublime spectacle" the best part of a century ago: ". . . the unwearied self-forgetful attention to every phase of the living universe reflected in our consciousness may be our appointed task on this earth—a task in which fate has perhaps engaged nothing of us except our conscience, gifted with a voice in order to bear true testimony to the visible wonder, the haunting terror, the infinite passion, and the illimitable serenity; to the supreme law and the abiding mystery of the sublime spectacle."[14] Without us, with only an infinite span of eras devoid of beings capable of appreciating the whole glorious jumble, what would "the sublime spectacle" matter? But we are here, and it does matter, and it is our job to take care of every creature.

As far as we know, we are unique in our ability to appreciate beauty and to elevate a sense of the aesthetic to divine heights. We need this gift in order to be human. And if we need the gift of appreciation to be human, nature needs us to celebrate it if nature and we are to survive together. I once had a spirited conversation with Dodge Morgan, a naturalized Mainer who sailed alone around the world, driven in part I am sure by a deep-seated urge to pursue the question of our rightful attitude to nature. I made the claim that nature was too beautiful not to have an audience, and that therefore not only was our rapture necessary, but without it the value of nature could not be fully realized. He countered my argument with the experiences of his voyage. "I have seen an albatross in the Southern Oceans, perfectly beautiful," he wrote to me later, "which perhaps no other man will ever see and [I] cannot understand the view that the bird exists simply for my pleasure." How could I propose so profligate a margin of aesthetics? I found myself replying that the albatross as a thing of grace and beauty had existed only while it was in his view. Before and after, the bird was an aerodynamic machine, handily adapted to its environment. But the revelation of its flight as a stupendous work of art, the satisfaction of seeing it at one with waves and wind, the awe at sharing the empty sea with only such a creature: these were emotions that the bird never knew it could produce based on

14 *A Personal Record.*

qualities it didn't know it possessed. Without the eye or ear (or con-science) of Homo sapiens, these qualities would not exist. If only it were not so!

Environmental organizations, just like most of the Western world, find such metaphysics hard to tackle. For the most part we have evolved as players in the legal and economic system addressing direct causes and effects. A river is polluted; we seek to identify who is doing it with what and then try to stop them. To ask a value-laden question such as how someone could turn clear water into crud calls for a wider frame of refer-ence that we as yet have few ways of even defining. While we may talk about them sincerely, the truth is that we are uncomfortable in dealing with values. This reluctance leaves us ill equipped to try to change deep-seated articles of faith. That has been the traditional place of religion. When environmentalists don priests' or shamans' robes, the world gen-erally views us with the same skepticism with which I viewed an Angli-can priest who held a "communion" service with bread and water, the words of the prayer book appropriately changed to reflect Earth as the deity. It was in the course of a discussion group on "spirit and nature" made up of doctors and environmental educators, as well as the clergy. We used to meet early in the morning, and each member of the group would take turns in opening our discussion with a poem or a reading of some appropriate text. It was not the paltering with the liturgy that dis-turbed me, although I could have made a case that it was blasphemous. It was rather the notion that one could simply take one ritual with a 2,000-year tradition and plunk it down on another willy-nilly that I found so wrongheaded. I am not convinced that the search for a way to give Earth and nature the honor they deserve will be successful through religious ritual, but if it should be, it will have to develop its own cere-monies based on its own values.

A couple of years ago, the local paper quoted a farmer taking issue with his town's wetland protection efforts as saying, "God made the earth for us, not us for the earth." The farmer's complaint is the incarnation of one side of a struggle over our natural heritage that has reached a crescendo in the last fifty years: the benefits of valuing it for its own sake versus the profits of exploitation. Paradoxically, as both "sides" come closer together in crafting a shared vision of environmental health, nothing stands out so much as the profound difference between the parallel visions of an emotionally nurturing landscape and ecologically sustainable development. One looks beyond protection towards restoration and reunion; the other aims to reduce environmental damage enough to prevent a total collapse of the system while we benefit materially from nature. We need both.

Of the two, sustainable development is enjoying a clear advantage. Values are infinitely more difficult to approach than pollution, even in parts per trillion. Public policy needs to be measured in terms whose importance is familiar: jobs, health and standard of living. They are the immediate currency of calculating the conflicting needs of six billion people. A night sky lit only by moon and stars, the loneliness of an empty beach, a field or orchard tended with love: these have a value that is beyond numbers, and so they are inevitably forgotten. Vitally important though it is in the practical day-to-day containment of the environmental crisis, sustainable development cannot be an end in itself because it addresses price, not value, and the heart is left out of the picture. Conservation must be "carried like music in the heart of people," wrote Edward Wolf. "The challenge is much more visceral than rational."[15] He was referring to people in the tropics. Closer to home, as president of Massachusetts Audubon, Jerry Bertrand made the same point when he said, "Effective conservation action must first be an affair of the head, but when it becomes an affair of the heart—that's when things really get moving." Our view of the blessings that nature showers upon us will remain dangerously narrow, the case for them dangerously weak, until the priceless and the priced stand on equal ground.

I am confident that Homo sapiens has the brains to find its way out of its present pass, but it is the capacity to carry nature like music in the heart that is the question. We have allowed the strength of valuing the earth in our hearts to atrophy along each step of the march to civilization. That said, we have no alternative but hope. (I cannot say optimism

15 "Arousing Biophilia," Orion Nature Quarterly, Winter 1989.

because the task of restoring the planet is, like its age, simply too huge to contemplate.) We are a hopeful species that looks to the light. We celebrate the winter solstice as a return to life, despite the terrors of the dark, but midsummer as the high noon of the year, not the beginning of the descent into death. Just as saving a fish left behind by the tide one long-ago evening bolstered my hope that the world could be spared a nuclear war, my contemplation of a wood leafing out in the spring sunshine annually restores it, as does the first snap of fall in the New England air. We have proved that we are superlatively good at turning our brains to destruction, and we might yet prove that we are even better at loving. But we need to find the will to turn back from our current path and "forswear our foolish ways," as the hymn goes.

Finding our way back to nature will involve making peace with the very branches of knowledge that brought us to this pass. With qualitative religion that encouraged us to dominate it; with quantitative science that tried to take away its mystery; and with philosophy that presided over our alienation from it, "The I-thou relation . . . destroyed to become the I-it," in the words of Islamic studies professor Seyyed Hossein Nasr.[16] It will be the most challenging and fascinating task for any environmentalist today.

Christian belief, if not religion itself, has found nature hard to deal with since the monks drove away the Mother Goddess. In the Old Testament, God gave man "dominion over the fish of the sea, and over the fowl of the air, and over every living thing that moveth upon the earth," and told Adam to "subdue" the land. But first he bade him "replenish" it. Over the course of two millennia, we have reaped the benefits of dominion and subduing, but have paid considerably less attention to replenishment. Above all, "God saw every thing that he had made, and behold, it was very good." If He was that gratified by His efforts, Genesis starts with an implicit assumption that should direct all believers to keep His creation whole. The Catholic theologian-environmentalist Thomas Berry has applied this assumption to our times in no uncertain terms.

16 *Man and Nature: The Spiritual Crisis of Modern Man.*

"We lose even the sacraments as we lose the natural world. If the water is polluted it cannot properly be used for Baptism since it is a sign of death rather than life. If our bread is denatured or contaminated with chemicals, it is to that extent inappropriate for celebration of the Eucharist." Whether we see our species as the crowning achievement of a Supreme Being or as having achieved this distinction by pulling ourselves up by our own evolutionary bootstraps, our obligation is to take care of the rest of life on Earth.

While applauding the spirit of the Romantics that rebelled against the materialization of nature in the nineteenth century, Nasr observes that it was more sentimental than intellectual. It is in a similar vein, especially in reaction to the effortless bonhomie of the New Age, that I find the rigor science can bring to bear the most convincing and comforting, like the back of a solid chair. At the beginning of her book *The Sacred Depths of Nature*, biology professor Dr. Ursula Goodenough introduces a reassuring point of view on this as she wonders at her own presumed lack of religious feeling: "What is being religious anyhow? What about the way I feel when I think about how cells work or creatures evolve? Doesn't that feel the same as when I'm listening to the St. Matthew Passion or standing in the nave of the Notre Dame Cathedral?" Dante called nature "the art of God."

At a conference that I attended on "The Good in Nature and Humanity," Dr. Goodenough told us that it is not enough to appreciate nature; "we must understand it to the marrow of our bones." Taking a tree for her example, she said that we have an obligation to understand how it works. How could we possibly appreciate its beauty fully without doing so? How could it be "not interesting?" she asked. She went on to suggest that resistance to scientific explanation often comes from the gut, a fear that it will reduce the impact of nature's beauty. We fear losing the spiritual moment and "wrecking the experience." I thought about my own conclusion that, as with the smell of an orange, I needed some form of intellectual stimulus to prolong the experience of aesthetic appreciation. Dr. Goodenough put it in perspective for me. She called scientific understanding a "glorious narrative," and illustrated her point by stating that we humans share 47 percent of the same genes as yeast, and 74 percent with a worm, which is fairly mind-bending to think about. "We must acknowledge nature's nature, and give her her due respect." Or, to condense her message into two words, witness and wonder. In the right hands, wonder is robust enough to survive its transformation into knowledge. Indeed, that is its logical pathway.

At the same conference, Gus Speth, a veteran at the center of the environmental movement in the United States, welcomed the participants. "What we have learned, after thirty years," he said, "is that the most important resource is human motivation—our hope, our caring, our feelings about nature and our fellow humans. In the end that is what will save us and sustain the world. . . . So put the lobbyists and litigators on hold for a while, and bring on the philosophers, the psychologists, the preachers, and the poets!"

In her lovely meditation on the Maine woods, my friend Nan Waldron watched a dragonfly and mused, "As a creature of earth do I have signals deep within? I cannot fly, my talent is to contemplate flight. But I wonder too if I might have gossamer wings already in place waiting to unfold—twin talents of insight and intuition."[17] If, as I believe, salvation will come first and foremost from rediscovered values rather than technology, insight and intuition are important. A Jungian might say that we gained our individuality at the cost of cutting ourselves off from our being's instinctive connection with nature, but in truth it has more likely only been banished. Our psyches are riddled with fragments of the old magic. Whose expectations are not improved by a splendid sunrise? Who doesn't believe in myriad little superstitions—that making a traffic light before it turns yellow on the way to work is a good sign for the rest of the day? And just as strands of magic survive in our daily lives, wonder, even if tarnished or uncared for, survives somewhere in all of us. As remnants of our undifferentiated past, insight and intuition are lying in wait for a general uprising like the Rhine-maidens waiting for Brünnhilde's ring, an invitation to work back to the stage of human consciousness before the rise of the Ego.

17 *North Woods Walkabout.*

Cut off or banished, it happened at the point in our prehistory when we opted for agriculture and settled existence rather than nomadic hunting and gathering. Assuming that the development of our consciousness as a species is reflected ontogenetically in the development of the individual mind, we should give special attention to children at the stage in their lives that shares the most with our prehistoric ancestors, the earliest school grades. Rachel Carson was fully aware of its transitory nature when she wrote, "A child's world is fresh and new and beautiful, full of wonder and excitement. It is our misfortune that for most of us that clear-eyed vision, that true instinct for what is beautiful and awe-inspiring, is dimmed and even lost before we reach adulthood." Her wish was that the good fairy bestow "a sense of wonder" on each child to last a lifetime. More practically, she went on, "The years of childhood are the time to prepare the soil. Once the emotions have been aroused—a sense of the beautiful, the excitement of the new and the unknown, a feeling of sympathy, pity, admiration or love—then we wish for knowledge about the object of our emotional response. Once found, it has lasting meaning."

Rachel Carson's reference to preparing the soil made me think that making peace with lowly things would be a symbolic step towards reconnecting with nature. Somewhere along the line, our capacity for aesthetic appreciation became overrarified. We sing, "All things bright and beautiful, / all creatures great and small," in praise of nature as God's handiwork. But stuff that is essential to the orderly workings of nature—the smelly, necessary harbingers of decay as well as the critters in which we see no redeeming value—we vilified and banished from civilized society. It is time to make amends and join Monty Python in their version of the same hymn: "All things scabbed and ulcerous, / All pox both great and small, / Putrid, foul and gangrenous, / The Lord God made them all."

One day I accompanied a group of children on a nature walk around Scarborough Marsh, Maine's most impressive salt marsh. As we tramped through the spartina, the teacher would stop to pick up objects of interest and discuss them with the kids.

"Do you know what this is?" she asked. "It's poop. We call it scat," she went on reassuringly, crumbling the dry material in her hands. "Scat's interesting because it tells a story. You can tell that an animal stopped here and what it ate. Do you know what kind of animal it was?" Several kids volunteered different ideas until someone guessed it was a muskrat. A little later, we were picking through lumps of algae, and one of the children asked about some pink stuff embedded in it. Our guide was delighted. "That's bacteria," she said. "You know that egg-farty smell you get in a marsh? That's what causes it. If you smell that smell, you know the marsh is healthy. Mm, mm, good," she added with satisfaction.

What struck me about these scatological references was the entirely natural way this basic knowledge was imparted to the children and how quickly they got over their initial titters. It was quite different when I was in third grade. I am sure I had never heard an adult utter the word *fart*, still less a teacher. However venerable the word's Anglo-Saxon heritage, the Oxford English Dictionary calls it vulgar. As the teacher knelt down talking casually about natural functions and smells, I had a brief image of my grandmother hovering over her saying, "Don't be vulgar, dear."

This seemingly insignificant change in attitude is a little shift towards the values we need if we are ever to live in harmony with the natural world again. Decay and bad smells are as much a part of nature as the scent of lily of the valley; they just appear at different points around the wheel of life. By ignoring them when we contemplate beauty, we effectively transform a cycle into a linear event; a process that constantly renews itself as it goes round becomes instead one with a beginning and an end. Being able to sense this continuity by sight or smell is a step towards getting back into the cycle. Making a personal connection with it—owning it—is the next step. We all create waste. Getting over the taboos of talking about it is in its own small way a milestone.

Looking through the other end of the ontological telescope, could we as a species have reached a place in our journey analogous to middle age, when, psychologists believe, we tend to open ourselves to intuition and "connectedness?" Intuitively, I think of the passion for gardening I and so many of my friends have developed at this stage in our lives: a desire to be *connected* with the earth and a cycle that may outlive us, made real by the dirt under our fingernails. Today, there are signs—the rise of the

environmental movement is but one of them—that the world collec-
tively has reached middle age and is ready to connect again with the
stream of nature. We do not have much time to apply the wisdom our
journey has taught us and reconcile it with the web of life once more. We
need to harness it with our other abilities and bind them into our intrinsic beliefs before our excesses set up their own runaway reaction and
bring us down.

We have a double duty: besides tending the "sense of wonder" like a
garden and reviving it where it has become parched, we need to ensure
that there is still something left to inspire it. Almost fifty years ago,
Rachel Carson was searching for "an unfailing antidote against the boredom and disenchantments of later years, the sterile preoccupation with
things that are artificial, the alienation from the source of our strength."
As a larger and larger proportion of the population grows up in a city, and
as the cities themselves overwhelm the open space around them, landscape that could nurture a sense of wonder is diminishing and slipping
ever further over the horizon. Not only are we losing ready access to the
woods and rivers and fields, but what is left is also being compromised,
even the special places. When I was a child, my greatest dream was to
visit the Grand Canyon. It is still a treat I have in store, although I am
told that the air is not so clear as it would have been back then, making
the colors more subdued.

Finding that nature's comfort has been driven from a place I once
knew comes as a rude shock. I think of Stonehenge, where we used to
play as children, not natural, perhaps, but in its prehistoric eloquence
still close to it, the high-water mark of a society still struggling to be
apart from nature. Today our games are a thing of the past. Stonehenge
is surrounded by a chain-link fence, and the magic circle is covered with
an asphalt path. How much magic could be left? I think of Amberley,
where the green velvet of the South Downs now has the look of a threadbare rug and a once dingly dell is gouged by motorbike tracks. There is a
special pain at such a loss.

If loss of place is pain, loss of species is nothing less than guilt. In his
extraordinary environmental novel, *Ishmael,* Daniel Quinn codifies a
golden rule of planetary survival: "You may compete to the full extent of

your capabilities, but you may not hunt down your competitors or destroy their food or deny them access to food. In other words, you may compete but you may not wage war." Being the sentient as well as dominant species has conferred upon us an additional ethical burden: responsibility. Despite this, we have broken all of Ishmael's taboos. Whether or not we have the right to decide the fate of the 30 million (or however many there are; we have nowhere near identified them all) other species with which we share the Earth, we have taken their fate in our hands. The question we are left to confront is whether we have the right to cause their extinction, and the answer to that is clearly "No!"

But another issue floats like a submerged log through the selfish humanist's argument: What would it be like never to know consciously what one was missing? Einstein said that "the joy of looking and comprehending is nature's most beautiful gift." Away from the complexities and spectacles of nature, what would happen to curiosity and creativity? In his opening remarks at the Good in Nature conference, Gus Speth quoted from a poem by W. S. Merwin: "I want to tell you what the forests were like / I will have to speak in a forgotten language." How mournful the poet's "forgotten language" sounds. We need to get all our kids into the out-of-doors and teach them how to watch and be while there is still time. Important as it may be to promulgate rules to save species and build barriers to preserve places, the struggle will be won "in the heart of people."

The knowledge of our natural systems that we have acquired, paltry as it may be, can also be transformed into wonder. But the gap between that wonder (how close we are to the earthworm and how far we have come) and adequately expressing it (beyond a percentage sign) is fearsome, beyond those group discussions that so easily degenerate into feel-good show-and-tell that I can only liken to self-gratification. When I was still at University, I saw a performance of Schoenberg's twelve-tone masterpiece *Moses and Aaron* at the Royal Opera, Covent Garden conducted by Maestro Solti. The opera, never finished, personifies the struggle between the idea and the word; Schoenberg composed Moses' lines to be spoken rather than sung to heighten the conflict of delving into the "inexpressible." I will never forget Forbes Robinson as Moses sinking to the stage at the end of the evening, horrified at the way the "Inexpressible, many-sided idea" of the infinite had been translated into images and idols. Nor the cadence of his final exclamation of despair, "O Wort, du Wort, das mir fehlt!"[18]

Regarding this inadequacy of words, Robert Donington writes that it is left to poetry and music to "call up feelings by the indirect but powerful workings of association. . . . Poetry . . . never explains; it simply presents images, trusting these images to do their own work on our imagination."[19] Where Mahler's Eighth hails the crushing majesty of terrestrial forces, it is the sensuous caress of nature that breathes out of the Song of Songs:

> *The flowers appear on the earth;*
> *the time of the singing of birds is*
> *come, and the voice of the turtle*
> *is heard in our land;*
> *The fig tree putteth forth her green*
> *figs, and the vines with the tender*
> *grape give a good smell. Arise, my*
> *love, my fair one, and come away.*

Neither appeal is readily described, nor can the source of its power be explained in rational terms.

One attempt to make science the touchstone for wonder in a poem is Robert Frost's "Choose Something Like a Star." I first encountered it in a Unitarian Church choir, set to the music of Randall Thompson. Commanding the star to reveal itself, the poet (and the composer) allows wonder and witness to play in a counterpoint of associations. From wonder—his star is "the fairest one in sight"—the poet descends to witness in the language of the laboratory:

18 "O word, thou word, that I lack!" That Schoenberg should have been unable to resolve this dilemma over the next twenty years of his life cannot help but strike me as telling, notwithstanding the difficulties he experienced as a refugee from Nazi Germany and in his later years from declining health.

19 At the beginning of his analysis of Wagner's *Ring*.

Say something to us we can learn
By heart and when alone repeat.
Say something! And it says "I burn."
But say with what degree of heat.
Talk Fahrenheit, talk Centigrade.
Use language we can comprehend.
Tell us what elements you blend.
It gives us strangely little aid,
But does tell something in the end.[20]

before being pulled back, almost resentfully it seems, into the star's glory:

Not even stooping from its sphere,
It asks a little of us here.
It asks of us a certain height . . .

To complete the circle of our separation and reconciliation, nature will "ask of us a certain height."

I started this Epilogue saying it was the tale of a quest. As I have put it down in writing, the exercise of making sense of my beachcomber's "polished stones" has turned out to have been more than a literary one. One night, after days of wrestling with the layers that separate conscious appreciation of nature from subconscious devotion, I dreamed I was in a crowded room and wanted to remove my clothes. Nothing seemed more natural, and then I was walking down an equally crowded street stark naked, not knowing how or whether to cover myself again. Next morning when I went running in the woods, the awe they inspired was harsher, less radiant with reflected joy; and the serried ranks of trees seemed bent on underlining my insignificance. It was as if they had rebuffed my

20 "Choose Something Like a Star."

feeble effort to approach them on their own turf. "It asks of us a certain height. . . ."

Ten thousand or so years, billions of men and women and who knows how many life-enhancing inventions later, our mental shield against nature's powerful splendor is a luxury we can no longer afford. The determination of how we mutually survive lies in the personal relationship each one of us has with our environment. Learning humility and respect anew is indispensable, whether we ascribe its wonder to a divine hand or feel its beautiful complexity to be awe-inspiring in itself.

If our quest for knowledge to "tell something in the end" is to help change our view, we must find a way to express our link to Earth in simple everyday terms, not just relying on the poets and meditation. If "the word" may have sealed the break with nature, it must also be pressed into service to cement a new bond with our roots. Just as something as common as breathing was the key to meditation, the language we use in our daily lives must be summoned to our aid. If I cannot do justice in words to what I sense, how can I investigate those feelings further, let alone share them abroad?

To become truly part of our culture, name and action have to evolve organically in tandem. On the linguistic evidence alone, we have had to invent the concept of "environment" and impose it on our lives full-blown. Therefore, by definition, a more convincing alternative cannot be pulled from a hat. But I would suggest some areas where a search might prove fruitful. I would give high marks to any word whose root had only one syllable. Given that I speak English, an Anglo-Saxon word would be preferable, and its connotations should be as broad as the horizon and as ancient as evolution. Could it be that the word is *Earth*? Earthly issues? Earthly quality? I submit that the word *Earth* provides an infinitely richer vein for inspiration than *environment*. It's not an original thought. After all, the rallying event that launched the environmental movement was called "Earth Day." Simpler than Schubert, four-square as the old organ in the church in Amberley where I first heard it as a child, the old hymn still says it all:

For the beauty of the earth,
For the beauty of the skies,
For the love which from our birth,
Over and around us lies,
Lord of all to thee we raise
This our hymn of grateful praise.

For the beauty of each hour
Of the day and of the night,
Hill and veil and tree and flower,
Sun and moon, and stars of light,
Lord of all, to thee we raise
This our hymn of grateful praise.

For the joy of ear and eye,
For the heart and mind's delight,
For the mystic harmony
Linking sense to sound and sight,
Lord of all, to thee we raise
This our hymn of grateful praise.

Amen

Bibliography

Prologue

Rachel Carson, *The Sense of Wonder*, New York and Evanston: Harper & Row, 1956

Johann Wolfgang von Goethe quoted on p. 80 of Theodore Schwenk, *Sensitive Chaos*, translated by O. Whicher and J. Wrigley, London: Rudolf Steiner Press, 1965

Richard Jefferies, *The Gamekeeper at Home*, London: Smith, Elder, 1914

Rudyard Kipling, "The Roman Centurion Speaks," Poems from History, in *The Writings in Prose and Verse of Rudyard Kipling*, New York: Charles Scribner's Sons, 1925

John Masefield, "Up on the Downs," *The Penguin Book of English Verse*, Harmondsworth: Penguin, 1956

Kenneth Newman, *Newman's Birds of Southern Africa*, Macmillan South Africa, 1983

T. H. White, *England Have My Bones*, New York: G. P. Putnam's Sons, 1936

Home

Richard Barringer, Editor, *Toward a Sustainable Maine*, Portland: Edmund S. Muskie Institute for Public Affairs, University of Southern Maine, 1993

Béla Bartók, "Folk Music, Haydn, and Beethoven," *The Music Lover's Handbook*, edited by Elie Siegmeister, New York: William Morrow, 1943

Wendell Berry, "The Wild," *The Broken Ground*, New York: Harcourt, Brace & World, Inc., 1964

Rupert Brooke, *Rupert Brooke, The Poetical Works*, London and Boston: Faber and Faber, 1946

Neville Cardus, *Gustav Mahler: A Centenary Appreciation*, London: Royal Festival Hall, 1960

C. P. Cavafy, *Passions and Ancient Days*, translated by Edmund Keeley and George Savidis, New York: The Dial Press, 1971

Susan Cooper, *Dreams and Wishes*, New York: Margaret K. McElderry Books, 1996

Antony W. Diamond, Rudolf L. Schreiber, Walter Cronkite, Roger Tory Peterson, *Save The Birds*, A PRO NATUR book, Boston: Houghton Mifflin Company, 1989

Robert Donington, *Wagner's "Ring" and Its Symbols*, London: Faber and Faber, 1963

Jean-Henri Fabre, *The Passionate Observer*, edited by Linda Davis, translated by Alexander Teixiera de Mattos, San Francisco: Chronicle Books, 1998

Ford Madox Ford, *Provence*, New York: Ecco Press, 1979

Viscount Grey of Fallodon, *The Charm of Birds*, New York: Frederick A. Stokes Company, 1927

Anne Harries, *Manly Pursuits*, New York and London: Bloomsbury, 1999

Katharine Butler Hathaway, *The Little Locksmith*, New York: Coward-McCann, 1942

James Huntington, *Forty Acres*, New York: Hastings House, Publishers, 1949

Richard Jefferies, *The Gamekeeper at Home*, London: Smith, Elder, 1914

Rudyard Kipling, *Puck of Pook's Hill*, London: Macmillan, 1906

Aldo Leopold, *A Sand County Almanac*, New York and Oxford: Oxford University Press, 1949

Alma Mahler, *Gustav Mahler, Memories and Letters*, edited by Donald Mitchell, New York: Viking, 1969

Thomas Mann, *The Magic Mountain*, translated by H. T. Lowe-Porter, London: Martin Secker, 1928

Roger Manvell and John Huntley, *The Technique of Film Music*, British Film Academy, London and New York: Focal Press Limited, 1957

Arvind Nehra, *Letters of an Indian Judge to an English Gentlewoman*, London: Peter Davies Ltd, 1934

Roger S. Payne, "The Music of Whales," Program, New York Philharmonic Promenades, June 11, 1970

Alan Pryce-Jones, *The Bonus of Laughter*, London: Hamish Hamilton, 1987

François Rabelais, *The Works of François Rabelais*, translated by Sir Thomas Urquhart and Peter Motteux, London: H. G. Bohn, 1851

Bernard Shaw, *Music in London 1890–94*, Volume II, London: Constable and Company Limited, 1932

Mary Taylor Simeti, *On Persephone's Island*, New York: Alfred A. Knopf, 1986

Robert Simpson, *The Essence of Bruckner*, Philadelphia: Chilton, 1968

Brian Urquhart, *A Life in Peace and War*, New York: Harper & Row, 1987

Ralph Vaughan Williams, "The Nature and Evolution of Folk Song," *The Music Lover's Handbook*, edited by Elie Siegmeister, New York: William Morrow, 1943

The Notebooks of Leonardo da Vinci, translated by Edward MacCurdy, New York: George Braziller, 1956

Alice Morehouse Walker, *Historic Hadley*, New York: Grafton Press, 1906

Gilbert White, *The Natural History of Selborne*, Garden City, N.Y.: Dolphin Books, Doubleday, 1978

The Story of Burnt Njal, author unknown, translated by Sir George W. DaSent, London, 1861

Abroad

Aucassin & Nicolete, "done into English by" Andrew Lang, London: George Routledge & Sons, 1905

Amadou Hampate Ba, *Kaidara*, translated by Daniel Whitman, Washington D.C.: Three Continents Press, 1988

Amadou Hampate Ba, *Amkoulel, l'Enfant Peul*, Babel: Actes Sud, 1991

S. Baring-Gould, *In Troubadour-Land*, London: W. H. Allen & Co., 1891

Ernle Bradford, *Ulysses Found*, New York: Harcourt, Brace & World, 1963

René Char, "Complainte du lézard amoureux," *Les Matinaux*, Paris: Editions Gallimard, 1950

René Char, "La Sorgue," *Fureur et Mystère*, Paris: Editions Gallimard, 1948

Alphonse Daudet, *Letters from My Mill*, translated by Katharine Prescott Wormeley, Boston: Little, Brown & Co., 1900

Alphonse Daudet, *Numa Roumestan*, translated by Charles de Kay, Boston: Little, Brown, 1899

Michel Droit, *Camargue*, translated by Ernest and Adair Heimann, Chicago: Rand McNally, 1963

Loren Eiseley, "The Lost Plateau," *Notes of an Alchemist*, New York: Charles Scribner's Sons, 1972

Ford Madox Ford, *Provence*, New York: Ecco Press, 1979

Johann Wolfgang von Goethe, *Wilhelm Meisters Lehrjahre*, translated by Thomas Carlyle, (1795–6) bk. 3, ch. 1.

Johann Wolfgang von Goethe, *Italian Journey*, translated by W. H. Auden and Elizabeth Mayer, London: William Collins, Sons & Co., 1962

Luc Hoffmann, *An Ecological Sketch of the Camargue*, British Birds, vol LI, 1958

Albert Lamorisse and D. Colomb de Daunant, *White Mane*, New York: E.P.Dutton & Company, Inc., 1954

Claude Léone-Chanot, *Fontaine de Vaucluse*, Chronique du Val-de-Sorgue, Avignon: A. Barthélémy, 1990

Alma Mahler, *Gustav Mahler, Memories and Letters*, edited by Donald Mitchell, New York: Viking, 1969

Marie Mauron, *Quouro la vido ero la vido / Lorsque la vie était la vie*, Pierre Rollet, Edicioun Ramoun Berenguié, 1971

Marie Mauron, *La Provence au Coin de Feu*, Paris: Librairie Academique Perrin, 1962

T. C. McLuhan, *The Way of the Earth*, New York: Touchstone, 1994

The Memoirs of Frédéric Mistral, translated by George Wickes, New York: New Directions, 1985

Leon Niangaly, "Motifs de couleurs," *Chant pour chant*, Bamako: Editions Jamana, 1994

Mungo Park, *Travels into the Interior of Africa*, London: Eland, 1983

Petrarch, *Selections from the Canzoniere and Other Works*, translated by Mark Musa, Oxford: Oxford University Press, 1985

Pliny, *Selections from The History of the World commonly called The Natural History of C. Plinius Secundus*, translated into English by Philemon Holland, Doctor in Physic, and now selected and introduced by Paul Turner, Carbondale: Southern Illinois University Press, 1962

James Pope-Hennessy, *Aspects of Provence*, London: Longmans, Green & Co., 1952

St. Francis, *The Little Flowers of St. Francis and Other Franciscan Writings*, translated by Serge Hughes, New York: New American Library of World Literature, 1964

Simon Schama, *Citizens*, New York: Vintage Books, 1989

Gertrude Slaughter, *The Amazing Frederic*, New York: Macmillan, 1937

Susan Sontag, *The Volcano Lover*, New York: Farrar, Straus & Giroux, 1992

Epilogue

Ray Anderson, *Mid-Course Correction*, Atlanta: Peregrinzilla Press, 1998

Rachel Carson, *The Sense of Wonder*, New York and Evanston: Harper & Row, 1956

Joseph Conrad, *A Personal Record*, New York and London: Harper & Brothers Publishers, 1912

e. e. cummings, "maggie and millie and molly and may," 95 Poems, in *Complete Poems 1904–1962*, New York: Liveright, 1991

Robert Donington, *Wagner's "Ring" and Its Symbols*, London: Faber and Faber, 1963

Riane Eisler, *The Chalice and the Blade*, San Francisco: HarperCollins, 1987

Robert Frost, "Choose Something Like a Star," Country Things and Other Things, in *A Pocket Book of Robert Frost's Poems*, New York: Washington Square Press, 1943

Gilgamesh, translated by John Gardner and John Maier, New York: Alfred A. Knopf, 1984

Ursula Goodenough, *The Sacred Depths of Nature*, New York and Oxford: Oxford University Press, 1998

Alma Mahler, *Gustav Mahler, Memories and Letters*, edited by Donald Mitchell, New York: Viking, 1969

Seyyed Hossein Nasr, *Man and Nature: The Spiritual Crisis of Modern Man*, London: George Allen & Unwin, 1968

Daniel Quinn, *Ishmael*, New York: Bantam, 1995

Yi-Fu Tuan, *Topophilia: A Study of Environmental Perception, Attitudes and Values*, New York: Columbia University Press, 1990

Richard Wagner, *Götterdämmerung*, translated by G. M. Holland, 1965

Nan Turner Waldron, *North Woods Walkabout*, Bethlehem, Conn.: Butterfly & Wheel, 1998

Acknowledgments

A FEW BITS FROM *For the Beauty of the Earth* have appeared under different guises. While in the Vaucluse on a three-month sabbatical from the Maine Audubon Society in 1998, I intended to compile some of the pieces I had written for *Habitat,* Maine Audubon's journal. The project quickly morphed into a very different book, but several passages originated in *Habitat,* and I owe a great debt to Bill Hancock for his fearless editing of my director's columns over a dozen years. Part of "Landscape with Man" appeared in BBC *Wildlife* magazine as "The Dome"—my appreciation to editor Rosamund Kidman Cox. And in his novel, *Flint's Law,* Paul Eddy borrowed some of the personal notes from the manuscript of "Make the Boy a Naturalist" to create not one, but two characters for his international spy thriller—neither of which, I am sorry to say, is a good guy.

Acknowledging all the people who by their impact on the author have shaped a book like this is an altogether different matter. I owe whatever insights my book contains to so many people and over so long a period of time that it would be quite impossible to name them all.

People like the old men of Amberley I knew as a boy—Amberley "yellow-bellies" they would have been called in an earlier age, tinged by the smoke from the peat dug out of the marshes below the village that heated their homes: Mr. Crowhurst, the blacksmith; Charlie Scutt and Mr. Plummer, the gardeners; old Mr. Newell and Mr. Reed, forever clipping hedges; and Farmer Chas. Herrington who owned the pub from which so many of their stories came.

Colleagues and mentors like Allen Morgan, Jim Baird and Jerry Bertrand at Massachusetts Audubon; Christoph Imboden at the International Council for Bird Preservation; Carl Straub and Walter Christie, board members at Maine Audubon; and the late Malcolm Sutherland, minister of the Unitarian Church in Harvard, Massachusetts. Roger Payne, who was kindness itself in explaining the dynamics of whale songs; and Roger Tory Peterson, who not only offered his assistance when I moved to Maine Audubon, but responded most generously when I took him up on the offer. Natural philosophers all, they have had an impact on me that is apparent in this book.

Among friends on both sides of the Atlantic, I should mention:

Humphrey Brooke, who introduced me to *The Gamekeeper at Home*, both in and out-of-doors; Jeremy Caulton, who more than anyone is responsible for my musical education, then and now; my cousin Peter de Brant, for teaching me to scour the Sussex Downs for fossils, shards and flints; Mike Rands, Peter Vickery, and Lindsay Hancock who—along with Bill and Jerry—were companions on some of the memorable birding expeditions described herein; Alain Crivelli, Alison and Patrick Duncan, and my sister-in-law, Gene MacDonald, all of whom have given me the benefit of their knowledge and love of the Camargue; Howard and Francoise Appel, Nick and Ana Livingston, Georges and Margit Leger, Jill and Dania Baikoff, who did the same for the Vaucluse; Randy Mickelson, whose unforgettable "magical mystery tour" of Venice instilled in me a love of that city that has only increased in the thirty years since; Dodge Morgan, the "bright-eyed mariner" who held me spell-bound with his tales of albatrosses in the Southern Ocean; Antonio Parisi who showed me Calabria and Sicily and who shares my admiration for Hadrian, Frederic II, and Lady Hamilton; and John Spritz, the only person so far who has trusted me enough to let me go on the air as a classical DJ.

Others made more specific contributions. Dan Abbott spent an afternoon taking author photographs. Peter Cox read several chapters and discussed them with me over divine Mediterranean lunches (even though we were in Maine). Bill Maxwell encouraged me with advice when I was at the very beginning of the book, one of the last of his many kindnesses. Mass Audubon's John Mitchell read the Italian chapters. Ken Newman introduced me to the jizz of World War II fighter planes as well as southern Africa's birds. Sean Palfrey, my oldest friend, with whom I have cultivated my "sense of wonder" from the beginning, made the beautiful double exposure on the jacket cover. Cal Snyder, serious scientist who nonetheless shares my anthropomorphic pleasure in the dioramas of the Natural History Museum, helped me track down photos of the most appealing ones. Saara Walden chivvied recalcitrant *fonctionnaires* in Provençal museums on my behalf.

My appreciation goes also to those who went above the call of duty, promptly and generously responding to my pleas for research help and finding just the right picture or quotation: Jim Berry at the Roger Tory Peterson Institute; Jiman Duncan at the Buckley School Music Department; Jane Fenton at Birdlife International; Ryan Jensen and Jennifer Belt at ArtResource; Mark Katzman and Gustavo Braga at the American Museum of Natural History; Susanna Kerr at the Scottish National Portrait Gallery; Susan Lisk at Forty Acres; and Marjorie Yesley and Pat Harris at the Bagaduce Music Library. My thanks to Gopa & Ted who kept coming across old friends in the text as they turned manuscript and pictures into their elegant form, providing delightful confirmation that it is a small world. Lastly, Norman MacAfee kept my feet to a very genial fire with his meticulous copyediting. None of them should be blamed for any mistakes in the book.

Of my family, my father, Brian Urquhart, gave me encouragement as I fed him the work in progress bit by bit and allowed me to rifle his photograph albums for illustrations. My daughter, Emily Urquhart Scott, not only kept my descriptions of life in Mali on track, but introduced me to the experiences in the first place. My sister, Katharine Urquhart, has been a fount of information on arcane points of music and family history. My cousin, Andreana Emo Capodilista, contributed helpful background about the Italian side of the family and especially Villa Emo.

Special thanks are due to my agent, Upton Brady, whose confidence kept me at it; Monica Wood, who took time from her own writing to read my manuscript and make invaluable suggestions; and to Jack Shoemaker and Trish Hoard, who have been unfailingly enthusiastic and a delight to work with.

Finally, without my wife, Amy MacDonald—my sternest critic, who taught me everything I know about the craft of writing—this book could not have been written.

Photo credits and permissions